Living Together

Living Together

Inventing Moral Science

DAVID SCHMIDTZ

OXFORD
UNIVERSITY PRESS

OXFORD
UNIVERSITY PRESS

Oxford University Press is a department of the University of Oxford. It furthers the University's objective of excellence in research, scholarship, and education by publishing worldwide. Oxford is a registered trade mark of Oxford University Press in the UK and certain other countries.

Published in the United States of America by Oxford University Press 198 Madison Avenue, New York, NY 10016, United States of America.

Library of Congress Cataloging-in-Publication Data
Names: Schmidtz, David, author.
Title: Living together : inventing moral science / David Schmidtz.
Description: New York, NY, United States of America : Oxford University Press, [2023] |
Includes bibliographical references and index.
Identifiers: LCCN 2022027395 (print) | LCCN 2022027396 (ebook) |
ISBN 9780197658505 (hardback) | ISBN 9780197658529 (epub)
Subjects: LCSH: Ethics, Modern.
Classification: LCC BJ301 .S33 2023 (print) | LCC BJ301 (ebook) |
DDC 170—dc23/eng/20220801
LC record available at https://lccn.loc.gov/2022027395
LC ebook record available at https://lccn.loc.gov/2022027396

DOI: 10.1093/oso/9780197658505.001.0001

Printed by Sheridan Books, Inc., United States of America

Years ago, my wife Cate and I were settling in to enjoy a baseball game. We sat immediately over the Arizona Diamondbacks dugout. The fan beside us, curious, asked how we scored the most perfect seats in the house. I said the tickets were a gift from the owner. The fan was eager for me to show reciprocal interest, so I politely asked, "What's your story?" The fan told me Ken Kendrick and Karl Eller would meet at a coffee shop in Scottsdale every Saturday morning. The fan made a habit of sitting next to their table so as to overhear the most amazing conversations. Karl and Ken got used to seeing the fan sitting there, and, a few days earlier, Ken had astounded the fan by leaning over and giving him a front-row ticket to tonight's game. So ended that story.

After a minute, the fan asked me how well I knew Ken, and whether I knew Karl. I answered, "I don't know either man well, but they're my best friends." The fan spent a long moment trying to decipher what I might have meant by that. Finally, quietly, he said, "I wish more people realized that those guys are their best friends."

This book is dedicated to Ken Kendrick, Randy Kendrick, Stevie Eller, and (the fond memory of) Karl Eller.

Contents

5 POLITICAL ECONOMY AND MORAL SCIENCE II

6 INVENTING THE SELF

7 THE POSSIBILITY OF CIVILIZATION

Preface

These essays follow my collection, *Person, Polis, Planet: Essays in Applied Philosophy* (2008), also published by Oxford Press. The focus on moral science is a new theme but not a new approach. For me, it goes back to the end of a disheartening first year of graduate study in philosophy, when (on the inspired advice of Jules Coleman) I transferred into economics. I worked as a research assistant in Arizona's Economic Science Laboratory and was mentored by Mark Isaac and Vernon Smith. I needed mentoring, too. I had no previous instruction in economics and only one year in philosophy. My undergraduate work was mainly in biology.

Animating the Economic Science Laboratory was a relentless interest in method. When I walked down the hallway, economists would emerge from their offices wanting to talk about, of all things, philosophy. They introduced me to coffee and filled my days with questions about what counts as a theory, an experiment, or a confirmation, and what transcends disciplinary boundaries. In the process, those wonderfully curious and collegial economists confirmed my love for the academy and for philosophy, ecology, and the study of the human condition.[1]

My first faculty position was in philosophy at Yale. Over the years, I sat in on courses at Yale Law School taught by Robert Ellickson and Carol Rose. They studied historical pressures to

---

[1] Behavioral economics at its best is a paradigm of moral science, treating rational choice models as having testable implications. (Which ways of making decisions raise quality of life? See Part 6.) But behavioral economics at its worst licenses the very hubris that it flatters itself for debunking. Having observed that people overestimate their competence as decision-makers, *nudgers* (Adam Smith called them "men of system") decide to run other people's lives, imagining they'll be better at that than their theory predicts they'd be at running their own.

which property rights are a response. From them, I learned that, while questions about private versus public property are important enough, the game-changing questions are more situated and more empirical: How big do parcels of land need to be (and what exactly do fences need to keep out) to give owners a workable base for projects from which communities grow?

Ellickson's and Rose's humble, entertaining, always illuminating economic analyses of law were a glimpse of what moral science could be. Moral science could be a history of communities identifying contingently practical solutions, keeping in mind this paramount fact about real solutions: they help communities to keep adapting to what will turn out to be an evolving problem.

Acknowledgments

This essay is substantially new work and remains work in progress. Yet it also pulls together what I've been thinking about for thirty years. The result is influenced by countless discussions spanning decades, especially with Jason Brennan and Cate Johnson. It is a continuation and reworking of the following:

Part 1 draws from Schmidtz 2018 and Schmidtz 2020.

Part 2 draws from Schmidtz 2016a.

Part 3 draws from Schmidtz 2011a, Schmidtz 2016d, and Schmidtz 2017b.

Part 4 draws from Schmidtz 2016c and Schmidtz 2015b.

Part 5 draws from Schmidtz 2011b and Schmidtz 2001.

Part 6 was originally drafted in 1997 as a sequel to Schmidtz (1992, 1994) and to "Why Be Rational?" in Schmidtz (1995).

Part 7 draws from Schmidtz 2016b and Schmidtz and Brennan (2010).

More generally, I also draw on Schmidtz (2000, 2006, and 2017a).

Special thanks to my editor, Peter Ohlin, two anonymous referees, and Ritwik Agrawal, Paul Aligica, Elizabeth Anderson, Jennifer Baker, Adrian Blau, Peter Boettke, Allen Buchanan, Gary Chartier, Billy Christmas, Peter DeMarneffe, Tyler DesRoches, Iskra Fileva, Valerie Franchitti, Chris Freiman, Harrison Frye, Luke Golemon, Robert Gordon, Chris Griffin, Stefanie Haeffele, Ryan Hanley, Ed Hall, Patrick Harless, John Hasnas, Mike Huemer, Mario Juarez, Max Kramer, Jacob Levy, Bob Lusch, Eric Mack,

Deirdre McCloskey, John Meadowcroft, Elijah Millgram, Carmen Pavel, Mark Pennington, Guido Pincione, David Poplar, Kaveh Pourvand, Enzo Rossi, Alex Schaefer, Lucy Schwarz, John Schwarz, Amartya Sen, Allan Silverman, Candace and Vernon Smith, Jacek Spendel, Virgil Storr, Vlad Tarko, John Tomasi, Bart Wilson, and Matt Zwolinski. I am grateful for extended visits and discussion at King's College London, Florida State College of Law, Georgetown School of Business, George Mason, Australian National University, and Hamburg University. Thanks to Doug Den Uyl and Liberty Fund for supporting the work of several of these commentators. Thanks to Subramanian Rangan, Ebba Hansmeyer, and the Society for Progress for their encouragement over the years and especially for commissioning my presentation on corruption at the Royal Society of London in 2014. Thanks above all to Tammi Sharp, Mary Dilsaver, Jeff Paul, Ellen Paul, and Fred Miller at the Social Philosophy & Policy Center.

Introduction

Moral philosophy begins with a question of how to live. Is moral philosophy more foundational than political philosophy? In other words, is "how to live?" more fundamental than "how to live together?" I was taught to assume as much, but there was never any reason to believe it.

Must rigorous reflection on how to live aim to derive necessary truths from timeless axioms, ignoring ephemeral contingencies of time and place? In the 1800s, philosophy left the contingencies to emerging departments of social science. How did that work out for philosophy? Did cutting ties to empirical reality checks leave philosophers with better answers? Better questions? Here, too, philosophy wants to say yes, but the truth appears to be no.

To recover a measure of relevance, theorizing about how to live might ask what has a history of demonstrably being organizing principles of actual thriving communities at their best. To an analytic philosopher, this approach has a cost. The cost is that what emerges from ongoing testing in the crucible of life experience will be mere evidence, not proof. Nothing is guaranteed. Nothing gets settled without remainder. Evidence may be suggestive, but it will not point to necessary truth; neither will it appear to do so.

Proof

Imagine that raising the minimum wage in Sacramento is followed by *rising* teenage employment. Impossible? Hardly. Still, my neoclassical economic training predicts the opposite: other things equal, as price of teenage labor rises, demand for teenage labor ebbs. My theory can be drawn on a blackboard, so you can plainly see that this is its implication. But, however clear and indeed well-confirmed my theory may be, it remains a conjecture about a relationship between two variables, while Sacramento is a sea of variables. The virtue of my theory is that it enables me to find my observation surprising and leads me to ask: Where in that sea of uncontrolled variables is the "dark matter" pulling Sacramento in that unexpected direction? If all else fails, I take a hard look at my seemingly air-tight theory. Meanwhile, Sacramento is teaching me that, to be properly accountable to my world, I must stand ready to find it interesting.

Adam Smith knew better than to turn his back on the fact that reality is a learning experience. To him, evaluating tariffs involved gathering information on relations between tariffs, prices, unemployment, and wages. Looking back, what did Smith prove? Given what philosophers now mean by proof, we could argue—indeed prove—that Smith proved nothing.

Yet Smith gave us something to think about. How often can we say that about our proofs? Smith aimed to observe, not prove. To identify covariance, not necessary and sufficient conditions. He observed a continent becoming famine-proof and wondered what was making it so.

Part 1 reflects on what moral science was becoming during the Scottish Enlightenment: an observation-based study of what members of a community find useful and agreeable. Parts 2 and 3 each contrast what might have been with what actually happened. Part 2 reflects on the oddly impractical exercise in calculating what to do that utilitarianism accidentally became at the end of the 19th century as questions about what works left philosophy to become the province of the emerging social sciences. Part 3 contrasts what "ideal theory" became with what a more realistic idealism might have been.

Parts 4 and 5 consider (a) Adam Smith and the rise of moral science; (b) political economy's core premise that administrators respond to incentives much like everyone else; (c) the ethics, politics, and economics of the rule of law; and (d) cost-benefit analysis as a tool for holding regulatory agencies of the administrative state accountable.

Part 6 picks up where Adam Smith left off in observing human agency as an achievement that starts from infancy, runs a gauntlet of maturation, and culminates in an agent who can grow an evolving constellation of adult targets over the course of a life.

Part 7 works toward reconstructing the preceding materials as an ecological justice. Ecological reasoning, like economic reasoning, is reasoning about competition, scarcity, consequences predictable and consequences unintended, and the logic of how systems respond to attempts to manipulate them. What if justice evolved as a real question about what people ought to be able to expect from each other?

These essays reflect on how we manage conflict—conflict between us and conflict within—as we define compartments in our lives that allow our pursuits to be projects rather than obsessions. To compartmentalize resources is to budget. If philosophy were the moral science that it could have been, it would focus on the role of budgets in a life well lived. Yet, Chapter 1 warns, when the compartmentalizing of intellectual resources is crude, such as when the academic unit that studies budgeting and the academic unit that studies life well-lived are not even in the same college, compartments tend to become artificial. Their contributions become vestigial—fading memories of a field that was once a response to questions that mattered.

1
THE RISE AND FALL
OF MORAL SCIENCE

1

Philosophy Lost

THEME: *Over the 1800s, moral philosophy had to reinvent itself as what was left after testable hypotheses became the turf of newly emerging departments of social science.*

For Scottish Enlightenment scholars, the mid-1700s was a heady time. Europe had never seen better prospects. Scholars knew they wanted to do what Newton was doing. Exactly what that meant was unclear, though, and determining how to conceive of science, then called natural philosophy, would take time. But natural science was rising, and Hume thought there ought to be a science of human nature as well. Hence Hume's attempt to "introduce the experimental method of reasoning into moral subjects" (the subtitle of Hume's *Treatise*).

Hume wrote his greatest work in his mid-twenties. He was trying hard to be notorious. Hume shook us (out of "dogmatic slumber" as Kant would put it) when he observed that nature's uniformity is an assumption, not something demonstrable.

If nature's uniformity is not a proven conclusion, then what is it? Is it a premise? Not exactly. We might state it as a premise so as to put an argument in deductive form, but in fact it enters scientific reasoning as neither premise nor conclusion but as something more like an inference rule.[1] Is it a guaranteed truth-preserving

---

[1] BACKGROUND: Premises are what deduction operates *on*. Inference rules are what deduction operates *with*. For example, take two premises

1. p
2. if p, then q

and turn them into a conclusion

3. q

Living Together. David Schmidtz, Oxford University Press. © Oxford University Press 2023. DOI: 10.1093/oso/9780197658505.003.0001

rule? No. Or rather, not *necessarily*, which is to say not all reasoning is deductive.[2]

Today, it is easy to read Hume as a skeptic, and maybe he was. However, we also can see Hume observing that scientific reasoning, although fallible, can be well-grounded in its way. While Hume's early work may have been written as much to dazzle as to enlighten, I read Hume as sensing his historic place as an expositor of scientific methods of studying the human condition. In sum, the Enlightenment view—Hume's view—was that there is such a thing as the human condition. It is lawlike, and it can be studied. Even when certainty is nowhere to be found, we can still make predictions and test them. To a scientist, having a basis for prediction does not mean that we will never be surprised.[3] Rather, science helps us know what to *count* as a surprise. Science is about listening to a world that never stops trying to tell us something.[4]

The ambition of Hume and Smith did not go according to plan. Their celebration of observation-based reasoning would lead, in

by using the inference rule *modus ponens*. Whereas premises p and if p, then q are explicit lines in the argument, modus ponens is not. Rather, modus ponens is a license to infer q from those premises.

[2] BACKGROUND: *Deductive* reasoning (e.g., geometry) treats axioms as premises from which a conclusion necessarily follows. *Inductive* reasoning (e.g., any empirical science) sharpens hypotheses by adjusting them so that what they lead us to expect better fits what we observe. Far from being necessarily truth-preserving, inductive reasoning is a learning process and hypotheses are subject to correction. Karl Popper (1963), seeing that induction proves nothing, proposed a "hypothetico-deductive" model of scientific reasoning. I find his model dubious but acknowledge that disconfirmation is never indisputable (Quine 1951). More precisely, when I worked in the Economic Science Laboratory, I often saw theoretical predictions disconfirmed, such as that players necessarily defect in a Prisoner's Dilemma (see Chapter 5). But an observation's interpretation was always an open question. Open questions will always be a problem for moral science.

[3] BACKGROUND: To formulate a natural law is to articulate a way of understanding the world. It is like drawing a map. Maps simplify. A map is not real in the way that the terrain is. Furthermore, a map provides a basis for knowing what to expect, but knowing what to expect is not the same as never being surprised. Chapter 4 elaborates.

[4] No one should worry about predictions of economic theory sometimes being disconfirmed. The problem would be if Economics were like astrology, with postulates too vague ever to be testable.

the 1800s, not to Philosophy becoming Moral Science but to the social sciences splitting from Philosophy and becoming their own siloed specializations. What remained of Philosophy was left to reconceive itself as a discipline whose specialty was anything but empirical.

Therein lies a story. Here is one way of telling it. Of course, telling a story entails choosing where to start, what to leave unsaid, and whom to portray as protagonists. Above all, the art and rhetoric of narration involve choosing to present a sequence of events in such a way as to invite readers to see cause and effect. I will mention other ways of telling the story as we go.

1.1 From Specialization to Fragmentation

John Stuart Mill aspired to work in the tradition of his father, James Mill, and his father's mentor, Jeremy Bentham. In some respects, Bentham was continuous with the Scottish Enlightenment. John Stuart Mill, too, aimed to take an observation-based approach to questions about how communities work and why some work better than others. In his day, Mill was a visible, influential expositor of empirical moral science as he interpreted it.

By 1848, Mill's ambition to make moral philosophy more scientific culminated in his *Principles of Political Economy*, wherein Mill separated questions about production from questions about distribution. Questions of production can be delegated to economists but questions of distribution are for philosophers: those who work on justice. Further, Mill thought, humanity had largely exhausted the frontier of technological progress. To be sure, the telegraph was invented in 1837, so electricity's potential was manifest even as Mill was writing (McCloskey, 2010, Vallier 2010). Yet, somehow, Mill expected the coming age to be an economic steady-state with relatively little news on the production side.[5] Progress would come via better distribution, not rising productivity—a thought that further encouraged us to see distribution as *the* topic for theories of justice.

Today, we do not remember Mill pressing that distinction, but the impact on our thought was so profound that we now can barely imagine not treating production and distribution as separate topics. As production became the turf of newly emerging departments of economics, philosophy was left to assume that, since questions of distribution are the questions left to philosophers, justice must be a question of distribution. This shift in focus turned moral philosophy into something so far removed from science that today calling it moral *science* could seem like an attempt at humor.

It was as if we had seen that "evening star" and "morning star" are distinct meanings, then inferred that hard-nosed astronomers would treat them as distinct phenomena. I am not sure how far to push that analogy, but it suggests a worry. Namely, what Mill pulled apart was not a pair of eminently separable questions of production and distribution. Rather, he unwittingly pulled one question into two half-questions that in fractured isolation had no proper answers and that would derail rather than facilitate our study of the human condition.

Today, philosophers conceive of society's total production as a pie. Consider not only how abstract but how deceptive it is to imagine a pie sitting there, inert, waiting for philosopher-kings to justify slicing it one way rather than another. Treated as an isolated quantity with no past and no future, there is no testable answer to how to divide it. We have only untestable, thus unresolvable,

---

[5] "It is only in the backward countries of the world that increased production is still an important object: in those most advanced, what is economically needed is a better distribution, of which one indispensable means is a stricter restraint on population" (Mill 1848, Book IV, ch. 6, titled "Of the Stationary State").

rivalries among intuitions—deeply felt, no doubt, but for all that, merely felt.[6] Students infer that it's "all relative" or "all subjective." We know they are mistaken, but we have no tools. Today, after a century of distancing ourselves from tools for constructing testable hypotheses, even our best attempts to steer students back toward truth seem clever rather than wise.

1.2 Moral Theory Repurposed

Hume and Smith studied what people observably expect from each other. What makes a pattern of mutual expectation (what Hume called a convention) stable? Why do some patterns of mutual expectation seem to have a robust (if not a demonstrably *causal*) connection to peace and prosperity? Why do some—but only some—patterns of mutual expectation accompany observable progress in building the wealth of nations? Hume observed that we approve of "every quality which is *useful* or *agreeable* to ourselves or others" (Hume, *Enquiry*, §IX, Part 1). What, then, are the features of some societies by virtue of which behavior that is useful or agreeable to oneself tends to be useful and agreeable to others as well? These were their questions. That was moral science.

Consequentialism as then conceived was about how things work. It was partly a study of incentive compatibility, capable of generating testable predictions.[7] Consequentialism veered in a different direction when Henry Sidgwick's *Methods of Ethics* (1874/1996) defined utilitarianism and egoism as alternative "Methods" of deciding what to do. Philosophy, now treating

---

[6] "Intuitions are appropriate to ethics because ours is an a priori, not an empirical investigation" (Kamm 1993, 7).

[7] BACKGROUND: *Incentive compatibility* is a matter of whether opportunities and incentives generated by institutional structures predictably lead people with interests of their own to act in ways that serve the common interest.

utilitarianism and egoism as decision procedures, moved away from studying the human condition. Studying what works—*how things work*—had been a utilitarian focus, but, by the 20th century, utilitarianism had become something else: a study of what to do *if you aim to maximize utility*. It was no longer a study of what has an observable history of leading self-interested agents to act in ways that are useful and agreeable to the people around them. How best to pursue one's self-interest was now the "Method" of egoism. Asking what reconciles incentives came to seem like a confused mush of two incompatible methods of deciding what to do.

By the end of the century, whether due to Bentham, Mill, Sidgwick, advances in formalization that were splitting political economy into two fields, or something else, professional philosophy was parting ways with the idea of moral science as a study of the observable human condition. Utilitarianism would come to be a question of what you have to do to count as a good person—specifically how much you ought to contribute to famine relief—whereas Adam Smith would have asked: How do some societies become famine-proof? Had we told Smith that annual deaths worldwide due to famine would fall from 500 per million in 1960 to 5 per million fifty years later, the magnitude might have surprised him.[8] But what would have staggered him is philosophers having almost nothing to say about it. Hypotheses about the impact of tariffs, once a central topic for Adam Smith, became unrecognizable as philosophy. Philosophers were no longer equipped or inclined to study what makes some incentive structures apt for reconciling self-interested behavior with the common good.

---

[8] https://ourworldindata.org/famines#long-term-trends-in-global-famine-mortality (accessed July 2021). But see de Waal (2018) for a less encouraging picture of post-pandemic developments. See also Pogge (2023).

1.3 Regarding What Works

As observers of human nature, we study how x is working. We study x's effects, disciplining observations by comparing alternatives and remaining alert to the explanatory potential of uncontrolled variables. Then we join Hume in observing a further fact: namely, we sometimes see what people find useful or agreeable—that is to say, we see what works for them.

By the end of the Scottish Enlightenment, we had been coming to see justice as a question about an ongoing process of living to-gether. When philosophy decided it was not philosophy's business to reflect on progress and the wealth of nations, philosophy cut it-self off from tracking what works—what drives people to invent new ways of making themselves useful.

By the mid-1900s, moral philosophy had painted itself into a corner. Philosophers were analyzing the use and meaning of words. They reflected on how to define terms and on how terms were used in ordinary language. This was work worth doing. It still is. Yet the idea that philosophy should not venture beyond linguistic anal-ysis was itself an idea that ventured well beyond linguistic analysis. Moral and political philosophy were in rough shape.[9]

1.4 Philosophy Found

Epistemology's Holy Grail—the Cartesian project—was the ego-centric project of proving (deductively) that I am not being deceived by an evil demon. Epistemologists eventually noticed an evidence-based alternative: working from outside-in rather than inside-out. We can observe how people acquire and process information. We can observe which ways of trying to stay informed are more reliable

[9] For a then-contemporary perspective, see C. L. Stevenson (1944) and, more recently, Bilgrami (2010).

than others. Alvin Goldman's (1967) move in this direction (we call it "reliabilism") was simple in retrospect but revolutionary. We start with the "is" of how we form beliefs then draw conclusions about which paths to belief are more useful than others.

Could something paralleling reliabilism's emergence in epistemology happen in moral philosophy?[10] Could moral science be a study of the human condition and of how things work?

---

[10] We can emphasize reliabilism's continuity with traditional epistemology by treating it as a new gloss on analyzing knowledge as justified true belief. To me, however, reliabilism was something bigger: a recasting of epistemology as a cognitive science unshackled by mid-20th-century conceptions of analytic philosophy.

2

The Is-Ought Problem

THEME: *Hume articulated the Is-Ought problem more as a way of defending scientific reasoning than as a way of attacking moral reasoning.*

After Mill separated production from distribution and Sidgwick separated egoism from utilitarianism, another towering philosopher, G. E. Moore, drove a comparably momentous wedge between "is" and "ought" in his *Principia Ethica* (1903). Moore transformed the Is-Ought problem into one of philosophy's core puzzles, stumping us to this day.

Here is the problem in one sentence: deductive logic cannot get us from premises about what is to conclusions about what ought to be. By the mid-1700s, Hume had precisely stated the problem.

> In every system of morality, which I have hitherto met with, I have always remark'd, that the author proceeds for some time in the ordinary way of reasoning, and establishes the being of a God, or makes observations concerning human affairs; when of a sudden I am surpriz'd to find, that instead of the usual copulations of propositions, is, and is not, I meet with no proposition that is not connected with an ought, or an ought not. This change is imperceptible; but is, however, of the last consequence. For as this ought, or ought not, expresses some new relation or affirmation, 'tis necessary that it shou'd be observ'd and explain'd; and at the same time that a reason shou'd be given, for what seems altogether inconceivable, how this new relation can be a deduction from others, which are entirely different from it. (*Treatise*: 3.1.1.27)

Living Together. David Schmidtz, Oxford University Press. © Oxford University Press 2023.
DOI: 10.1093/oso/9780197658505.003.0002

Hume had a genius for identifying skeptical problems, and, in this case, he was showing that scientific methods of observation and testing are not like geometry's method of deriving necessary truth from indubitable axioms. Even Hume at his most notoriously skeptical—noting that we observe correlation, not causation (as statistician Karl Pearson put it)—was more observant than skeptical. Scientific reasoning is very roughly a process of collecting data then speculating about what could make data look like that. Much of what we think we know is inferred from experience: Events have causes. People have minds. People make choices. What Hume was attacking was not an idea that we know things but a presumption that deduction is *the* model of good reasoning. To Hume, this presumption is not deduced from anything, and here there really is a gap. There is no reason—no *deductive* reason, indeed no reason of any kind—to believe it.

So Hume saw that observed correlation proves nothing about *cause*.[1] But the target of Hume's withering skepticism was not the idea of causation so much as the idea of proof, at least as philosophers had come to interpret proof. Hume was observing that we do not learn about our world by proving. And somewhat as we leap from observed correlation to inferred causation, we also leap from *Is* to *Ought*. Even as toddlers, when we experimented with touching the red glow on top of the stove, we learned fast to process information and jump to a conclusion based on experience.

PREMISE: Hand is burning!
CONCLUSION: Ought to move that hand!

Not valid, yet not a mistake. On the contrary, it is a paradigm of how we learn (i.e., from experience).

---

[1] Hume's *Enquiry Concerning Human Understanding* (sec. VII) would later toy with reducing cause to correlation by definitional fiat, but, even in that passage, Hume acknowledges that causation is more than correlation. A cause somehow makes a difference to whether an effect occurs (see also Lewis 1970).

Hume seemed to articulate the Is-Ought problem partly to flag a resemblance between the inference patterns of moral and scientific reasoning. Hume was not attacking morality. He was defending science. He was, as he said, attempting "to introduce the experimental method of reasoning into moral subjects." We missed his point.

Marchetti and Marchetti (2017, 3) describe the is-ought problem as an argument that "nothing is objective outside the sphere of natural science." Marchetti and Marchetti reject this, but what they reject is not Hume. Hume's explicitly stated target is thinking that moral reasoning can be *deductive*, which to Hume was almost the opposite of thinking it can be scientific. Hume's world still needed to learn that deduction is not an all-purpose model of logical rigor. To Hume, again, "a reason shou'd be given, for what seems altogether inconceivable, how this new relation can be a deduction" (*Treatise*: 3.1.1.27).

Of course, we do make mistakes. The conclusions we jump to— that even the greatest scientists jump to—often are mistaken. What we need to avoid is not mistakes per se so much as being slow to *admit* mistakes. Being quick to admit mistakes, thus quick to learn, drives progress. It is in our nature to experiment, guess, make mistakes, get burned, and learn fast.

Proof and evidence are related, yet distinct. Proof is rare; evidence is everywhere. We look at facts and see reasons. We derive reasons from facts a hundred times a day, but not by deducing.

2.1 Jump

Science is a realm of contingent rather than necessary truth. The same is true of any ethic disciplined by the logics of economics and ecology. The best we can do is to jump to a conclusion from solid information about how expectations and institutions affect opportunities for people to make themselves useful and live agreeable lives together in a given time and place.

Hume saw moral philosophy painting itself into a corner, losing sight of how we get to Ought. Hume realized that what we find useful or agreeable is not a conversation stopper, but also that it is a place to start. If we resist the tide of necessary and sufficient condition that analytic philosophy became a century ago and give up on deducing what people *ought* to find useful and agreeable, then we can simply observe what people *find* useful or agreeable and move in the direction of being empirical. We can of course ask, "why should we fully trust people's perceptions of what is useful and agreeable?"[2] Indeed, we should not *fully* trust it. If people find fentanyl useful on the strength of a false hope that fentanyl is safe, that won't count for much.[3] Yet observing what people find useful or agreeable is observing what matters to them. So suppose people matter. If people matter, then it matters what they find useful or agreeable. A person of good will at least tentatively prefers that people find their situations agreeable and approves when they find ways to make themselves useful to each other.

Suppose we observe people expecting drivers to slow down in school zones then observe accident rates falling from levels prevailing before establishing the lower-speed convention. We have no reason to call this new convention ideal, but we do have reason to call it progress. Our reasoning is not formally valid and is subject to correction as scientific reasoning always is, but (so long as we do not pretend to be deducing necessary truth from indubitable axioms) it is not a mistake. A moral science would study when the jumps that get us to *Ought* are not mistaken despite being deductively unsound. It would involve acknowledging that we can always respond to empirical claims by saying, "Not necessarily," which leaves us needing to learn when what we want to track is a relationship not of necessity but of covariance. Formulating a counterexample takes

---

[2] Enzo Rossi, personal communication (2022).
[3] See Brennan (2011) on how (in the context of voting) gaps emerge between expressed preference and true satisfaction.

cleverness; distilling genuine insight from a counterexample takes maturity.

Moral science requires humility, of course. Competent scientists are not scientistic. Neither do they fool themselves that their branch of science is the one true answer to all questions. They realize that arriving at plausible answers will always be as much art as science. A scientist's job is not to explain away what we cannot yet explain, but to take phenomena at face value. Some yet undiscovered synthesis may turn out to be more illuminating, but there is no recipe.

3

Justice as Traffic Management

THEME: *Justice concerns what we ought to be able to expect from each other. Moral science observes what happens when people expect one thing rather than another.*

As G. A. Cohen (2008) notes, not everything is contingent. Justice has fact-insensitive features implicit in the meanings of the words themselves. For example, justice is about people getting what they are due. That much is true no matter what the context, which is what it means to call it fact-insensitive. Exactly what a given person is due is a different question; when we ask that question, context matters.[1] But here, too, there are fact-insensitive features. For example, punishment may be a given person's due, but not by virtue of a person being innocent. No contingency could ever imply otherwise. It is no mistake for Cohen to stress this much, and to this extent he is in good company.[2]

Still, many intuitions about justice are somewhat testable. Reality after 1989 seemed to condemn the socialism that G. A. Cohen had spent his life defending. The test was not clean. Empirical tests

---

[1] If Sue is an infant, you may suppose her "due" is a matter of what Sue needs. In different contexts, the answer might have to do with whether she deserves a reward, whether she deserves a chance, what treatment she is due as an equal citizen, or what would count as returning a favor (Schmidtz 2006).

[2] Chapter 19 finds a parallel between Cohen's view and that of Barbara Herman, Christine Korsgaard, and others who say there are fact-sensitive (hypothetical) imperatives of the form

If [*x* is our end] + [*y* is a means to *x*], then [we rationally ought to *y*])

but who believe that this fact-sensitive imperative schema presupposes a more fundamental fact-insensitive (categorical) imperative: namely, we rationally ought to seek means to our ends.

Living Together. David Schmidtz, Oxford University Press. © Oxford University Press 2023.
DOI: 10.1093/oso/9780197658505.003.0003

never are. But empirical tests are the kind of tests we have. Cohen seemed to acknowledge that socialism had been tested and found wanting qua policy while insisting that underlying his socialism is an intuitive principle of justice that can never be touched by worldly experience.

David Hume, as I now read him, thought otherwise. Hume may not have pictured applying the experimental method of reasoning to moral questions as we would understand that method and those questions today, but he did say justice has to do with conventions—patterns of mutual expectation—that we find useful or agreeable to ourselves or others. Although doing as justice requires can often seem disagreeable or even useless, knowing what to expect from each other is useful, as is coming to have reason to trust each other.

Hume thus treated justice (so oddly to a contemporary reader) as bound up with property rights. Why? Because property rights manage traffic. Truths that manage traffic are truths about whose turn it is. Someone says, "no trespassing." Someone decides to manage traffic with lights rather than signs, overpasses, or roundabouts. It can seem arbitrary, but the profoundly liberal insight remains: the truth that manages traffic is *not* truth about who has the superior destination. We seldom reach consensus on who has the superior destination, yet we seldom *fail* to reach consensus on who has the right of way.

But wait. Seriously, what if your destination is superior? If your mission is more important, then shouldn't drivers with second-class destinations defer regardless of whose light is green? Actually, no. Hume's insight, and Western liberalism's insight, is that the task of justice is not to rank destinations but to settle whose turn it is. What we now call utilitarianism wants to be a decision procedure that says what to do. To utilitarianism thus construed, Hume's respect for property rights is puzzling since it will always be a plainly observable fact that nearly everything you own would have more utility in someone else's hands (a point Peter Singer makes in a uniquely memorable way, as per Chapter 5). But moral theorizing as theorizing about decision procedures was foreign to Hume and Smith. To Hume, the usefulness of property conventions is not that they settle what to do (or how to slice the pie) but that they settle who should decide. Hume understood that any given settling of who has right of way may end up being an inefficient result in a given case yet remain useful or agreeable as a general practice.[3] How? By helping us know what to expect. Once we know whose turn it is, we can get on with our journey. What frees us from the tyranny of a class-based pecking order is freedom from needing to decide which destination (or which religion) has higher status.[4] Sometimes what liberates is not needing to prove anything.

Something evolves among human beings as a set of devices for managing traffic. We call that something justice. Wanting to *know* about justice means wanting beliefs about justice to be not mere intuitions but somehow to be tried before the court of observable fact. Possible? Maybe not. I was trained to not expect to derive much from bare facts. Yet basic both to ecology and to what I call moral science is this observation: an ecology comprises parts that are adapting to each other. Justice is our way of adapting to a miraculous feature of our ecosystem; namely, our ecosystem is populated by beings with ends of their own—highly plastic animals

---

[3] An underappreciated fact: a principle of utility competently applied to one subject matter never "collapses" into the principle as applied to some other. If we ask how *rules* work, a theory about what to *do* will be off topic as an answer. Note: while such matters often cannot be settled by thought experiments, this one can. Imagine baseball umpires doing case-by-case utilitarian calculations regarding how many more strikes they should allow any given batter (as per Rawls 1955). In fact, baseball as a rule-governed practice has utility by virtue of prohibiting case-by-case reasoning about what the rules are. Or imagine drivers wondering, at every intersection, which color is the optimal signal for "stop." A principle of utility prohibits even asking. Motorists need to trust each other not to treat whether to stop as calling for case-by-case reasoning. As a way of helping people to know what to expect from each other, a rule of "stop if stopping has utility" is inferior to a rule of "stop if the light is red."

[4] Of course, in an emergency, even disciples of law and order might urge us to run a red light. Disciples insist on two points only: first, an emergency trumped the fact that the light was red; but second, even in emergencies where red does not mean what it normally means, it still means something. But what? See Chapter 15 on property versus liability rules.

who choose (and sometimes second-guess) not only means but ends themselves. Sometimes, x persists by virtue of being right for the social animals we are and also right for the responsible free agents we have it in our veins to be. Liberalism's defining insight is that effective traffic management is not about agreeing how to rank destinations. Liberal justice does not task travelers with even knowing other people's destinations, much less with ranking them.

Justice enables people to navigate a social world. In Hume's terms, justice is an artificial (in particular, a non-maximizing) virtue: a serviceable feature of a process, not an optimal feature of an outcome. It makes justice an egalitarian rather than aristocratic virtue.[5] Justice is artificial also insofar as its content (what people are due in a time and place) depends on conventions (i.e., emerging mutual expectations). In that way, justice fosters shared understandings of whose turn it is that enable everyone to see their turn coming.[6] To Hume, that is as far as justice goes, but that is enough to make justice a key to a community's progress.

When travelers respect each other in that easily understood and profoundly egalitarian way, implicitly treating the values of their respective journeys as presumptively (even if not necessarily) on a par, they do what it takes to constitute their society as a place that promotes value. Society depends less on people knowing how to promote value than it depends on people who share the road reading the signs, seeing whose turn it is, and in that way knowing how to *respect* value.

A system of justice that misses this crucial fact about justice, and why we approve of it, is missing a lot. The justice that helps people to make progress together does not invite us to imagine we know

---

[5] We might call it a bourgeois virtue. See McCloskey (2006), elaborated in McCloskey (2010) and (2016).

[6] If I am kept waiting for service because someone else has been waiting longer, that isn't injustice. It's traffic management. I needn't resent arbitrary distinctions that manage traffic; someone had to be first, and drawing random distinctions beats having to decide which of us is lower class.

better than others what their destinations should be. Humean justice is not everything—not even close—but almost everything depends on it. Justice so conceived is potentially something we can know, tested by (if not deduced from) observable fact.

3.1 Liberalism

I supposed in passing that we are highly plastic social animals. Realists are supposed to be skeptical about utopian overconfidence in our ability to reshape human nature (Galston 2010, 409). However, I agree with utopians that human nature is highly plastic. The trouble is that historically observable plasticity is no friend of utopian visions. Suppose we decree that crops belong to the People and that accordingly, Ukrainian farmers must resist the impulse to feed their children. Problem: because Ukrainian farmers are indeed plastic, our decree will reshape them with a vengeance. Where a utopian *imagines* farmers learning to stop feeding their children, realists observe farmers learning to stop farming.[7] We are not in a realm of necessary truths, of course, but this is the thing to predict.

Realists see the most primordial political fact of all: that I am not alone. I live among beings who decide for themselves. Even in an ideal world, Ukrainian farmers are not pawns that I move and sacrifice at will. I may think people cannot reasonably reject my deepest convictions about justice. But they can, and they know it. This fact makes politics what it is, and justice what it is.

Some ideals are political, not moral. We see that people with whom we are going to live, and with whom we'd rather not be at war, have moral ideals unlike ours. So we make an essentially political decision. We ascertain where we will not agree. Then we work to ensure that, on those issues, *we don't need to*. We have different

---

[7] BACKGROUND: The reference here is to the Holodomor. See https://www.britannica.com/event/Holodomor

views about how to live, but a liberal political ideal is about not having to go to war over differing destinations. Regarding religion, we learned from experience, not from theory, that moral and political ideals are not the same. The political ideal is to manage traffic, not impose the correct destination. Even if coordinating on a utopian vision were a *moral* ideal, minimizing the need to coordinate would be the corresponding *political* ideal.[8]

We learned (haltingly and still imperfectly) to be liberals in matters of religion. Liberalism is the name for a consensus: not on what to believe but on who gets to decide. You need not decide whether my religion is a good choice but only whether it is *my* choice. So, too, with freedom of speech. These are signature successes in learning how to live together. Liberalism is in part an optimism that the greater the range of ideas made to feel at home in a society, the more vibrant, prosperous, and progressive a society will be. Another aspect of liberalism is an insight that community life is not zero-sum. One person's gain does not imply another's loss. Typically, we are neither worse off when others succeed nor better off when others fail. Typically, we can mind our own business, wish others well, feel no need to meddle, and be content to defer to whoever is next in line. The zero-sum mindset, by contrast, is the seed from which grows xenophobic fear of the other.

We can afford to disagree. If we can disagree without feeling threatened, then we can feel comfortable simply listening and learning. When disagreement is robust, the political ideal is to make disagreement non-threatening—to make it safe to disagree. The adult political ideal is not to avoid losing but to avoid needing other people to lose.

Real cooperation consists of people with different conceptions of justice learning to live together and make their communities better—better even for people with different conceptions of justice. When we check how things are going, here is what we see: we see

---

[8] For recent views, see Hope (2016) and Mason (2016).

people who don't agree on how to live, and we see how they are getting on with their lives.[9]

The term "ideology" was coined around the time of the French Revolution. Adam Smith witnessed liberal and conservative ideologies rising as twin reactions to monarchy's twilight. To Smith and Edmund Burke, it was plain that democracy might be better and mob rule might be worse. To simplify considerably, and with a bow to Judith Shklar's reflections on a "liberalism of fear," we can see liberalism and conservatism ascending in the late 1700s as complementary responses to a "populism of fear" wherein tyrants weaponize fear of the "other" to muster support for dictatorial power.[10] Against a populist yearning for authoritarian governance, conservatism was a word to the wise about respecting traditions that often endure for a reason, while liberalism was a vision of free choice in a society without hereditary class. At the time, someone speaking of liberty, equality, and fraternity would not have been heard as speaking about a tradeoff. Seeing liberty versus equality as a tradeoff is a 20th-century idea. In the 19th century, if you saw women fighting for a right to have bank accounts, patents, or property deeds in their own name and asked them whether they were fighting for liberty or equality, they may well have been puzzled by the implication that there is a tradeoff. Equality was about *status*, not *slices*. Fighting for equal status was fighting for freedom. Likewise, in the 18th century, declaring, "We hold these truths to be self-evident, that all men are created equal. . . ." prefaced a pledge of life, liberty, and sacred honor to a fight *for* freedom, not against it.

I noted that narrators make inevitably controversial choices about how to tell the story. I choose Hume and Smith as a point

---

[9] See Sleat (2013) and Andy Sabl's insightful review. Sleat sees our system's legitimacy as grounded not in our arguments but in how we live. The ideal is to "extend freedom and equality to the non-liberal minority not by offering them arguments they can accept— that's impossible—but by ruling them with decency" (Sabl 2015, 1143).

[10] "Liberalism of fear" (1998) was Shklar's memorable way of describing a distrust of concentrated power that comes from seeing power used to scale up cruelty.

of departure, but every starting point has a history of its own. We credit Descartes with launching modern philosophy, but it was his contemporary, Francis Bacon, who did much to craft the scientific method that Hume later would run with. Meanwhile, Bacon's secretary, Thomas Hobbes, would plant seeds of what would become liberalism by daring to ask a then-scandalous question about why citizens have any duty to obey kings (scandalous because it dared to presume that kings did not own their subjects). Later, in the early 1700s, Mandeville would tell his own scandalous tale of private vices with public benefits. Today, many people lazily equate Mandeville's story with Adam Smith's. But see Chapter 13.

Before that, Martin Luther's credentials as a liberal are mixed at best, yet his work in the 1500s culminated in Protestantism and accidentally set the stage for Roger Williams (one of liberalism's underrated co-inventors) in separating church and state.[11] What grew in the soil of religious freedom was more than religious toleration; it was liberalism itself: the idea that we need not presume to run other people's lives. Liberalism is a dream not that people learn to agree but that they learn to let everyone decide for themselves.

When consensus is unneeded, that is a triumph. While people need to share the road, they *ideally* need not share, rank, or even discuss destinations. Above all, no one must accept relegation to a class of persons whose destination is less important.

Thriving communities minimize our need to justify our destination. Indeed, a traffic system's utility lies in our not needing to justify ourselves. We need not stop at intersections to justify ourselves. When we need to stop, it is because it is someone else's turn. That is all we need to know.

---

[11] As Roger Congleton notes, American liberalism's emergence as a practical response to frontier realities predated the tide of European liberal theorizing (2018, 138). The Massachusetts Body of Liberties, in 1641, codified women's rights and restricted state monopolies, takings, and cruel, unusual punishment. Congleton says, "Liberalism emerged in the United States because it worked, rather than because of abstract ideological or theological theories (Congleton 2018, 141).

3.2 Starting with Politics

John Rawls launched his greatest work with the thought that justice is the first virtue of social institutions (1971/1999, 3), suggesting (as Rawls would stress) that a theorist's first task is to articulate principles of justice. Rawls's sentence resonates. It is lyrical, poetic, compelling.

But it is not right. To Bernard Williams, the first institutional question concerns not justice but "the securing of order, protection, safety, trust, and the conditions of cooperation. It is 'first' because solving it is the condition of solving, indeed posing, any others" (2005, 3). Historically, we make progress when we acknowledge that the first virtue of social institutions is that they enable us to be neighbors. Being neighbors is, before anything else, about knowing where the boundaries are and respecting them.[12] That isn't everything, but it's a start.

In practice, the first thing we need from institutions is a settled framework of mutual expectation that keeps the peace well enough to foster conditions that enable society to be a cooperative venture for mutual benefit. As communities answer the first question and become cooperative, only then can a second question arise: How to distribute cooperation's fruits?

Of course, even if this picture is illuminating, it is not the whole truth. (No picture ever is.) Theorists rushing to familiar ground can note that what resolves conflict need not guarantee fairness. Yes, of course! When Bernard Williams said peace comes before justice, he could hardly have been unaware that peace and justice are different things.

Thomas Fossen interprets Williams as holding that "peace ought to take precedence over a commitment to justice. It is more

---

[12] Robert Frost's "Mending Wall" quotes Frost's neighbor as saying, "Good fences make good neighbors," although Frost himself is thoughtfully ambivalent. I thank Deirdre McCloskey for the reflection.

important that we find some way of getting along without resorting to violence, than that we specify the terms according to which we do so in the morally right way" (2019, 111). I read Williams as saying something different. Williams never says peace is *more important*. When he says peace needs to come first, he means literally first. In societies that achieve peace, justice is not guaranteed. But the point is, those are the societies that have a chance.

Or, let me rephrase, because that isn't quite right either. The real question is not which comes first, peace or justice. Instead, achieving peace and justice is a back-and-forth learning process. A common interest in peace is a common interest in tolerably respectful terms of engagement. To be durable, peace must seem fair enough, even if peace comes first. Conversely, fairness must seem peaceful enough, even if fairness comes first. We still need to go back and forth to make sure that what we *call* fair does not implicitly assert a right of conquest over those who disagree. Conceptions of peace and justice *both* mature in the back-and-forth process of mutual adjustment that Rawls calls reflective equilibrium.

Williams saw political realism as giving greater autonomy to distinctively political thought by contrast with a "political moralism" that sees political reasons as reducible to moral reasons (2005, 2). To me, by contrast, the key insight here is not that the political realm *is* autonomous but that the moral realm *isn't*. People negotiating what to expect from each other are creating social niches within which they hope to flourish. To Hume, flourishing meant living in ways useful and agreeable to self and others—loved by others and lovely by the light of self-inspection. So, as people embrace mutual expectations, what is taking shape is their morality and the morality of their community. They are witnessing the birth of a dimension of morality that begins life as politics—useful and agreeable terms of engagement that emerge when social and political animals figure out how to live together.[13]

---

[13] See Rossi (2019b). For a recognizably Humean realism predating the topic's emergence, see Sayre-McCord (1994).

3.3 Consensus Is Overrated

Consider how idiosyncratic our personal visions of perfection are, thus how unfit they are as blueprints for a community. Part of the essence of toleration, of mature adulthood—of being fit to live in a community at all—is acknowledging that personal visions do not obligate others, not even if we are so gripped by confirmation bias that we can fool ourselves into believing that our destination is the important one and that *our* vision is the one that cannot reasonably be rejected.

Truly taking diversity into account comes down to asking: "What terms of engagement are apt for people who do not even agree on what terms of engagement are apt?" Rushing to treat our personal intuitions about ideal justice as uniquely reasonable is a classic way of failing to rise to the level of seriousness that justice demands. When you start seeing what you call justice as licensing you to ram your agenda down the throats of people who see things differently, you are crossing a line that should not be crossed. Whatever is on the other side of that line, it is not diversity. It is not justice. It is not a cooperative venture for mutual benefit. It is not even peace.

I recently read about a woman whose husband had died of covid-19. She posted a photo of herself getting vaccinated. The online chatter vilified her for not waiting for her priority category. She replied that she was a newly widowed single mother. Not wanting her newborn baby to be an orphan, she felt a duty to see whether the clinic had a spare dose at the end of the day that otherwise would go to waste.[14] As the chatter revealed, some saw priority categories as ways to expedite people getting vaccinated, while others saw the categories as reifying entitlements against lower priority people jumping the queue. Rawls stipulates that "In justice as fairness, men agree to share one another's fate" (1971, 102). In reality, far from agreeing to share

---

[14] See https://people.com/tv/amanda-kloots-covid-vaccine-backlash-took-away-from-emotional-moment/.

one another's fate, people do not even agree on the point of getting in line. Incredibly, people still figure out how to manage traffic.

Anyone who wants peace must acknowledge a fact at the heart of the human condition: justice is not, even ideally, about any of us getting what we deem ideal. Justice at its most ideal is traffic management among people who see the humanity in each other even when their respective moral ideals border on being mutually unintelligible.

Perhaps no one will find that thought satisfying. I don't. It does not vindicate my personal vision. But the justice of a real community won't be the justice of anyone's vision. It will be a political compromise.

Institutions that let us lay down our weapons and have a conversation are the ones that make it safe to show up. Yet Rawls's first question is about distributing fruits of cooperation. It is hard to avoid suspecting, with Williams, that distribution is not the first institutional question, or even the first question of justice. Before we start distributing what separate persons brought to the table, fairness starts with acknowledging that they brought it. Getting that acknowledgment right is a prerequisite of people trusting each other enough to risk bringing anything.

The first question of justice is not how to treat the pie, but how to treat bakers. Losing sight of this was part of the price of Mill separating questions of production from questions of distribution. When the question of why bakers bake became social science, philosophers were left to ponder how to *distribute* what bakers bring to the table rather than how to *respect* what bakers bring.

I expect Smith would have deplored the hollowing out of esteem implicit in describing what bakers achieve—describing even their character and willingness to work hard—as morally arbitrary accidents of a genetic and social lottery for which bakers can claim no credit (Rawls 1971/1999, 104).[15] To questions about

---

[15] Responding to this notorious passage in Rawls, "Two Kinds of Arbitrary" (Schmidtz 2006) notes a fateful ambiguity. Distributions can be arbitrary, meaning *random*. Or

how to respect bakers, it is hard to imagine a worse answer. We are supposed to imagine bakers won't mind being hypothetically represented with such surreal incompetence. We are invited to stipulate that bakers (because they have a sense of *justice*!) will strictly comply with whatever we condescend to distribute to them. But the pie is not a thing from nowhere. Indeed, it is not a thing at all, but work: embodied hopes, dreams, and lives of separate persons.

Rawls's thought experiment, meant to pump intuitions about distributive justice, has us facing each other as adults from nowhere, meeting to divide a pie from nowhere, free of baggage. In fact, we arrive at different times, each one of us a latecomer, to a world knee-deep in baggage. When we see a pie, it won't be up for grabs. It will be a pie produced, divided, claimed, and already part of someone else's plan.[16] To people who got there first, there will be only so much we latecomers can insist they owe us while still plausibly claiming to have come in peace.

When we settle disputes, it is not by presuming a right to condescendingly dismiss rival visions as unreasonable. To be gripped by a vision—*any* vision—is problematic. What we need is not to dream but to listen. That is, we need politics.

Here then, is another reason to doubt that what Rawls calls justice is the first virtue of social institutions: in practice, what any theorist calls justice is his or her vision. But, among diverse people, the

---

choices can be arbitrary, meaning *capricious*. Rawls wants us to see anything arbitrary as unfair. Not so. On the contrary, *fair* lotteries are the ones where winners are chosen at random. A *rigged* lottery is unfair because it *fails* to be arbitrary. Rawls's natural lottery is arbitrary in this benign sense. Nothing about unfairness follows. Rawls would insist that it is how we *respond* to the natural lottery that is fair or unfair. Maybe, but that doesn't change the fact that when we respond to the natural lottery, we are responding to something that is not unfair. If we ever pay for an operation to fix a baby's cleft palate, what will be motivating us is knowing that cleft palates are *bad*, not that they are improperly distributed.

[16] To be clear, regarding Rawls's theory that the smallest slice should be maximized: while I find it hard to imagine a worse answer to how to treat bakers, I also find it hard to imagine a *better* answer to how to *slice pie to which no one has a prior claim*, if only real questions were that ahistorical.

true first virtue of institutions, the political virtue, is that they curb our hunger to impose a vision on people who see things differently.

3.4 When Reality Is the Exception to the Rule

Foundations are not deducible from anything logically prior. Yet we judge foundations all the time. How? By judging what gets built on them. When we look at what is built on a foundation, we enter a realm of fact-based empirical contingency. What is built on a foundation does not *prove* anything. Still, we give ourselves a chance to observe robust covariation and to learn lessons, including when to see an experiment as a mistake that humanitarians would not want to repeat.

G. A. Cohen (2008, 316) asks us to imagine a world of two persons. They receive manna from heaven in one of two possible distributions: (5,5) or (7,6). The first vector of numbers is equal but the second is better for each. Cohen invites us to see the second as obviously better but also obviously unjust. To Cohen, the second vector might be the right one to choose, all things considered, but not because (7,6) is more just; indeed, it is less so on Cohen's intuition that justice is a matter of avoiding accidental inequality (2008, 8).

Let's put flesh on the bones of Cohen's example. Let Cohen's vectors be units of life expectancy, as extended by alternative cancer treatments. Treatment (5,5) extends two lives by five good years each, whereas treatment (7,6) extends one patient's life by seven years and the other's by six. Imagine saying, "It's a tradeoff. Justice requires treatment (5,5), but (7,6) would be better on humanitarian grounds." Imagine saying "Compared to (7,6), (5,5) is *bad* because the second patient has one year less, but (5,5) is *just* because the first patient has two years less."

Political theorists ponder how to form a community, keep it together, and make it worth keeping together.[17] If I am terrified by

---

[17] Cohen warns against confusing rules of regulation with fundamental principles. So, to avoid confusion, let's be clear. To say political theory asks what makes communities

a prospect of my children growing up in what I call a just society, then I need to rethink what I call justice. I accept Cohen's premise that growing up in a just society guarantees little. Still, the *prospect* should be better than the prospect of growing up in an unjust society. (5,5) can't be what justice amounts to. Even when justice is cruel, it isn't *petty*.

Again, Cohen concedes that what he calls justice should sometimes be compromised for humanitarian reasons (2008, 271–2, also 302–4).[18] There is a nugget of truth here, obvious to any judge. Namely, we can have reason to temper justice with mercy in exceptional cases.

However, if the human condition is the exceptional case—if *reality* is the exception to the rule—then what we were calling justice is an imposter. Of course, we can imagine an exceptional case where, on humanitarian grounds, demanding justice would be wrong.

But we should not need to be *imaginative* to come up with a case where demanding justice would be *right*.[19]

---

worth keeping together is not to propose a regulation; it is to identify political theory's subject matter.

[18] Oddly, from his premise that humanitarian values sometimes trump egalitarian ideals, Cohen does not deduce that egalitarian ideals are fact-sensitive. Why not? I lament not having a chance to ask him. He would have had an interesting answer.

[19] A remark about the grand conversation that is philosophy. Years ago, on a hike, a graduate student told me she had me figured out. She said my arguments in class were so strangely inconclusive (she may have used the word "flimsy") that it seemed I was not even trying to win. What she suddenly realized, she said, is that it's actually true that I don't try to win. I simply give students something to think about.

The point is, I discussed Gerry Cohen's work often but never thought Cohen and I were having a debate that would end with Cohen saying, "Okay, you win. I concede." In fact, Cohen gave me plenty to think about and always treated me as if I were returning the favor. My dealings with him were unfailingly cordial, constructive, and even warm. In some unstated Canadian way, we were fellow travelers. His untimely death was a real loss. I still feel it today.

4

What Is a Theory?

THEME: *Seeing moral theories as decision procedures makes it look as though we can permit only one procedure lest multiple procedures conflict. But construing moral theory as decision theory is a mistake worth correcting. Theories are maps: nothing more, nothing less. It is fine to have more than one.*

To theorize is to draw a map with words. Here is a crucial fact about theorizing, expressed as a point about maps: there is no such thing as *the* correct way to draw the map. Consider how astounded you would be if two cartography students, working separately on mapping a terrain, drew identical maps. It would not happen.

So, too, with drawing theories. Theorists choose how to represent terrain. A crucial fact about this activity is that terrain underdetermines choices we make about how to map it. A truism in philosophy of science: for any set of data, indefinitely many theories will fit the facts. Even if we agree on particular cases, it will remain a somewhat open question what general theory to extract from the particulars. Theorizing per se does not lead to consensus (Gaus 2016a, 2016b; Schmidtz 2006, 5).

Why not? Either an argument is sound or not. Why isn't a theory compelling to all of us, if sound, or none of us, if not? My answer: theories are not arguments but maps. Maps, even good maps, are not compelling. No map represents the only reasonable way of seeing the terrain.[1]

---

[1] W. D. Ross (1930) understood this despite treating moral theory as theorizing what to do.

Living Together. David Schmidtz, Oxford University Press. © Oxford University Press 2023. DOI: 10.1093/oso/9780197658505.003.0004

The truth is, the optimal number of maps to have in the glove compartment is not necessarily one, and having more than one is not enough to convict us of inconsistency. For one thing, having more than one purpose can leave us needing more than one map. (Do I want to know whether South Sudan shares a border with Uganda? Do I also want to map a route to campus from the nearest airport?) Moreover, cartographers try to represent three-dimensional truth in two dimensions, which makes distortion inevitable. (Analogously, expressing theories as sentences represents in linear form thinking that is not necessarily linear.) Part of the art of cartography is choosing, on behalf of an anticipated user, the least of evils in terms of distortion. (Mercator Projections can make Greenland look as big as South America. When is that distortion acceptable?) In any case, there remains a three-dimensional truth. The point is not to be skeptics about the terrain but to be realistic about how much we can expect from the activity of theorizing.

When maps represent moral terrain in different ways, they show us where being moral is not straightforward. If various things matter without always pointing in the same direction, that is good to know. Admittedly, if you have two maps (one defines progress as fostering excellence, another defines it as empowering the least advantaged), they may conflict. Possible response: get rid of one. Yet if you find that conflict cannot be resolved without discarding information, that itself is valuable information. Seeing that various things matter without always pointing in the same direction is not a mistake. When different values point in different directions, that is life. Complexity and ambiguity are not theoretical artifacts. Knowing where maps clash is knowing where formulaic thinking isn't good enough. That is how we know when life is asking hard questions.[2]

---

[2] "Experience leads us to form a theory about what to expect under conditions not previously observed. If morality were a neighborhood, a moral *theory* would be a map of that neighborhood. The best theory will be incomplete, like a map whose author declines to speculate about unexplored avenues, knowing there is a truth of the matter yet leaving

4.1 In the Details

In practice, to begin with a problem is to begin with a description of a problem. A theorist, aiming to express an understanding, makes judgment calls about what can be ignored. As Peter Godfrey-Smith observes of biological theories, "ignoring some features in a description of a system is inevitable to some extent in any description" (2009, 48). Or, as Alan Hamlin observes, a map of the London Underground sets aside nearly everything about London, even distances and scale, in order to distill the one kind of information that the map's anticipated users will be seeking: the sequences of stops making up the network's lines (2017, 196).

Descriptions are idealizations. Well-handled idealizations simplify by setting aside variables that do not bear on the question at hand, thus helping anticipated users focus on what brought them to the map. Every idealization is a risk and a tradeoff. Idealization per se is no mistake, yet not every tradeoff is well-handled.

Rawls assumes our economy is self-contained. He assumes people can take for granted that others will comply with what we end up calling justice. That sort of assumption is "a considerable abstraction, justified only because it enables us to focus on certain main questions free from distracting details" (1993, 12). Yet what makes x merely a "distracting detail" is that it makes no difference to the question at hand. Nothing changes when we set it aside. Therefore, whether x is a mere distraction is a matter for discovery, not a stipulation.

For example, suppose we aim to determine water's boiling point. To keep it simple, suppose we classify altitude as a distracting detail and set it aside. That idealization may sound reasonable, but it would, as a matter of contingent fact, be incompetent. Why?

those parts of the map blank. A theory evolves toward representing the neighborhood more completely, in the hands of future residents with more information and different purposes, even as the neighborhood itself changes" (Schmidtz 2006, 3).

Because altitude is no mere distraction when determining water's boiling point. As it happens, boiling point is a function of atmospheric pressure, and atmospheric pressure is a function of altitude. Thus, to set aside details is to exercise fallible judgment. It takes experience to know whether altitude is a mere detail.[3]

Simplifying is risky. It is fine to set aside details to reveal an underlying logic operating across worlds. But if we set aside the fact that incentive structures affect behavior in law-like, robustly predictable ways, then we aren't setting aside details to reveal a system's underlying logic. We're setting aside the underlying logic. Rather than setting aside what makes no difference, we are setting aside what changes everything.

It is easy to slide from ignoring to ignoring with prejudice: setting details aside not because they don't affect the argument but precisely because they do. If we must set aside circumstance x to have circumstances where y would be ideal, what does that tell us? It tells us that y is *not* ideal—not under circumstance x—plus it suggests that x is a problem. Although we set aside details to focus on the problem, one thing we must never set aside as a detail is *the problem*.

Here is a parable to illustrate a problem being set aside. Tucson's city government once tried to manage traffic flows by designating inner lanes of major roads as one-way lanes toward the city center during morning rush; during evening rush, those lanes reversed and became one-way lanes *from* city center. At off-peak times, inner lanes reverted to being turn lanes.

In a world of ideal drivers, it might have worked. But in Tucson, with its daily influx of "snowbirds," where it takes only one bewildered driver to create a dangerous mess (and giving drivers a few days to learn won't help because new drivers arrive every day), the system was a recipe for traffic jams, accidents, and road rage.

---

[3] Chris Freiman (2014) observes that it takes empirical inquiry, not mastery of language, to know whether water and H_2O are the same. See Quine (1951).

One way to describe the mistake is to say that traffic managers set aside the problem. Another way to describe the mistake is to say that they responded to a hypothetical rather than real problem. Traffic management's proper aim is to minimize collisions, not to be a system that *would* minimize collisions between ideal drivers. Therefore, proving that a scheme would work for ideal drivers says nothing in its favor *even as an ideal.*

Ideal gas law idealizes when it supposes gas molecules take up no space, thus setting aside a detail that is a mere distraction for practical purposes (Ismael 2016). Onora O'Neill (1987, 56) distinguishes (1) setting aside truth that changes nothing from (2) adding falsehood that changes everything. I accept O'Neill's distinction while emphasizing what might be seen as a third category: setting aside truth that changes everything—that is, setting aside the problem.

In Tucson, traffic managers got feedback and undid their mistake. Unfortunately, the academy gives no analogous feedback to philosophers who mistakenly equate what *is* ideal with what *would be* ideal in response to an idealized problem.

Yet, egregious though this sounds, it is not always a mistake. Sometimes, idealization helps us to focus on the importance of what we set aside. Thus, physics can demonstrate friction's importance by modeling frictionless systems. Likewise, Ronald Coase won a Nobel Prize for showing how crucial transaction cost is, and he did this by modeling an economy without the friction of transaction cost.[4] What justified setting transaction cost aside is not that transaction cost is a distracting detail, but that it is the opposite. This was no mistake; it would, however, be a colossal mistake to think solving idealized economic problems yields even approximate

---

[4] BACKGROUND: *Transaction costs* include costs involved in delivering products to end-users: marketing, storage, time waiting in line, etc. Economic progress often consists of innovations that lower transaction cost (steamboat, railroad, airplane, telegraph, telephone, internet, bar code reader, "apps" that enable Uber and AirBnB) plus organizational models (FedEx's "hub and spoke" system, or "containerization" of truck trailers that eliminate what had become the most time-consuming step in commercial transportation: transferring the contents of trucks to ships and trains).

solutions to real economic problems. It would be almost comical to see Coase's exercise—showing what would be efficient in a world without transaction costs—as showing what is approximately efficient in a world like ours. Nothing of the kind follows. It likewise is almost comical to see Rawls's exercise—showing what would be fair in a world without compliance problems—as showing what is approximately fair in a world like ours. Here, too, nothing of the kind follows. In both cases, what is set aside is no mere detail. (On compliance, see Chapter 10. On transaction cost, see Chapter 15.)

Conclusion

Neither Hume nor Rawls represented their maps of the human condition as complete. Maps supplement rather than replace good judgment. Maps *represent* a problem. They do not *constitute* it. Moreover, maps can mislead. So, a challenge for any theorist is to distinguish what can safely be set aside as a distracting detail from what cannot.

Theories are tools. One thing we cannot build into tools is a guarantee that they could never be misused by evil geniuses. Still, although much can go wrong when tools are useful enough that it becomes possible to misuse them, simplifying per se is no mistake. Simplifying serves a purpose when it amounts to setting aside distractions to clarify what works rather than to hide what doesn't. Knowing the difference is an achievement. There is no formula. It takes insight.[5]

How do some societies make it normal that people mind their own business and avoid getting in each other's way? What enables

---

[5] For more on simplicity, see https://plato.stanford.edu/entries/simplicity/ My view: Having posited that justice consists of four "elements" (desert, reciprocity, equality, need) I ask, Would a more elegant theory reduce the multiplicity of elements to one? Would a monist theory be simpler? The Periodic Table would in one sense be simpler if we posited only four elements—even better, only one—but would that make for better science? No. Astronomers once said planets *must* have circular orbits. When they accepted the reality of elliptical orbits, which have two focal points, their theories became simpler, more elegant, and more powerful. So, simplicity is a theoretical virtue, but when

most people to be amazingly adept at knowing what others will count as minding one's own business? It is not because they have a theory. Theory does not help. When we stand in the parking lot deciding which car to try to drive home at the end of the day, we never consult the theory of justice we spent all day perfecting, except in jest. Theorizing is not what teaches us how to avoid triggering people's sense of injustice. We navigate the terrain of mutual respect with a compass far older than any theory.

When Rawls (1971/1999, 281) agrees with Hume that we live in a world of real but limited generosity, it is a simplification yet we see the truth in what they say. They are not saying everything. They simplify. But neither are they making it up.[6] Second, Hume and Rawls (Rawls 1971/1999, 127) agree that we live in a world of scarcity but that we can manage scarcity if we cooperate. Third, we are intelligent; cooperation is possible. No one can know everything, decide everything, or do everything. Yet we anticipate, respond, communicate, and give our word. By our deeds we make our word count for something and, in time, learn to trust one another. These enduring features of the human condition motivate us and ultimately enable us to become a kingdom of ends.[7]

a phenomenon looks complex—when an orbit seems to have two foci, not one—the simplest explanation may be that it looks complex because it is (2006, 4).

[6] Simon Hope (2010, 135) warns against working on idealized constructs with cherry-picked features rather than on situated problems of real people. But as Hope also notes, the simple fact of asking a question is not enough to convict us of begging the question: we can describe a problem without setting it aside. While there is no uniquely accurate description of the human condition, there are descriptions that do not mislead.

[7] BACKGROUND: The phrase has been part of philosophy's technical vocabulary since Immanuel Kant's *Groundwork of the Metaphysic of Morals* formulated a moral imperative never to treat anyone as a mere means to an end but to instead always treat each person as an autonomous member of a kingdom of ends. See Chapter 8.

2

AFTER SOLIPSISM

5

Strategic Consequentialism

THEME: *Utilitarianism as it came to be done in the 20th century does not work. It does not solve problems baked into the human condition that give us reason to theorize about morality.*

Here are three mundane facts. First, we are social beings. Second, we make decisions. Third, decisions affect other people. These facts make morality what it is. They also make morality unlike what our current moral theories say it is.

People decide for themselves. Outcomes, however, often depend on what *others* decide. Therefore, because we are social animals living in a world of other people, we typically do not choose outcomes in the way that we do choose actions.

If we could choose outcomes in the way we choose actions, act-utilitarian morality would be a simple matter of choosing the utility-maximizing outcome. A buried premise that choosing acts is the same as choosing outcomes quietly lies beneath what utilitarianism became in the 20th century. The premise is false in ways that matter.

Consider that what you do affects people. You affect their payoffs, as we say in game theory. But we misunderstand the human condition if we suppose our ways of affecting people are all ways of affecting their payoffs. We also affect their behavior.

Scottish Enlightenment philosophers cared enough about humanity to ask what works, meaning: What has a history of leading people to act in ways that they and others find useful and agreeable? Today's act-utilitarianism, by comparison, can seem remarkably

Living Together. David Schmidtz, Oxford University Press. © Oxford University Press 2023.
DOI: 10.1093/oso/9780197658505.003.0005

inattentive to which of our ways of interacting have a robust history of good consequences. A prominent strand of today's utilitarianism is useless—not because it is obsessed with consequences but because it largely ignores them.

5.1 Sacrifice

In the words of philosopher Peter Singer, "If it is in our power to prevent something bad from happening, without thereby sacrificing anything of comparable moral importance, we ought, morally, to do it" (1972, 230). This principle requires something. But what? On what Singer calls his favored interpretation, the principle requires us to give everything we have to famine relief efforts or more generally to whoever needs it far more than we do. A bit more technically, Singer says, his principle requires "reducing ourselves to the level of marginal disutility," which means, "the level at which, by giving more, I would cause as much suffering to myself or my dependents as I would relieve by my gift. This would mean, of course, that one would reduce oneself to very near the material circumstances of a Bengali refugee" (1972, 241).

Singer's critics typically see it as common sense that morality does not ask so much. Morality, they say, is demanding but not maniacal. To be clear, *this is not my concern.* Instead, what I find odd is that a principle specifying how much we should aim to accomplish would come to be reinterpreted as specifying how much we should aim to sacrifice. In practice, the call to maximize benefit morphs into a call to maximize . . . cost.

Heretics who have the nerve to ask for an argument find in Singer two thoughts. First, Singer says, suffering is bad, and those who disagree need read no further. Second, we should minimize suffering whenever we can (1972, 231). Singer offers the latter as a "point" that is nearly as uncontroversial as the first. He presents his "point" as an intuition, not an argument, but defies readers to deny that it resonates. In fact, it resonates powerfully indeed with my Catholic upbringing. We are sinners by nature. Ethics is about proving to God that we have sacrificed enough to be forgivable. I learned to do penance so that I'd be lovable, so that God would know I was serious.

Another temptation to equate what we accomplish with what we sacrifice is that we are trained to brutally oversimplify utilitarian morality. Singer circa 1972 had a theory. Namely, we have two options: give or don't give. Regarding these options, we have one question: Which has more utility? Regarding this question, there is one answer: if giving has more utility than not giving, then give. *Keep* giving until stopping would have more utility. Give regardless of whether you've already given. What you gave five minutes ago means *nothing* when deciding what to give now.

5.2 Theorizing About Consequences

Here, then, is my question. What else matters, besides how much you can give at this moment? What matters more? I preface one answer with a distinction between parametric and strategic games. *Parametric games* like solitaire involve one decision-maker, one player. *Strategic games* like poker involve several decision-makers. Why does the distinction matter? Because, in a parametric world, outcomes are straightforward consequences of the acts we choose. You choose an outcome. In a game of chess, you choose whether to move your pawn to *D4*, and that is the end of it.

Wait. Did moving *pawn to D4* give the other player a reason to move *knight to D4*? Answer: in a parametric game, you are the only player, so the question cannot arise. You picked *pawn to D4* as the utility-maximizing outcome and that was the end of it. By contrast, in a real strategic game, as soon as the other player moves, it stops looking like you can simply choose an outcome.

In a strategic world, your action constructs another player's situation. If your opponent moving *knight to D4* to capture your pawn is not ideal, then your moving so as to make that your opponent's best option is not ideal. Indeed, the fact that I do not choose for everyone is *the* political fact of life. To preview Chapter 11, if I live among other players, then whether my move is ideal—whether it's even competent—depends on what it leads other players to do.

I may imagine that *pawn to D4* would be ideal, but chess players will see such so-called imagination as a paradigmatic *failure* of imagination. True imagination for chess players has everything to do with anticipating the other player's best response, and this is not merely a fact about chess. In a strategic world, solipsistic ways of identifying ideals are grossly unimaginative.

It takes imagination to be a realist. The player who anticipates what can go wrong is the player whose imagination chess players admire. Imagining what *would* be ideal in a parametric world is no substitute for being able to see what *is* ideal in a strategic world.[1] Chapter 9 extends the point. Meanwhile, the conclusion here is that, in a strategic game, if we can get to an ideal outcome, getting there won't be as simple as simply choosing it.

5.3 A Strategic Game

Some of our moral reasons stem from the fact that ours is a strategic world: people *respond* to us as if we were agents. They anticipate how we respond to circumstances; they treat our anticipated response as part of *their* circumstances and react accordingly. Wanting to make a difference in our world, true humanitarians do their homework.

---

[1] See Schmidtz (1995, 167). See also Woodward and Allman (2007, 185).

	Jane	
	Betray (AKA *defect*)	Keep Silent (AKA *cooperate*)
Betray	1, 1	10, 0
You		
Keep Silent	0, 10	9, 9

Figure 5.1 Prisoner's Dilemma.*

* ILLUSTRATION: In the definitive example, you and Jane face criminal charges and up to ten years in jail. You can betray Jane by testifying against her. The prosecutor makes you an offer: If Jane keeps silent, you get a ten-year sentence reduction if you testify, or a nine-year reduction if you also keep silent. Alternatively, if Jane testifies against you, you get a one-year reduction for testifying, or zero reduction if you keep silent. Jane has received the same offer.

The Prisoner's Dilemma typically is represented as a matrix, as in the 2 × 2 matrix of Figure 5.1. The payoffs are ordered pairs (Yours left, Jane's right). Numbers in this example are years of sentence reduction.

Seeing millions on the edge of famine, a result-oriented humanitarian acknowledges that this story is not a story about her. She is not trying to impress God. True humanitarians ask how some societies made famine a thing of the past. What leads farmers (in some societies) to develop and successfully act on an ambition to feed customers by the millions?

The intuitive case for 20th-century utilitarianism, as taken to its logical conclusion by Singer, involves a hidden empirical premise: there is a straight shot from the *act* with the highest payoff to the *outcome* with the highest utility. This premise is not realistic. It is not a priori; in strategic settings, it is not even true. In strategic settings, result-oriented morality is not an imperative to pick the action with the biggest number. Instead, it is about standing ready to walk away from the biggest number. Why? Because what counts is not numbers attaching to acts, but numbers attaching to outcomes. Outcomes are consequences not of particular acts but of patterns of cooperation.

The Prisoner's Dilemma (Figure 5.1) models this core feature of the human condition.

5.4 Interlude: Action Versus Outcome

In a Prisoner's Dilemma, players are collectively better off cooperating, but individually better off defecting.[2] Game theory predicts that rational players defect in such games and thereby fail to realize their potential as cooperators. In real life, people identify this as a problem and respond by building communities that hold partners accountable for their choices. In particular, we contrive repeated games. In a repeated Prisoner's Dilemma, you still choose to cooperate or defect, but repeated play enables strategic play. If a partner cooperates, you'll gladly do business with them again. We do this so naturally that we don't even think of it as a strategy, but it is. Defecting has a higher payoff than cooperating in a one-shot game, yet reciprocated cooperation ultimately has a higher payoff than reciprocated defecting (Axelrod 1984).[3]

Observe that in Figure 5.1 *outcomes* are cells in the matrix, but the only *act* available to you is a choice of row. Given that Jane (your partner) must decide how to respond, and given that her ideal response is cooperative, a result-oriented consequentialism would hold you responsible for doing what you can to *encourage* her cooperative response. You cannot simply *choose* it.

If there is an ideal strategy in a Prisoner's Dilemma, it is because of three factors:

(1) it matters whether your partner cooperates, yet

(2) you do not choose whether your partner cooperates. However,

(3) you can make it pay for your partner to cooperate.

---

[2] BACKGROUND: In this definitive case, for each of you, keeping silent optimizes your collective sentence reduction while testifying optimizes your individual sentence reduction. Testifying is what game theorists call a *dominant strategy*: each of you is better off betraying the other (one year better off in this example) regardless of what the other does.

[3] As a theoretical point, the latter idea is controversial. See Pettit and Sugden (1989) and Axelrod (1984). But what I have in mind here is the emergence of empirically observable cooperation. See Elinor Ostrom (1990).

In strategic settings, it does not pay to work on Jane's *payoff* by unconditionally giving. What pays is working on Jane's *strategy* by reciprocating. If you aim to do some good, you want to act in ways that lead Jane to cooperate rather than to free ride.[4]

The Prisoner's Dilemma illustrates the difference between choosing an act and choosing an outcome. It is the difference between choosing a row in the matrix—an act—and choosing a cell in the matrix—an outcome. The former is within your power in a way that the latter is not. The point is not that you lack the will to pull the lever that would result in mutual cooperation, but rather that unconditional giving is no such lever. You hope for, aim at, or work toward outcomes, but you do not choose outcomes.[5]

[4] There are, of course, nonstrategic problems—early child rearing, say—where allowing a free ride is the point.

[5] There are harder problems than the Prisoner's Dilemma. In a tragic commons, we can face an influx of new *players*, which can make it far more difficult to teach partners to cooperate (Schmidtz 2008, chaps. 11 and 12).

6

After Shallow Pond

THEME: *Moral theory as conceived by Hume and Smith was consequentialist, but their consequentialism was not a theory about what to do. The lesson of Peter Singer's Shallow Pond is not that utilitarianism demands too much but that theorizing about what to do is no substitute for theorizing about what works.*

Peter Singer says, "If it is in our power to prevent something bad from happening, without thereby sacrificing anything of comparable moral importance, we ought, morally, to do it" (1972, 230). To motivate this principle, he offered a thought experiment that we now call SHALLOW POND. It is among the most fertile thought experiments in the history of philosophy.

> SHALLOW POND: If I am walking past a shallow pond and see a child drowning in it, I ought to wade in and pull the child out. This will mean getting my clothes muddy, but this is insignificant, while the death of a child would presumably be a very bad thing. (1972, 231)

Most people (including me) find this compelling. Many scholars hedge Singer's utilitarianism with contrary intuitions. We all have contrary intuitions—regarding separate personhood, personal projects, and so on. However, for argument's sake, let's forget our contrary intuitions. Forget all of the contrivances philosophers use to hedge utilitarianism. Instead, let's start at the start by asking: What can an uncompromising utilitarianism say about SHALLOW POND?

Living Together. David Schmidtz, Oxford University Press. © Oxford University Press 2023. DOI: 10.1093/oso/9780197658505.003.0006

Here is what uncompromising utilitarianism needs to say: SHALLOW POND is a parametric situation. There is one player. The game is not repeated. Cooperation is not at issue. Reciprocated cooperation pays better than reciprocated withholding in the long run, but there is no long run in SHALLOW POND. Strategy is moot, and therefore what you need to do in SHALLOW POND is obvious. Wade in. Save that baby. Then get on with your life. You most likely will never be in that situation again. Hardly any of us have been in that situation even once.

Singer wants to apply the lesson of SHALLOW POND to world famine. Does it apply? In one way, the answer is no. In SHALLOW POND, you know exactly what the world needs you to be in that one moment, handle a crisis, then get on with your life. By contrast, the story of hunger will never be a story that ends with you wading in, saving the day, being the hero, then getting on with your life. If the challenge were literally to save a drowning baby, one key fact would be this: if I ever pull a drowning baby out of a pond, I will get up the next morning to a life of my own. So, yes, being moral is about stepping up when the world deals us a SHALLOW POND. A pivotal disanalogy is that with world famine, the facts of the case impose no inherent limit on a duty to save the hungry, so you need the skill and maturity to craft artificial, self-imposed limits.

6.1 Managing a Crisis Versus Managing a Life

Consider a feature of the human condition never (to my knowledge) made explicit by moral theorists: we solve problems, but we do not have (and cannot solve) problems except as defined by sets of constraints. Most strikingly, external constraints tend not to be sufficiently constraining to give us well-defined problems (Schmidtz 1992). That is why we continuously impose constraints on ourselves: so that we can have well-defined problems.

Limiting any given pursuit enables us to have *projects* rather than obsessions. Limits create room to breathe. So we give ourselves budgets, adding details as we go. We complement our one-month home-hunting budget with a further constraint that, for example, we look at houses within walking distance of school. We pick limits somewhat arbitrarily, as we must, precisely because there is nothing arbitrary about our need for limits. Operating within self-imposed limits that enable us to have well-defined problems is at the core of the daily business of living a life. Budgets of time, money, and distance acknowledge that we have other things to do and that we would not be better people if we were instead consumed by a single goal.

There is a reality here from which moral theory is well-advised to begin. Namely, we wake each morning to a frontier of new opportunities and decisions. What we do to cope with this frontier is hard to explain in standard rational choice terms, but it works. We stipulate budget limits that help us fabricate compartmentalized structures of separate pursuits that add up to what is recognizably a life. These self-imposed constraints are the heart of humanly rational choice. They limit us even while liberating us to pursue goals that come into focus within those constraints.

It would be grossly counterproductive to think each day needs to focus on the same thing as the day before. The optimal number of projects for human beings is not necessarily one; neither is it typically one. Furthermore, it would be brutish to act as if everyone has a duty to join me in focusing on the single target that obsesses me at this moment. You have no such duty, and you know it, regardless of whether you can prove it.

Projects that make up our days are pursued within compartments defined in part by budgets. Singer himself inhabits multiple compartments: he gets up on a given day and his heart tells him that today is for railing against factory farming. Tomorrow will be about laboratory animals. The day after that is for his mom. Another day will be for famine relief. Some days, instead of helping the poor, he writes about doing so. And it's hard to see any of these as days when Singer is being immoral. Singer has a life. If the option of living a life is invisible to a moral theory, then shame on the theory. So, what makes it right for Singer to find his own way—to find *fistfuls* of ways—of making it good that he lived? Which theory can draw lines such that good people like Singer have room to breathe? Singer's utilitarianism is not that theory.[1]

It is striking that Singer circa 2022 asks people to give not to a point of marginal disutility but to an arbitrary limit such as one percent of their income. Then, Singer suggests, donors can recalculate if, as Singer plausibly predicts, giving that much turns out to enrich their lives. Needless to say, act-utilitarianism entails that giving one percent has nothing to do with how much we truly ought to give. On the other hand, if Singer's quest is to maximize how much he can get us to give, one percent may be his maximally influential request.

Without meaning to criticize, I observe only that moral theorizing as usually understood is an attempt to articulate truths about morality, not to be maximally influential. If it is *true* that one percent works as a way to compartmentalize what we should be giving, then that truth fits well with morality as I conceive it. It does not, however, fit with act-utilitarianism.

We discover, inherit, and fabricate a matrix of limited expectations (of each other and of ourselves) so that we can afford to inhabit a social world. Between nothing and "too much" is where we are responsible for choosing our own way, or *ways* (Singer is allowed more than one, as are we all) of making sure our world is better off with us than without.

---

[1] Note: this is not an ad hominem argument. I have no problem with Singer. I observe only that utilitarianism is not the theory that defines the compartments that make up Singer's life. If he spends ten minutes replacing a printer cartridge so he can finish his editorial on factory farming, it is not because he calculates that this is his best chance of saving a famine victim. Rather, finishing *this* editorial on *this* day is the project that defines *this* compartment in his life.

Morality requires us to operate within constraints that compartmentalize projects that make up a life, thus preventing any given project from becoming an obsession that sucks the life out of us. These constraints often are self-imposed, somewhat arbitrarily. To be living a moral life means we do not take marching orders from anyone's theory, certainly not Singer's and, really, not even our own. (Maps can illuminate, but maps do not choose destinations.) I have no duty to be in Singer's compartment, or even in the compartment I myself was in yesterday. Even so, self-imposed and relatively stable constraints are key tools for giving ourselves frameworks for coping with one of the human condition's core challenges: figuring out habitable limits on what to expect: from each other and from ourselves. (Chapter 17 reflects further on the rationality of compartmentalized pursuits.)

6.2 What Morality Demands

Whatever we make of accusations that utilitarianism demands too much, I am struck by what Singer's Principle fails to demand. It doesn't demand that we figure out what has a history of solving the problem. It demands only that we give. For those who care about consequences, that isn't good enough.

Whatever social morality turns out to be, it does not go to heroic lengths to fool me into thinking morality revolves around me.[2] I cannot learn what morality demands by asking what I need to do to have a clean conscience. Instead, I learn what morality demands by observing and evaluating the traffic

---

[2] Shelly Kagan acknowledges that, according to utilitarianism, "neither my time, nor my goods, nor my plans would be my own" (1989, 2). Paul Hurley sees utilitarianism so conceived as failing to make a case for rationally caring about what it calls right and wrong (2006, 685). My worry: by failing to ask what has a history of actually feeding people, Singer's Principle not only fails to engage with *rationality* but with properly consequentialist *morality* as well.

management scheme in which I live. If that scheme is making our world famine-proof, that is a big deal. Aiming to be part of that is aiming high.

How much should we give? Singer's theory gives a simple answer: more. He says, "taking our conclusion seriously means acting upon it" (273). Indeed, but to get something we can take seriously in Singer's sense, a theory needs to do better than that. Theorists need to realize that moral theorizing isn't a game you win by demanding the biggest sacrifice. Moral theorizing is more demanding than that. It needs more imagination than that.

Conclusion

There is a literature on whether Singer's interpretation of utilitarian morality demands too much and whether utilitarianism as a decision procedure leaves room for personal projects. If I had nothing to say beyond joining that fray, I would not bother.

I am not saying Singer made a small, obvious mistake. If Singer made a mistake, the mistake is so huge that we need to step way back to see it. I am not saying Singer is giving the wrong answer. I'm saying he is asking the wrong question. We need to step back to see how different it would be to stop asking what to do and start asking how things work.

Observably, some basic structures have a history of enabling and empowering people to mind their business in ways that yield a famine-proof society. In general, I see functional structures as tending to tread lightly when it comes to dictating destinations. Morality has a social strand, which demands that we respect patterns of mutual expectation in our society that serve the common good by helping us to know what to expect from each other, thereby helping us to anticipate, first, how to stay out of each other's way and, second, how to be of service.

Yet morality is not one-dimensional. Whatever the interpersonal strand demands of us in our situated circumstances, morality's personal strand, only alluded to here, demands more. The personal strand, whose content we largely self-author, demands that we choose a goal and throw our lives at rising to the challenge it poses. It concerns what I need to do to be treating myself with respect, as someone of whom it is reasonable to have high expectations, while operating within demanding yet not suffocating confines of morality's interpersonal strand—that is, mutual expectations emerging to constitute our community at its functional best. The latter, of course, involves not simply observing what our community is but evaluating what our community is at its best.

Philippa Foot once said, "When anthropologists or sociologists look at contemporary moral philosophy, they must be struck by a fact about it which is indeed remarkable: that morality is not treated as an essentially social phenomenon" (1978, 189). Many philosophers might not recognize themselves as targets of Foot's critique. They might ask, "If my work does not count as studying social phenomena, what does?" First, to study social phenomena is to study phenomena. That entails observation. Second, studying social phenomena entails observing such things as what people expect from each other and themselves, how people respond to falling short of expectations, what people find useful and agreeable, and how responsive people are to opportunities to make themselves useful. We study a kind of *Is* that suggests *Ought* when we shift from studying what people expect to studying which expectations have a history of helping people stay out of pits of misery. On my view, expectations historically vindicated in that way are the ones that make up morality's social strand.

You try to see what is good in whatever mutual expectations make your community tick. Then you respect the spirit and letter of that goodness. The social part of morality is the decent part—the part that respects the rule of law. The other part, the personal part, is the heroic part.[3]

---

[3] To Judith Shklar, liberalism offers no "*summum bonum* toward which all political agents should strive, but it certainly does begin with a *summum malum*, which all of us know and would avoid if only we could. That evil is cruelty and the fear it inspires" (1998, 10–11). Politics has a point, I imagine Shklar saying, but its point is not to substitute for morality's heroic part so much as to set the stage for it (see also Den Uyl and Rasmussen 2017).

I am left to wonder, has anyone done better than Peter Singer at focusing on justice as avoiding cruelty rather than on justice as chasing a dream of perfection? Maybe not. Shklar might accept the point while conjecturing that Singer 1972 had a dream—and a cruelty—insofar as Singer 1972 (unlike Singer today) failed to accept how our humanity should lead us to *own* our projects rather than be owned by them.

7

What Works

THEME: *Our task as students of moral science is partly a task of deciding what to expect from ourselves. But that task is constrained and disciplined by a more inherently social task: to discover which of the evolving patterns of cooperation and coordination that we inhabit are observably making our world a better place.*

What has enabled billions of people to work their way out of pits of famine? Adam Smith inquired into the nature and causes of the wealth of nations. Smith set aside the egocentric question "what does morality ask of me?" and instead asked what was making the world so prosperous. (Singer has been studying this too, to his credit.) What I call social (as opposed to personal) morality is not about deciding what to expect from ourselves. It is about discovering which of the evolving patterns of cooperation and coordination that we inhabit are observably making our world a better place. The question that raises is about what to respect, not what to do.

If welfare depends on variables other than how you choose to act, those other variables could be more important. We have no reason to assume morality's natural subject matter is deciding case by case what to do next. The question is whether anybody's case-by-case decision-making matters much; the answer will depend on circumstances.

A consequentialist might care enough about famine to *theorize about famine* (why it begins, why it ends) rather than about acts. Instead of asking what to do, we might ask: Why are fewer people

Living Together. David Schmidtz, Oxford University Press. © Oxford University Press 2023.
DOI: 10.1093/oso/9780197658505.003.0007

starving today than when Singer was writing about famine in 1972? Which ways of organizing communities have a history of making famine a thing of the past? History is a complex, poorly controlled experiment, but its lessons seem hard to miss when it comes to detecting which communities have a history of securing reliable access to food in the face of periodic shocks that otherwise have lethal consequences.

Consequentialism so construed tracks histories of improving global trends. Regarding world hunger, we were trending in a good direction. But happy trends are stories about what induces, expands, and sustains patterns of cooperation in a social world. Singer acknowledges (without prompting, in conversation in 2013) that the percentage of people starving (even the absolute number of people starving) has fallen since 1972.[1] More recently, the UN estimates that the number of undernourished fell to 795 million as of 2015, and to 678 million (8.9 percent) as of 2018.

Number and percentage of world's undernourished

1990–1992	1,015 million (19%)
2000–2002	930 million (15%)
2006–2008	918 million (14%)
2009–2011	841 million (12%)
2012–2014	805 million (11%)

When there are billions of people, there will be hundreds of millions of problems. Yet where there are hundreds of millions of problems, there will be millions of solutions, too. Between 1990 and 2018, continuing a decades-long trend, food production ramped up;

[1] Data originally gathered in 2015 from the United Nations (see http://www.fao.org/hunger/en/). COVID-19's disruption of global supply chains will interrupt progress on this front. For up-to-date information, see http://www.fao.org/news/story/en/item/288229/icode/.

furthermore, supply chains got better at getting food to consumers who need it. Society as mutually beneficial cooperation scaled up. There were advances in finance (micro-finance), communication (cell phones, Internet, the "app"), transportation (global container shipping), and so on.

Some institutions are created with good intentions. Other institutions help. Truly good intention implies wanting to know the difference—wanting to know not which institutions are well-intentioned but which institutions help.

How do we learn what helps? Consider this: *empirical research is the kind of research people do when they actually care.* What do you do when you want to help your child choose a car or college? What do you do when deciding whether to decline chemotherapy? Answer: you gather information.

Amartya Sen gathered information. He earned his Nobel Prize partly for his work on 20th-century famines, showing that not one was caused by lack of food. Natural disasters can push a population over the edge but do not force a population to live on the edge in the first place. Famine is caused by eroding rights, not eroding soil. When local farmers lose the right to choose what to grow or where to sell it, they lose everything, and that is when people starve.

Sen learned that laws and customs of famine-proof countries don't stop farmers from producing and shipping food to wherever they can get a good price. A famine-proof rule of law respects farmers who have, for generations, been gathering and revising information regarding how to produce, store, transport, and sell particular crops in particular places. A famine-proof rule of law doesn't take decisions out of their hands. It doesn't route decisions through administrative offices of distant "Zamindars" who may never have met (or imagined caring about) a farmer.[2]

In many societies, famine is a thing of the past. Why? Sen conjectures that a human rights ethic might be better at

---

[2] I thank Ritwik Agrawal for the terminology.

famine-proofing a society than a utilitarian ethic would be (2010, 362). True? If so, *which* rights are keys to a society becoming famine-proof? One answer: farmers must be able to count on their crops not being confiscated. Where farmers cannot count on that, they don't plant crops, and famine results. People survive droughts, floods, and fires. But what kills people by the millions is making it illegal for people to produce for purposes of their own.

Sen reported that "No famine has ever taken place in the history of the world in a functioning democracy" (1999, 16). Sen's report was stunning, and there was pushback. Michael Massing, writing for the *New York Times* in 2003, said "About 350 million of India's one billion people go to bed hungry every night, and half of all Indian children are malnourished. Meanwhile, the country is awash in grain, with the government sitting on a surplus of more than 50 million tons."

Indeed, Sen realized, there were famines in nominal democracies, but the key is not that leaders nominally are elected but that they can be held accountable. As a matter of observation, elections as such are not enough to hold leaders accountable in countries that lack stable constitutions, reliably independent courts, reliably independent media, and reliably independent markets (Pennington 2011).

A further point. Here I take myself not to be disagreeing with Sen so much as saying out loud what Sen left unsaid. Namely, there is something democratic about the marketplace. To acquire a sack of wheat, you need not be the one with political connections. All you need is to be one among millions willing and able to pay the price. Of course, there is no positive price that everyone is guaranteed to be able to afford. Yet the observable history of markets is the closest thing the world has seen to a guarantee that millions will be able to afford the price. Why? Any explanation will be more speculative than observing the plain fact. Still, profitably unloading 50 million tons of grain is bound to involve getting the grain to millions of paying consumers. The world has never seen a retailer sitting on a

50-million-ton surplus in the way that Massing accuses India's government of doing. Retailers aim to move merchandise, not hoard it.

It would be easy to misinterpret this as a necessary truth. It is not. To belabor the obvious, the fact that retailers aim to move merchandise is an empirical regularity, not a necessary truth. The rule will have exceptions, and contrary evidence will be to the point. In his own time, Adam Smith observed real-life cartels arising from deals between crony capitalists and corrupt monarchs. We can easily imagine a cartel of private retailers amassing 50 million tons of grain on world markets then belatedly realizing they have no plan for getting it to customers. Improbable though this may seem, it is enough to lead us to speculate that, ideally, no one would have *economic* power to control 50 million tons of grain. But however hypothetical that speculation might seem, the corresponding and not remotely hypothetical point is: ideally, no one would have *political* power to control 50 million tons of grain.

When we entrust production and distribution to a central planner, the result is not that there are no mistakes, but that there are no small mistakes. It is fine to talk about holding central planners accountable, but the fact remains that, like everyone else, central planners operate under limited and inevitably biased information, often supplied by lobbyists. When farmers are deciding on the ground, a bad mistake results in their needing to ask neighbors for help. When, instead, central planners are managing 50 million tons, a bad mistake results in famine. Where responsibility is big, mistakes are big. Saying central planners should be held accountable ignores the problem.

Sen might agree but, arguably, he needed to leave the above unsaid. Had Sen said there was never a famine in a country with a Wal-Mart, readers would have rolled their eyes, yawned, or, worse, sought to "cancel" him. What happened instead was that Sen made the world notice something monumentally important by circumspectly hanging his thesis on the most politically correct ingredient of the secret recipe that seemingly makes Western, constitutional, democratic, market societies famine-proof.[3]

As Sen might also agree, feeding people has saved countless lives in dire emergencies. However, when the time comes to explain why many countries no longer experience famine, it is hard not to notice that the secret correlates far more robustly to securing a right to produce than to securing a right to be fed.

---

[3] See Henrich (2020) for experimentally tested conjectures about what makes people in some cultures more adept at finding mutually beneficial solutions to common problems.

8

Strategic Deontology

THEME: *We need to think strategically not only to promote the good but also to respect it.*

Peter Singer concludes his essay by saying, "What is the point of relating philosophy to public (and personal) affairs if we do not take our conclusions seriously? In this instance, taking our conclusion seriously means acting upon it" (1972, 243).[1]

Suppose we take seriously Singer's idea that "If it is in our power to prevent something bad from happening, without thereby sacrificing anything of comparable moral importance, we ought, morally, to do it." Suppose we take the idea *very* seriously: sending goods to where goods do more good and for the same reason sending "*bads*" to where bads do less harm. We ship food to wherever it extends life expectancies more than it would ours. We also ship toxic waste to wherever it reduces life expectancies less than it would reduce ours. Wrong? By what standard? What is the other part of morality—the part that sometimes trumps Singer's imperative to "prevent something bad from happening whenever we can do so without sacrificing anything of comparable moral importance"?

---

[1] The essay is as clear as any philosophical essay ever written, leaving no doubt that these quotations accurately reflect Singer's view. But Singer adds that, even if we replace his favored interpretation with something more moderate, "it should be clear that we would have to give away enough to ensure that the consumer society, dependent as it is on people spending on trivia rather than giving to famine relief, would slow down and perhaps disappear entirely. There are several reasons why this would be desirable in itself" (1972, 241). I am at a loss regarding how to interpret this remark charitably.

Living Together. David Schmidtz, Oxford University Press. © Oxford University Press 2023. DOI: 10.1093/oso/9780197658505.003.0008

Here is one answer. First, suppose we had a duty to minimize the number of murders. Would that be a duty to minimize the number of murders even if that would involve committing a murder? You can imagine how the question could seem like an unresolvable dorm room debate if we start from theory. But suppose we instead start from empirical observation that we have laws against murder rather than laws requiring us to minimize the number of murders. Why? Moral science has a straightforward consequentialist answer: because that's how *legal institutions* minimize the number of murders, not by requiring ordinary citizens to minimize the number of murders but by *making murder illegal*.

Functional institutions seldom try to dictate goals. Instead, typically, they specify constraints. When they impose constraints, they do so as a means to an end: the end of making it safe for people to trust each other. If we investigate, we observe that, in the typical run of recurring cases around which we construct a rule of law, there is little tension between citizens respecting value and communities promoting value. Communities promote value by promoting respect. In our thought experiments, we stipulate that actions don't have unintended consequences, but real-world surgeons know precisely the opposite. And real-world morality takes its shape partly as a response to that fact. Hospitals save lives not by standing ready to sacrifice one patient whenever that looks optimal but by instead enabling us to trust our surgeon to be on our side when he or she picks up that scalpel.

Some philosophers find it mysterious that morality would incorporate any constraints beyond a duty to maximize the good (Kagan 1989, 121–7; Scheffler 1982, 129). But this is only a mystery from the inside, where an agent ponders what to do.[2] From outside, where moral science observes how principles work as responses to the human condition, there is no mystery regarding why moral

---

[2] In what is generally an impressive book, Sophie Chappell says, "We want to know what to do. Moral theories of the classic systematic types, such as consequentialism and deontology, are supposed to tell us" (2014, 29).

institutions constrain individual action. Institutions help, when they help, by positioning persons so that their pursuit of the good in a predictably partial manner is conducive to the good in general.

Historically successful experiments in building functional societies treat rights as durable enough that people can count on their rights precluding case-by-case utilitarian calculation. Thus, surgeons lack the right to sacrifice the optimal number of patients and thereby collapse the ceiling of our global potential by turning surgeons into people whom we could not trust. We likewise lack a right to dump our toxic waste on places where we calculate that it will do less harm. Institutions that work don't treat respecting human life as an obstacle to getting things done.

The respecting, more than the promoting, enables us to trust each other enough to work together in a way that is truly, not just conceivably, mutually beneficial. A morality that serves purpose x in institutional operation does so by inducing the game's genuine players—human agents—to act in ways that serve purpose x. Institutions make themselves useful by leading human agents to make themselves useful. The only institutions with a history of doing this are those that position people to pursue their separate goods in peaceful, constructive ways. Those institutions are the "other parts" of morality that limit the scope of Singer's Principle (rendering moot the license it otherwise would give to export toxic waste).

8.1 Universalizability for a Kingdom of Players

This leads to further speculation, in this case about deontology, the other main protagonist in our family of theories about what to do.[3] Deontologists regard "What can be universalized?" as

---

[3] BACKGROUND: There is no easy way to explain deontology. The basic idea is that the right act manifests good will. Good will is manifest not in consequences we achieve but in the maxim (principle) we follow when we act. A moral maxim embodies respect

foundational. My point: in a strategic world, we cannot univer-salize a solipsistic *interpretation* of universalizability. In a Prisoner's Dilemma, we can will that everyone reciprocates. Can we will that everyone cooperates unconditionally? The difference between the two strategies is momentous, so the difference cannot be invisible to a universalization test we are supposed to take seriously. But un-conditional giving will seem as universalizable as reciprocity if we interpret universalizability by imagining a single chooser choosing for everyone, as if ignoring our separate agency (and strategic dimensions of morality that separateness creates) were the essence of moral choice.

Deontology acknowledges that moral deliberation's point is to identify maxims fit for members of a kingdom of ends. *Strategic* deontology clarifies: a kingdom of ends is a kingdom of *players*. You choose how to live among ends in themselves. But ends in themselves are agents. They decide for themselves. Therefore, in a strategic world, imagining yourself unilaterally choosing be-tween everyone cooperating and everyone defecting is nothing like imagining yourself choosing for everyone in situations *relevantly like yours*. The *essence* of your situation is that you are *not* choosing for everyone. Therefore, I propose to treat *strategic* deontology as an alternative to "act-deontology" and accordingly to envision choosing among strategies, not among actions.

So, forget about action-maxims "I should cooperate" versus "I should free ride." Instead, picture your relevant choice as the choice between alternative *strategy*-maxims "I should encourage partners to cooperate" versus "I should encourage partners to free ride." Now even the most hard-core utilitarian can see the profound moral truth in strategic deontology: what is universalizable is acting so as to teach your partners to grasp their place in a kingdom of ends and

for all persons as ends in themselves—sovereign members of a kingdom of ends. Kant thought he could express this same categorical imperative in different words by saying true moral worth involves acting on a maxim we could will to be universal law. For more information, see https://plato.stanford.edu/entries/kant-moral/.

thereby mature in the direction of true moral worth. Teach them to cooperate.[4]

---

[4] I do not suppose this move solves all imaginable puzzles for the deontological approach. It does, however, hint at a way past certain "indeterminacy of description" problems in articulating the proper form of maxims as the subject matter of the universalizability test. See also Chapter 19 on reasons to embrace a categorical imperative.

3

TOWARD A REALISTIC IDEALISM

9

Ideal Theory: What It Was

THEME: *Philosophers and political theorists recently have had a common project: to reflect on the merits of realism and idealism in political theory. No one opposes being realistic or idealistic per se. The serious question is, what would make one attempt to articulate ideals better than another?*

Let's say *realism* studies the human condition as it is, while *idealism* studies the human condition as it could be. Thus described, realism and idealism are compatible. No one objects to studying the human condition—as it is or as it could be. What divides scholars is not *whether* to theorize about ideals, but how to do it competently.[1]

If we say, "x would be ideal!" listeners will suppose we have identified x as an ideal response to a problem. If x is untested, then our dream may turn out to have been utopian, but listeners will infer that we have reason to believe that the logic of x makes x worth a try. Or so we can believe until the actual trying teaches us otherwise. An important point: if being worth a try is implicit in

---

[1] Extending Chapter 4's discussion of maps, let's say realism posits that the human condition is a reality that a map can represent more or less usefully. A meteorologist commissioned to draw a weather map and a neighborhood realtor trying to give directions over the phone will produce utterly different constructs, but it is a feature of reality that choices have to be made about how to represent it, and differences will not entail that someone made a mistake. Moreover, 'the best theory will be incomplete, like a map whose author declines to speculate about unexplored avenues, knowing there is a truth of the matter yet leaving those parts of the map blank. A theory evolves toward representing a neighborhood more completely, in the hands of future residents with more information and different purposes, even as the neighborhood itself changes' (Schmidtz 2006, 3)

Living Together. David Schmidtz, Oxford University Press. © Oxford University Press 2023. DOI: 10.1093/oso/9780197658505.003.0009

being ideal, then rival hypotheses about ideals need not be untestable intuitions. Experience can sort them out.[2]

Utopian idealism equates "what could be" with what is logically possible or, more narrowly, what is metaphysically possible. Still more specifically, utopians focus on what we could do if we try—try *hard*—with unreservedly shared purpose. That is what makes their idealism utopian.

Realistic idealism parts ways with utopian thought at this point. Realistic idealism works in a different space, what realists call the realm of *politics*. Simplifying considerably, where a utopian asks what can be imagined, a realist asks what can be predicted.

9.1 Adult Reality Checks

Realistic idealism aims to identify real possibilities, then see whether an ideal response is among those possibilities. It need not be. Sometimes the best we can do is cope. Clearly, being ideal goes beyond mere coping. But to imagine *not needing* to cope with reality falls short of theorizing even about what it takes to *cope*. So it cannot count as competent theorizing about what it takes to be ideal.

Intuitively, we call the best available response "ideal" only if we believe in some fairly robust sense that we could not have done better. Suppose I have an inspiration that lasagna is the perfect dish to serve my guests tonight. Lasagna seems ideal as a response to the problem at hand. So what changes when ransacking my kitchen confirms that a key ingredient is missing? Sometimes we ask what is best under the circumstances, realizing how different that is from asking what would have been best under better circumstances (i.e.,

---

[2] Many things are not worth a try. If we are on the roof of a tall building and I say, "Ideally, I would fly like Superman" and you reply, "Well, it's worth a try," you will be saying something false. Not being worth a try makes my vision of Superman a daydream or a throwaway remark, not an ideal. Where *x* is not even worth a try, it is not an ideal. It

had I possessed the ingredients). Facts about available ingredients do not affect whether lasagna *would have been* perfect (that is, if only we had possessed the ingredients), but when a reality check reveals that lasagna is not feasible, I switch to Plan B.

While Plan B is the best I can do under the circumstances, it is not ideal. The difference, although intuitively obvious, is hard to define. The idea, however, is that when I switch to Plan B, I do so with regret about what seemed within reach and what would have been better. If I restock the missing ingredient to make sure lasagna will be a real option next time, that confirms that Plan B is merely the best I can do under the circumstances. All this is compatible with telling my guests later that evening that lasagna would have been ideal. However, if I instead tell them lasagna *is* ideal, they won't know how to make sense of that. They will think I must have misspoken.

Let's separate cases where lasagna turns out to be infeasible from cases where lasagna turns out to be undesirable. In the case just imagined, lasagna has turned out to be infeasible. In a different case, suppose I mention that I am making lasagna for our dinner tonight, and you mention that you are gluten intolerant. My best reply is: "Oops! Your intolerance makes it an empirical fact that my plan for tonight is not ideal."

But imagine I instead reply with, "So far, there is no discernible defect in my plan to make lasagna. Gluten intolerance is a defect in you, not in my lasagna."[3] Why does this sound ridiculous? Answer: Because my presumably adult intention was for my plan to be perfect for you, not for you to be perfect for my plan.

---

does not imply reasons for action and is not worthy of aspiration (Schmidtz 2011a). See Edward Hall (2016) on what it takes for idealizations to have political implications.

[3] I here reflect on (and will return to) David Estlund's remark that a plan can go awry without revealing a "discernible defect in the theory, I believe. For all we have said, the standards to which it holds people might be sound and true. The fact that people won't live up to them even though they could is a defect of the people, not of the theory" (2009, 264).

The realist lesson here: whether my plan is ideal is as fact-sensitive as whether my plan is feasible. You (my guest) have supplied a decisively relevant fact: there are people for whom my lasagna would not be ideal, and you are one of them. Your gluten intolerance does not affect my plan's feasibility. It affects the plan's desirability. It speaks directly to whether lasagna is an ideal answer to the question of what to make for tonight's dinner. Your gluten-intolerance makes it false to say lasagna, if only it were feasible, would be ideal. The truth: lasagna is an unworthy answer to a question about what to serve a gluten-intolerant guest. Feasibility is not the issue.[4]

If modern markets give me an option of making lasagna with gluten-free noodles, that may be ideal (not second-best, but genuinely ideal) for a gluten-intolerant guest. But the only way for x to be ideal in *this* reality is for it to be ideal as a *response* to this reality. Imagining a world so unlike ours that what one wishes were ideal actually would be is not a way of seeing what *is* ideal. There is nothing ideal in setting aside features of reality that embarrass the vision we long to find believable.

Reality checks bring us down to earth. One kind of check reveals limits of what is *feasible*. Another reveals limits of what is *desirable*. Again, hypotheses about desirability can be as testable as hypotheses about feasibility.

Suppose we are hiking, and we spy a beautiful spot some miles off, down the slope, across the valley. It isn't just beautiful, it looks

---

[4] Edward Hall concludes that a realist's "insistence that political philosophy must start with the acceptance of various facts, such that in politics people do not display the sort of unity of purpose that they do in Cohen's camping trip, is not a 'feasibility' concern at all, but rather the more fundamental requirement that we actually address the practice with which we claim to be concerned" (2013, 180).

BACKGROUND: What Hall calls "Cohen's camping trip" is the centerpiece of G. A. Cohen's *Why Not Socialism?* In that work, Cohen likens ideal communist society to a camping trip in which whatever camping gear campers bring is meant to be available for anyone's use. See also Ronzoni (2012), Jubb (2012), Forcehimes and Talisse (2013), and especially Brennan (2014).

like a great place to stay, or even to live. Alas, it is not yet clear whether we can get there . . . (Estlund 2020, 10, also 2009, 269).

Correct. Whether a spot would be ideal will not depend on whether we can get there. Ravines affect the feasibility of getting there, not the desirability. We can bracket questions of feasibility and still be discussing ideals. Still, there needs to be some reason to call a spot ideal.

Thus, a rule of thumb: what it takes to *get* there is a question of feasibility. What it would be like to *be* there is a question of desirability. The second reality check (learning that a spot is crawling with fire ants) teaches us something important: not that we can't get there, but that we don't want to. x can be ideal even if x is not achievable, but not if x is not worth wanting.

Utopians concede that what will happen if we try x bears on whether we should try x, yet insist that even if x's failure is predictable, that has no bearing on whether x is ideal. To Estlund, weak-willed Professor Procrastinate proves the point. As the story goes, Procrastinate is invited to review a book. He knows he ought to accept and that accepting will establish a duty to deliver. Problem: Procrastinate knows he has a bad habit of not following through and knows himself well enough to know that this will be no exception. Thus Procrastinate knows he ought to decline while also knowing he ought to accept. Estlund addresses the paradox by analyzing Procrastinate's duty as a conjunction: [promise + deliver]. If Procrastinate can't [promise + deliver], he should decline. Yet it is false that Procrastinate literally cannot [promise + deliver]. He simply foresees that he won't. We infer what Procrastinate should be, and ideally would be, from what he could be, not from what he predictably will be.

Then Estlund exports this point to strategic contexts. In a *Carens Market*, everyone is taxed in such a way that everyone ends up with equal after-tax income; yet, despite this, everyone keeps working hard to maximize gross income (Carens 1981). Conceivable? Yes,

although not what a realist would predict. But Estlund takes this to
show how supposing "we shouldn't institute the Carens Market because people won't comply with it doesn't refute the theory" (2011,
217). The idea seems to be that, just as Procrastinate's predictable
failure does not refute a theory that ideally Procrastinate would
[promise + deliver], the Carens Market's analogously predictable
failure cannot refute a theory that [work doesn't pay + workers keep
working] would be ideal.

Yet I wonder, if the undisputed fact that the Carens Market predictably won't work is off target as a critique of the supposition that
the Carens Market is ideal, could anything be *on* target? To a realist,
an ideal—an institution worth wanting—is one that brings out
the best in people. Bringing out the worst is not ideal. The Carens
Market's flaw is *not* that it would need people at their best but that it
would need people at their best even as its logic predictably brought
out the worst. This is not a concern about feasibility. The lesson is
not that we can't get there, but that we don't want to.

10

Justice Is Not a Peak

THEME: *The biggest problem with current utopian thought is not that it ignores how hard it is to **achieve** ideals but that it ignores how hard it is to **identify** them.*

Suppose we define a perfectly just world as one that could not be more just. What else would it be? Utopian idealism, imagining a world so perfect that nothing remains for justice to demand, is one alternative. Let's add another aspect to previous characterizations by saying realistic idealism is theorizing about an ongoing process, whereas utopian idealism is theorizing about an outcome: a "peak" where the process stops and from which further progress is inconceivable.

That may sound fine. But what if (as utopians would admit) utopian peaks are imaginary theoretical constructs while pits of injustice are historically situated observable realities?

10.1 Rawls

It was John Rawls whose characterization of ideal theory launched our current debate.

The intuitive idea is to split the theory of justice into two parts. The first or ideal part assumes strict compliance and works out the principles that characterize a well-ordered society under favorable circumstances. It develops the conception of a perfectly just basic structure and the corresponding duties and obligations

Living Together. David Schmidtz, Oxford University Press. © Oxford University Press 2023.
DOI: 10.1093/oso/9780197658505.003.0010

of persons under the fixed constraints of human life. My main concern is with this part of the theory. Nonideal theory, the second part, is worked out after an ideal conception of justice has been chosen. (Rawls 1971/1999, 216)

It seems innocuous to split theorizing about justice into two parts. Still, as with Mill's separation of production and distribution, it would not be the first time that philosophy split a real question into two half-questions that in retrospect should never have been separated. That may have happened here, too. Let's see.

What would split a theory of justice into two parts? Rawls supposes we need to settle what justice demands first, then think about how to handle people who fail to comply with its demands. He says,

> With the presumption of strict compliance, we arrive at a certain ideal conception. When we ask whether and under what circumstances unjust arrangements are to be tolerated, we are faced with a different sort of question. We must ascertain how the ideal conception of justice applies, if indeed it applies at all, to cases where rather than having to make adjustments to natural limitations, we are confronted with injustice. The discussion of these problems belongs to the partial compliance part of nonideal theory. (1971/1999, 309)

As Rawls conceded, "the problems of partial compliance theory are the pressing and urgent matters" (1971/1999, 8). Yet, Rawls adds, "I consider primarily what I call strict compliance as opposed to partial compliance theory" (Rawls 1971/1999, 8). Why? "The reason for beginning with ideal theory is that it provides, I believe, the only basis for the systematic grasp of these more pressing problems. . . . At least, I shall assume that a deeper understanding can be gained in no other way" (1971/1999, 8).

To Rawls, ideal and nonideal theory are not rivals; each has a place. Yet to Rawls, where we start is critical. Assuming perfect compliance leads down one road, realistic assumptions down another. We assume perfect compliance not because realistic assumptions go nowhere but because they don't go where Rawls wants his theorizing to go. He says, "We want to define the original position so that we get the desired solution" (Rawls 1971/1999, 122).

So, what is the desired solution? Can we distinguish true ideals from idle daydreams?[1] One might expect this to be the focus of ideal theory as a genre: crafting testable hypotheses about what would be worthy of aspiration then judging alternatives by the robustness of their tendency in practice to produce ideal responses to real problems. Not so.

10.2 First, Objectives Are Not Ideals . . .

To Rawls, ideal theory comes first because "until the ideal is identified, at least in outline—and that is all we should expect— nonideal theory lacks an objective" (1999a, 90). John Simmons glosses this as saying, whereas "ideal theory dictates the objective, nonideal theory dictates the route to that objective from whatever imperfectly just condition a society happens to occupy" (2010, 12).

Simmons's distinction seems obvious and seems to make perfect sense on its own terms. However, from the premise that we need *objectives*, it does not follow that we need ideals. Alexander Graham

---

[1] As Iris Murdoch (1970, 78–9) describes human nature,

> The psyche is a historically determined individual relentlessly looking after itself. In some ways it resembles a machine; in order to operate it needs sources of energy, and it is predisposed to certain patterns of activity. The area of its vaunted freedom of choice is not usually very great. One of its main pastimes is daydreaming. It is reluctant to face unpleasant realities. Its consciousness is not normally a transparent glass through which it views the world, but a cloud of more or less fantastic reverie designed to protect the psyche from pain.

Bell had a sense of the prospects for using electricity to transmit sound in his day. Thomas Edison had a sense of the possibility of recorded sound. They had objectives. Their objectives were rooted in their sense of what was possible. Would *ideal* sound transmission be faster than the speed of light? They didn't ask and didn't need to know.

At realism's core is an insight that progress is like sailing on the open sea and making repairs as we go, one plank at a time. To see a need to replace a plank is to have an objective. Envisioning a perfect boat may be worth doing, but it is not something we need to do to have an objective.[2]

Realistic idealism starts with nonideal theory because that is what it takes to make hypotheses about ideals responsive to at least something. Starting with problems—how to patch that leak—can discipline theorizing about what to count as an ideal response. Starting instead with ideal theory (and treating it as analogous to picturing a perfect boat) may have lulled Rawls into a kind of theorizing that treats problems as things to set aside.

Much of our best legal reasoning comes from judges aiming not at peaks but at solving problems—disputes brought to their bench by real litigants (as per Chapter 15). It is not law's purpose to be the ideal answer to all possible questions. Systems evolve, new conflicts emerge, and judges will one day need to say more than has yet been said about what would make a newly emerging dispute easier to resolve or avoid in the future. Real solutions do not track perfection; instead, judges play a perpetual game of catch-up with evolving problems, learning as they go what needs patching.

Solutions to real problems exhibit twists of historical contingency that armchair philosophy cannot anticipate. Driving on the right-hand side solved a problem in some societies. It makes no difference whether driving on the right is a necessary condition for solving a problem; it makes no difference whether philosophers can imagine a scenario where driving on the left would be better.

---

[2] BACKGROUND: See https://plato.stanford.edu/entries/neurath/.

All that matters is that when a convention of driving on the right emerges and durably solves a problem, drivers become warranted in expecting each other to drive on the right.

This is not to say ideal theory is hopeless. Realistic idealism identifies x as worthy of aspiration, starting from a sober assessment of problems here and now. Suppose we hear a rumor that x is ideal and pause to wonder whether we have reason to believe it. What would a reason be like? Suppose I say, "I have a dream that our after-tax incomes will be equal some day; I also dream of a world without carnivorous plants." My dreams presumably are internally consistent, but consistency is cheap. After the dreaming comes the part that takes discipline. What separates worthy ideals from idle daydreams is not internal consistency but information— facts—about how conceptions comprise evolving rules of engagement from which we build communities where life is worth living.

That suggests three concerns. First, when I hear Rawls say, "until the ideal is identified, nonideal theory lacks an objective," what am I supposed to think? Am I supposed to think that "until we identify an ideal destination at which all traffic aims, nonideal theory of traffic management lacks an objective?" No. Even if there were an ideal destination, a theory of ideal traffic management would not presume it. Traffic management is a response to each of us having lives of our own. *So is justice.* Justice as it pertains to process more than to outcome does not specify a peak destination so much as how to share the road.

A second concern is that there is a cost to seeing ideal theory as a stage of theorizing temporally prior to nonideal theory. When Rawls says, "until the ideal is identified, nonideal theory lacks an objective," he seems to be saying we need to identify a settled ideal before moving on to nonideal theory. That cannot have been Rawls's considered judgment. According to Rawls's own method, moral reasoning is a back-and-forth process of working toward reflective equilibrium. So, even if we start by imagining an ideal, that is a stage where we are entertaining a hypothesis. Then, at stage two, we check how a *hypothesized but not yet confirmed* ideal fares in nitty-gritty application. At stage two, it is false that we have finished and left behind the task of identifying ideals, and the only question still in front of us is how (or as humanitarians *whether*) to apply them. The truth is, stage two tests hypotheses produced by stage one. If a hypothesis proves inoperable in practice, then we go back to stage one, having learned that we need a better hypothesis. It is a dark day for philosophy if we are reduced to saying, "If my ideal cannot work with the crooked timber of humanity, then I reject humanity." Back-and-forth adjusting of hypotheses cannot be reconciled with Cohen's idea that principles are fact-insensitive, but it can be reconciled with Rawls's method of reflective equilibrium.[3] Indeed, the back and forth *is* Rawls's method of reflective equilibrium. What *cannot* be reconciled with Rawls's method is treating ideal theory as a task to finish first, treat as settled, then apply to nonideal cases.

My third concern, again, as per Chapter 9, is that we need to distinguish between what is ideal and what *would be* ideal under different conditions.

In these three ways, fact-insensitive utopian idealism fails not only to sort out what is feasible but to sort out what is worth wanting. Utopian idealism's problem is not that it fails at stage two. It fails at stage one by failing to identify a worthy objective. Stage one's proper task is not to settle what *is* ideal but to identify a testable hypothesis regarding what *might* be. A hypothesized ideal is disconfirmed when we find that it could not withstand a close encounter with the human condition.[4]

---

[3] The scientific method analogously works back and forth from observation to somewhat testable hypotheses in search of interesting anomalies, so that, with testing, a theory becomes less tautological, more accountable, and more useful. Luke Golemon (in conversation) dubs this my "method of scientific equilibrium."

[4] BACKGROUND: Pennington (2011) is currently the most sustained discussion of "robust political economy." Although the phrase seems to have been coined by Boettke and Leeson (2004), the concept appears full-blown in Boettke (1997). An economy's logic has predictable consequences under both favorable and unfavorable conditions. To be *robust* is to exhibit resilience—a tendency to stay on a path to progress—despite less than ideal conditions.

10.3 Second, Ideals Are Not Peaks . . .

When evaluating the status quo, Amartya Sen says, we consider available alternatives. We distinguish better from worse but need not postulate a standard of perfection (Sen 2010, 16). This is no mere platitude. Indeed, John Simmons considers it false. Sen says knowing the height of Mount Everest is not a prerequisite of being able to compare lesser mountains (Sen 2010, 101). Simmons's retort: "We can hardly claim to know whether we are on the path to the ideal of justice until we can specify in what that ideal consists" (2010, 34). Simmons interprets Sen as saying that, although justice is the high peak on an uneven terrain, we need only concern ourselves with local gradient climbing; so long as we climb, we reach the highest peak sooner or later. Not so, Simmons observes. Blindly groping for local high ground is as likely to lead away from Everest as toward.

The metaphor is Sen's. If it misleads as astute a critic as Simmons, as it appears to have done, Sen has only himself to blame. Sen scarcely gestures at an argument, but to me, what Sen needs to say is that the terrain's outstanding landmarks are injustices: pits in an otherwise featureless plane. Why don't we need to theorize about peaks? Answer: Because peaks don't exist. Justice has no peak form. There is no climbing to be done, no destination to seek, no problem to solve, unless people are in one of those pits. All we need to know about is the pits: what counts as being in, what counts as climbing out. It is only when our situation has features that make for injustice that we need to be somewhere other than where we are. Justice is not a property so much as an absence of properties that make for injustice. This is not Sen's view, but it is a charitably radical way of explaining how Sen could think that theorizing need not postulate peaks of perfection.[5]

---

[5] A less radical departure for Sen would be to deny that our climbing is a history of blind groping. Human alertness is not as *terrestrial* (to borrow a term from Ritwik Agrawal) as Darwinian natural selection is. Human innovators, unlike natural selection,

The peak metaphor is a theoretical construct corresponding to nothing ever observed. It is fine to postulate theoretical constructs that elegantly explain observations, but the peak metaphor has never done that. (We might have some excuse for supposing peaks must exist if we could not imagine an alternative, but we can. We just did.) Pits, by comparison, are documented tragedies, not theoretical postulates. Justice is about avoiding pits. Avoiding pits is a realistic ideal, a manifestly worthy aspiration, but it is not a peak.

10.4 And Third, Peaks Are Not Liberal

Political ideals are not points of convergence. The liberal political ideal is not that we embrace the same religion but that we don't need to. The ideal is everyone choosing for themselves. Actual progress, when it occurs, is toward an open future. To imagine that progress is toward a point of convergence would be incongruent with our experience. Thomas Edison and Alexander Graham Bell were problem-solvers, working on recording sound and on transmitting it over a distance. What drove them was a problem. Again, objectives need not be visions of perfection. Pretending we can discern progress only when chasing an imaginary theoretical construct can blind us to opportunities for real progress.

An implication worth stressing: Although there is no political peak, the fact remains that we can each have our own mountain to climb—our self-chosen moral peak—in which case justice is not well illustrated by a metaphor of us all climbing toward the same peak. Climbing out of the same hole is an image that better reflects the liberal insight that we don't have to be converging to be escaping injustice.

---

do not get stuck on local peaks. They hop. Instead of inventing ever-better buggy whips, innovators can see that a city is no place for mountains of horse manure, so they ponder what a horseless carriage would be like.

This is not to debunk climbing but to observe what real climbing is. When societies climb, it is not toward a peak. When we climb toward a more just society, we climb toward an expanding, not converging, horizon of human possibility. Our actual historical experience is that truly climbing is not toward being on the same page so much as toward *not needing* to be on the same page—toward learning to be at peace with the humbling fact that we live among people who have destinations of their own.[6]

We exaggerate how compelling our personal moral peaks can be to others and thus exaggerate how central our own visions can be as organizing principles of other people's lives in a diverse community. We each have our visions. Even if one of our visions were a moral ideal, it would not be a political ideal. Visions are too personal to be the mutually understood and accepted terms of engagement for political animals who inhabit a social world. It is implausible that justice is *any* of our idiosyncratic peaks. None could ever be good at managing traffic among diverse people.

The "peak" metaphor obscures the political element of ideals. Realistic political ideals are not about reaching a pinnacle where our story comes to an end and there is no more climbing to be done. Political ideals pertain to a process that does not end. Analogously, since Darwin, the idea of a species having an Aristotelian telos gave way to a different understanding. It is possible for populations to adapt to an ecological niche so long as the niche is relatively stable across generations, yet there is no ideal peak at which gene pools aim.

We would need to have a peak in mind just in case there were a destination such that arriving at that summit is just while arriving anywhere else is not. More realistically, justice is not a distribution that we need to get to. The essence of it is like the essence of "non-circle." The task of characterizing it directly, as if it were a destination, will never reach closure. The way to get closure is to

---

[6] See also Larmore (2013).

characterize it indirectly by characterizing its logical comple-ment: injustice. Justice is not a presence of particular features so much as an absence of particular marks of injustice.

None of this denies that there is such a thing as justice. However, wrestling society toward our imaginary peak and away from someone else's is neither useful nor agreeable. Insisting that justice is a peak, meaning someone's idiosyncratic conception of a peak, gets us into pits, not out.

In closing, imagine bargainers having a strict sense of jus-tice plus a will to fully comply with it. Problem: even if everyone were motivated by a sense of justice, they would not all have the same sense.

So, if strict compliance were a given, would people complying with their personal visions be able to trust or even *tolerate* each other? Imagine diverse conceptions of what is morally tolerable. Imagine diverse people each strictly complying with what *they* call justice. Imagine that compliance, to them, means being determined to impose their own vision no matter what the cost.

As a matter of observation, people can trust their imagined pin-nacle to a point of feeling entitled to persecute those who have dif-ferent destinations. To avoid those pits of persecution, we must learn to be okay with not being at—and with not even aiming for—an imaginary peak.

Treating justice as a duty to avoid pits, rather than to converge on some utopian's imagined peak, allows us to be liberals. Life among separate persons who decide for themselves is not a peak but nei-ther is it unjust. Negotiating with, adapting to, and learning from people who see things differently is a characteristically human sur-vival mechanism. Diversity is a feature of the human condition, not a bug. Embracing that reality is a political ideal, not a moral compromise.

11

Compliance Is Not a Detail

THEME: *We cannot set compliance problems aside when imagining what is ideal. Compliance is an endogenous variable. To choose an institution is to choose the particular compliance problem that goes with it.*

11.1 Compliance Unearned

The concept of compliance has a confusing place in the literature on ideal theory, as every reader of that literature knows. On one hand, we understand that achieving perfect justice would entail everyone complying with its requirements. On the other hand, there is room to observe that *if* compliance is ideal, then taking it for granted cannot be. In fact, compliance is an ongoing achievement. To set aside that we live among *agents*—beings whose fate as social animals hangs on making it safe to trust each other—is to set aside politics itself.

Rawls stipulates that ideal bargainers comply with principles of justice. Consider what an incredible further stretch it would be to infer that bargainers, on the strength of a stipulation that their own compliance is given, will forget that their job is to pick principles for a world where their clients cannot assume other people's compliance is given.[1]

---

[1] Rawls says, "We include in the first principle of justice the proviso that the equal political liberties . . . are to be guaranteed their fair value" (1993, 327). We cannot trust ideal public officials to figure it out later but must guarantee good behavior on the part of public officials *as they are* (Rawls 2001, 143). Realistic worries about compliance are central to the question of what can count as ideal in the first place (Orr and Johnson 2018, 6).

Living Together. David Schmidtz, Oxford University Press. © Oxford University Press 2023.
DOI: 10.1093/oso/9780197658505.003.0011

Hamlin and Stemplowska (2012, 57) nicely summarize Cohen's objection.

> If we assume, following Rawls, that individuals are motivated to comply with justice, then the need to trade off equality and well-being disappears. It only arises in the first place because talented people demand incentive payments to become more productive. But people who are motivated to realize justice fully would not demand incentive payments but rather increase productivity without them.[2]

What Cohen misses is that Rawls's contractors accept a tougher assignment: they contract for a world populated by agents other than themselves. Furthermore, contractors *represent*. To represent competently, contractors identify basic structures apt for the human condition their clients actually face. In particular, for contractors to know psychology, as Rawls assumes they do (1999, 137, 145), is for contractors to know that psychologies of citizens are exactly what they are. Therefore, consistently egalitarian representatives don't care whether *consistently egalitarian representatives* would need incentives. If you *care* about the people you represent, you don't bet their lives on people around them not needing incentives. By hypothesis, qua Rawlsian contractor, you are behind a veil of ignorance, and behind this veil, you do not even know whether you personally need incentives. But you do know (and have a fiduciary duty to care about the fact) that compliance is an achievement, not a given. Contractors would grasp that the relevant political ideal is to create conditions where people can afford to expect their fellow citizens to comply.

---

[2] Cohen's idea that a sincere egalitarian would give to a point of not having more than the least advantaged seems to parallel Singer's view (as per Chapter 6) that a sincere utilitarian would give to a point of marginal disutility.

Rawls also says, "An important feature of a conception of justice is that it should generate its own support" (1971/1999, 119). A few pages later, Rawls doubles down. "If a conception of justice is unlikely to generate its own support, or lacks stability, this fact must not be overlooked" (Rawls 1971/1999, 125). Whether a conception lacks stability needs to be *checked*, not set aside. Bargainers who take for granted not only their own but other people's compliance are committed to *failing to check* whether an alleged ideal can generate its own support. They imagine what it would be like not to need to check—not to have a political problem (Farrelly 2020).

11.2 Choose an Ideal Compliance Problem

To choose an institution is to choose an incentive structure. To choose an incentive structure is to choose a compliance problem. The compliance problem that turns out to be *our* problem will be the one we chose when we chose a basic structure. When we choose a package of principles out of which to build a basic structure, we *choose* that package's characteristic compliance problem. We choose it!

Compliance problems are baked into the human condition. The exact nature of a situation's compliance problem is a variable. It is, moreover, an endogenous variable. That is, whether we can assume others will do as we ask will depend on what we ask. Whether psychologically normal people comply with what we call justice will depend on what we call justice.

Rawls says contractors "are rational in that they will not enter into agreements they know they cannot keep" (1971/1999, 145). But here, too, whether *contractors* can keep an agreement is not the question. The question is whether *the citizens they represent* can keep it. Whether citizen x can keep it depends on whether citizen x can afford to keep it. That question goes beyond whether contractors are asking too much of citizen x. The harder strategic question is whether citizen x sees contractors asking too much of citizen x's fellow citizens—too much more than citizen x can safely expect.[3]

Compliance cannot be set aside as a problem that we take up after we identify an ideal. To pick an ideal is to pick a compliance problem. To set aside our chosen compliance problem as a detail best ignored is to set aside *the nature of what we are choosing* as a detail best ignored. It is to set aside what we are leading people to expect from each other. It is to set aside whether we are making opportunities to cooperate resilient or fragile.

We can conceptually distinguish a basic structure from the compliance problem that goes with it, but if we imagine they are two things that can be picked separately, we are mistaken. There is only one thing to pick: to pick a structure is to pick a problem. If you picked a bad problem, then you picked a bad structure.

---

[3] Andrew Mason observes that we are not always sensitive enough to whether theorizing has "identified a principle of justice for a different kind of being rather than a more ultimate principle of justice" (2012, 539). See also Miller (2013).

12

High Standards

THEME: *We need higher standards for what to call a high standard.*

Failing to engage real problems is not a way of having high standards. Here is the argument. Consider what Estlund calls a puzzle of plural obligation.

> What a person morally ought to do on a given occasion often depends on what others will do. It may be that, under the circumstances, Dr. Slice, a surgeon, ought to make an incision and remove a tumor if and only if Dr. Patch (or someone) will be there to stitch up the wound. If Patch will not be stitching, then (since neither will anyone else), it is not the case that Slice is required to cut (and she is probably required not to cut, which is a separate point). What Slice is required to do depends on what Patch will do. In its structure (if not in the stakes), this is familiar in daily life.
>
> . . . But suppose that Slice will not be doing the surgery. Patch might as well go golfing. Ought Slice to cut? Well, no, because Patch will not be there to stitch.
>
> . . . [So, how can it] be true both that something is morally wrong, and also that there is no agent for whom there is any relevant obligation? . . . The puzzle is to give, if we can, an account that would vindicate the common response of moral offense or outrage when the patient is left to die. . . . I will not tackle these questions. (Estlund 2017, 54)

Estlund may not tackle these questions, but he should. Suppose your job is to promise a service and then make sure your staff delivers as promised. Of course, if you know a key employee won't deliver, then don't promise. If we need to vindicate our outrage over Slice and Patch going off to golf, here is a suggestion. Suppose Slice and Patch are members of an emergency clinic's surgical team. In that case, they have duties in the same way Procrastinate has duties by virtue of being a professor. They are obliged to be what they represent themselves to be. They have no duty to work themselves to death or even give up golf. But if they *advertise* themselves as a 24/7 emergency service, then they have a duty to make sure the incoming shift stands ready. So they need to communicate. They are like a quarterback and pass receiver who acquire specific assignments as soon as a play is called. When a play is called, it becomes true both that the receiver should run to a particular spot and that the quarterback should throw to that spot.

In the case of Professor Procrastinate, there is nothing ideal in [promise + deliver] until we put it in context. What makes it ideal to promise and then deliver? Answer: Procrastinate is a professor. It's his job. Why is it ideal for Slice and Patch to coordinate? Answer: It's their job.

Yet, realistically, plans go awry. If a quarterback sees the receiver run a different route, the plan is moot, and part of a quarterback's job is to understand that the plan is moot. A quarterback's assignment is fixed by the calling of a given play, but that is only because a quarterback's job is more general: throw to that spot *to help the team win* unless throwing to that spot will not help. That is why plays get called: to facilitate winning coordination. But part of winning coordination is players improvising when they see that a play is not going according to plan.

As per Chapter 6, morality's interpersonal strand is not the part that requires heroism, but it does require decency, which includes being what we advertise ourselves to be. If the plan goes awry and the morning shift does not show, then Slice and Patch, like a quarterback scrambling to salvage a busted play, need to improvise, work overtime, and replace team members who prove unreliable. This is the nature of a high standard. If Slice and Patch promise customers "you can bet your life on our team," that is a big commitment. They may have no duty to *make* that promise, but if they do make it, they had better stand ready to keep it.

12.1 Realism About the Status Quo

Imagine me saying in traffic court, "Your Honor, ideally we would not need to drive defensively. Admittedly, my driving looks incompetent in this world, but that's because my standards are too high. The world isn't ready for them." A judge might respond, "Sir, the existence of drivers like you is precisely the reason why this world's ideal is to drive defensively."

Utopians worry that realists make concessions to the reality of the human condition that are premature when the task is to articulate ideals.[1] In one way, realism is indeed concessive. A realistic political ideal involves noticing when other drivers have the right of way. Even if others only *think* they have the right of way, that is reason enough for a defensive driver to slow down. Note: this is a metaphor for something crucial. Namely, we want to coexist in peace with all our neighbors, not only the ideal ones. Believing your neighbor is right is not a prerequisite of having reason to defer.

We can entertain forms of idealism oblivious to the strategic ideal of standing ready to concede the right of way when navigating

---

[1] Alison McQueen (2019, 27) conjectures that utopians feel they must reject realism on pain of resigning themselves to the status quo, but being realistic about where we start is not an arbitrary bias. Realists focus on reality because reality is what needs work. Realists acknowledge where we start because that's what it takes to be *starting*. They hear utopians talking about what "doesn't refute the theory," but they don't see utopians offering a theory. It is as if needing to know what to count as progress starting from here could be set aside as a distracting detail.

the shoals of unshared intentions. But being concessive with respect to rights of way is operating to a high standard.

An ideal traffic manager's idealism rises to a level of seeking ideal responses to real problems. If a proposed solution would not help, there is no further question about whether we can imagine it helping under utopian circumstances. One view: unrealizable ideals "may play an inspirational role" (Stemplowska and Swift 2012, 387), yet it can seem "naïve, and ineffective, to hold existing societies to account on the basis of such demanding moral standards" (Valentini 2012, 659). On this view, a norm like unconditional giving is too much to ask. It reaches too high. On the contrary, I would deny that realistic idealism asks *less* than utopian idealism asks. In fact, realistic idealism asks more. It demands that we do not shrug and call people defective just because *our theory* is unfit for the world they live in.

Estlund supposes utopian standards can be unrealistically high.

> Actions in pursuit of what will never be achieved can be wasteful or even disastrous. A theory that counsels action in pursuit of high standards that are not sufficiently likely to be achieved, where the costs of failing are very high, often deserves to be chastised as utopian. On the other hand, some people might be led by unrealistically high standards to improve themselves or their institutions. (2014, 7–8; also 2020, 118)

My claim: what makes utopian standards every bit as dangerous as Estlund says is how low they are, not how high they are. As per Chapter 5, to come to the table as a reciprocator is to demand cooperation, whereas to come as an unconditional cooperator is to demand nothing. As per Chapter 8, imagining that x would be ideal *if* it could be willed to be universal law has nothing to do with whether x is ideal in a world where the antecedent does not hold. If we must imagine universal compliance in order to be imagining a situation where an alleged ideal would even be habitable, that is a shockingly low standard for what to regard as ideal.

Suppose I advise my chess protégé to move to *D4* and her opponent promptly check-mates her. I shrug and say, "*D4* may not work in practice, but that isn't relevant to whether *D4* is the ideal move in theory. The real lesson is that my standards are too high; the world is not ready for them." Chess players would recognize my statement as a parody of "high" standards. They know that predictable failure is not merely a distracting detail.

Pablo Gilabert says, "It is part of the job of political philosophy to keep ambitious ideals clear and visible, and to criticize a political culture when it becomes complacent and superficial" (2017, 112). Indeed, "ivory tower" indifference to the details of real problems is complacent and superficial, not ambitious. The way to avoid complacency is to be cautious about judging people according to whether they fit our vision and relatively quick to judge our vision according to whether it fits people.[2] If our vision is poisonous for people as they are, then we need to stop blaming people for being ill-equipped to survive what we want to give them and start wanting something else.

12.2 Realism About Complacency

Returning to Estlund's case of Slice and Patch, suppose Slice and Patch finish their midnight shift. They are enjoying morning coffee just before leaving for their golf date, but the morning shift has not arrived. What should Slice and Patch do? Suppose they find that the incoming shift's building access is blocked by a picket line, which explains why the incoming shift did not show up. To Slice and Patch, the incoming shift could cross the picket line, should cross it, but predictably will not be able to bring themselves to cross it.

---

[2] Rousseau's (1762) *Social Contract* opens by asking about prospects for legitimate civil order, taking men as they are and laws as they might be, and treating justice as consistent with utility. We can see why Hume would befriend Rousseau in 1766, mistaking him for a fellow traveler on a road to realistic idealism and moral science.

Estlund might say (as he said about the Carens Market) that the defect is not in the plan but in the staff of the incoming shift.

> People could be good, they just aren't. Their failures are avoidable and blameworthy, but also entirely to be expected as a matter of fact. So far, there is no discernible defect in the theory, I believe. For all we have said, the standards to which it holds people might be sound and true. The fact that people won't live up to them even though they could is a defect of the people, not of the theory. (2009, 264)

Estlund has a point, theoretically, but it would be complacent for Slice and Patch to put any weight on it. It's their plan. If it doesn't work, it needs to change.

Estlund says "that a standard won't be met might count against people's behavior rather than against the standard" (2009, 209). For example, Estlund says, we may predict that students will fail our exam without blaming our exam. True. People responding poorly to a standard does not entail that the standard is faulty. Still, noncomplacent reflection on a predictably bad outcome begins with the role we see ourselves playing in making it happen. That students misread double negations is not a defect in our exam but littering our exam with double negations is.

Again, to avoid complacency, don't judge people according to whether they fit your vision. Judge your vision according to whether it fits people. If your double negations confuse students in a way that defeats your exam's purpose, then your exam is not ideal. It's broken and you need to fix it.

12.3 Realism About Optimism

A final thought: Feasibility is dynamic; what cannot be done today may some day be within reach. It is realistic to anticipate shifts in the ceiling of possibility.[3] In 1789, William Wilberforce could not muster the votes to abolish England's slave trade. Yet Wilberforce's faith that England would one day have the will to abolish proved every bit as realistic as it was noncomplacent. Working toward that day was the personal strand—the heroic part—of Wilberforce's morality.[4]

Was Wilberforce overconfident in the justice of his cause? Actually, his *opponents* were overconfident in *their* cause. Majorities are not always wrong, but they are the last to know when they are holding back progress. We underestimate prospects for change more than we overestimate. Visionaries overlook possibilities whose realization was around the corner. Indeed, we can scarcely imagine potentials *already realized*. Many people have a sense that food quality has drastically improved over the years while having no idea that innovations in container shipping reduced from days to minutes the time that food sits rotting at a dockyard while awaiting transfer from truck to ship. For all our theorizing about distribution, utopian imagination pales compared to innovations in our systems of distribution that some shipper is dreaming up as you read this sentence.[5]

---

[3] To Bernard Cohen, Benjamin Franklin's "invention of the lightning rod was the first major or large-scale example in history of Francis Bacon's prediction that advances in science should lead to practical innovations of benefit to mankind" (1987, 182). Asked about the invention's practical potential, Franklin reportedly said, "It is a child who is just born; one cannot say what it will become" (Cohen 1987). I thank Deirdre McCloskey for the example.

[4] A different point: Martin Luther King had a dream that his children would one day be judged by the content of their character. King was dreaming not about legislation but about the humanity of individual people with whom his children would live. King's dream is nowadays rejected by both the extreme right and the extreme left but remains a realistic ideal.

[5] On the contingencies of realistic feasibility, see Prinz and Rossi (2017) and Rossi (2019a).

4

POLITICAL ECONOMY AND
MORAL SCIENCE I

13

The Moral Science of Adam Smith

THEME: *Adam Smith aimed to observe what sort of freedom commercial society makes possible, and what sort of challenge this freedom poses. He also sought to explain why opportunities created by commercial society are as liberating as they are, yet not more so.*

Chapter 1 reflected on the ambition of Hume and Smith to develop an observation-based approach to moral philosophy. The emergence of economics as an autonomous discipline was an unintended consequence of their success. It was only in the late 1800s that theorems became the field's Holy Grail as the mathematical power of neoclassical theory split economics from political economy. Smith produced no theorems about guaranteed market efficiency, and, in this respect, he was no part of the neoclassical tradition he inspired (Hargreaves Heap 2020).

What Smith called self-love was not a simple drive to maximize profit that is so unrealistic yet so apt for cranking out theorems. On Smith's model of a social animal's self-love, pro-social attitudes don't *correct* self-interest; they *define* it. Neoclassical economists equate self-interest with profit maximization when that helps them crank out theorems, but Smith was not in the business of cranking out theorems. He was describing the human condition.

Had Smith been asked what guarantees efficiency, he would have been puzzled and might have said the question is what observably fosters progress, not what logically guarantees it. Had Smith been asked to prove that public regulation is never needed, the implied failure to read what he wrote would have appalled him. Smith's

Living Together. David Schmidtz, Oxford University Press. © Oxford University Press 2023.
DOI: 10.1093/oso/9780197658505.003.0013

actual worry was that people who become referees are themselves players of the game. Smith never doubted that we *need* impartial referees; what he doubted was whether we can *get* them.[1]

Smith's reflections on prospects for autonomy and self-esteem in commercial society inspired its critics almost as much as its defenders. Smith explained how commercial society liberates people in two ways: from starvation and from servility. Smith also observed that commercial society's liberating impact is not guaranteed. For two reasons, commercial society is less liberating in practice than it ideally would be in theory. First, crony capitalism—merchants and monarchs buying and selling political privilege—corrupts the polis. Second, lack of imagination leads people to overlook opportunities for a better life that commercial society offers. Beyond clichés about people wanting too much, Smith's more subtle worry came from observing people wanting too little.

One way to understand Adam Smith's place in history is to see Smith as, arguably, the greatest practitioner of a philosophical approach that Hume was preaching. Smith was a forerunner of what philosophy could have been. Hume and Smith were practicing the art of being observant, but Hume was preparing philosophy to become something more: a moral science guided by controlled experiment. It would not yield theorems. It would not culminate in certainty. Neither would it lay bare the universe's causal structure. At its best, it would identify robust correlation and thus feel its way toward a more informed view of the human condition. Smith evaluated trade barriers by asking whether they correlate

---

[1] Adam Smith did not take for granted the incentive compatibility of market processes. He seemed to see how impartial referees could make market processes incentive-compatible in principle, but he also saw that incentive compatibility for players was not the same thing as incentive compatibility for the game's all-too-human referees. That's why Smith wrote a book (TMS) exhorting public officials to look in the mirror and make sure they like what they see. Smith's discussion is the most insightful I've ever read on how an adult might outgrow a child's way of wanting to be esteemed and thereby rise above corruption.

in lawlike ways to price changes. I imagine Smith saying, "Given how trade barriers and monopoly licenses seem to drive rising prices and rising unemployment, I would not want the world to remember me as defending trade barriers. Observable correlations may not *disprove* the claim that trade barriers are just, but they sure do embarrass it." Smith was as cynical as anyone regarding corporatism's corrupting tendencies, but that did not stop Smith from observing that commercial societies of his time were becoming famine-proof.

13.1 Freedom from Starvation

Ryan Hanley says, "the fundamental departure point for Smith's defense of commercial society is its capacity to provide for the poor" (2009, 18). Smith observed commercial society liberating the poor from desperate need and held that "no society can be flourishing and happy, of which the far greater part of its members are poor and miserable" (WN I.viii.36).

In a village, a poor man's son might grow up to be a doctor, but no one will push the frontier of oral surgery. Why not? Because in villages there aren't enough customers. Specialized trades emerge only where a customer base is large enough to sustain them. To find specialists, we go to a commercial hub such as London. In London, someone who might otherwise be the village carpenter can specialize in crafting violins. Economies of scale make possible fine-grained specialization, thereby fostering new heights of excellence. In port cities, arts proliferate and people innovate because ports are hubs of commerce; they are where cultures meet and where entrepreneurs come looking for ideas (Cowen 1998). When trade goes global, enabling trade with customers by the millions, someone can get rich by inventing the window envelope. Wal-Mart becomes spectacularly profitable not by extracting millions from each customer, but by netting pennies each from untold millions of transactions per day. The trading volume is so huge that Wal-Mart can net billions even if Wal-Mart's customers capture nearly all the surplus value of the individual transactions.

How would we ensure that when London needs more carpenters, more carpenters appear? Smith's answer is one of his signature insights. Given price signals, we check whether there is a problem by checking the price of a carpenter's wage. This simple mechanism, intuitively grasped by everyone who buys and sells, coordinates the productive efforts of people who may share neither a religion nor even a language and who indeed are only dimly aware of each other's existence. A spike in wages of carpenters, in a uniquely reliable way, tells consumers that the community needs them to be more economical in their use of carpentry services while also alerting potential suppliers to a rising need for carpenters. Falling prices, again in a uniquely reliable way, signal suppliers that a community already has all it needs. From such coordination, mediated by freely adjusting price signals, a nation's wealth is made. What any given generation calls poverty will be what previous generations would have called opulence, so that even poor people will have life expectancies exceeding fifty years. Or sixty, seventy, eighty. Perhaps ninety some day.

Where Plato supposed the wealth of nations must depend on a guardian class assigning to each worker tasks appropriate to that worker's nature, it was obvious to Smith that no guardian class could ever know enough to handle such a task. Only a price mechanism can track the incomprehensibly vast flood of daily feedback from buyers and sellers regarding whether x is worth producing and if so where x needs to be shipped to reach consumers to whom x is worth what it costs to get it to them.

Smith concludes (in one of the few explicit uses of the metaphor for which he is most notorious) that high achievers "are led by an invisible hand to make nearly the same distribution of the necessaries of life, which would have been made, had the earth been divided into equal portions among all its inhabitants" (TMS IV.1.10).

13.2 Freedom from Servility

A second freedom transforming Europe's economy by Smith's time was the freedom of ordinary people to contract with persons other than their lord. In a feudal system, if you are born a serf, you are entitled to your lord's protection, but you lack many rights that we take for granted today. In a feudal system at its worst, you live where your lord tells you to live. You grow what the lord tells you to grow. You sell your harvest to the lord *at a price of the lord's choosing*. When you meet your lord, you bow. Your lord does not see you as his equal. Neither do you. As market society supplanted this system, the effect was liberating for all, especially the poor. As Hanley puts it, "commerce substitutes interdependence for direct dependence and makes possible the freedom of the previously oppressed" (2009, 20). Your dependence on a particular lord is replaced by your autonomous interdependence in a loose-knit alliance of customers and suppliers (WN 3, esp. 3.3).

If you choose to work for an employer instead of launching your own business, then you delegate many key decisions to your employer and relegate much of the risk that comes with those decisions. You remain a free agent in the crucial sense that when you decide to leave, you will not need permission. Even as an employee, you are in crucial ways a partner, not a possession. You may not *prefer* being a partner to being a serf. You may feel less secure than you would like. You may feel more responsible than you would like. But you will be free.

In Smith's mind, the strong have subjugated the weak throughout history, but commercial society changed the frontier of possibility in such a way that the strong now care less about social class and more about potential trading partners. To Hanley, "this fascination with and gratitude for the harnessing of the powers of the strong for the relief of the weak is the fundamental fact uniting Smith's seemingly separate defenses of commercial society and of his specific vision of virtue. [Commercial societies] promote not only universal opulence but also a universal freedom of which the weak are the principal beneficiaries" (2009, 19).

Bottom line: freedom in commercial society involves *depending* on many yet being at the *mercy* of none.

13.3 Freedoms Threatened

Yet the clarity of Smith's insight into the liberating power of markets notwithstanding, Smith is no cheerleader but is instead among history's most probing critics of commercial society even as he so insightfully defends it. That is, a society of free and responsible persons must solve a twofold problem. First, people tend to be too intent on running other people's lives. Second, people are insufficiently intent on properly running their own. One problem corrupts the city; the other corrupts the soul. This pair of problems is a focus of Smith's two major works.

13.3.1 Corrupting the City

Smith sees the soul of a community as vulnerable in two ways. First, crony capitalists end up being pirates rather than producers. Protectionists lobby for tariffs and other trade barriers. Mercantilists lobby for export subsidies. Monopolists pay kings for licenses to be free from competition altogether. Partnerships between big business and big government lead to big subsidies. These ways of compromising freedom inevitably are touted as protecting the middle class, but their true purpose will be to transfer wealth and power from ordinary citizens to well-connected elites. Smith still sees commercial societies as the ones where "the person who either acquires or succeeds to a great fortune does not *necessarily* acquire or succeed to any political power" (WN I.v.3, emphasis added). But Smith also remarks on how it pays crony capitalists to stifle competition:

To widen the market and to narrow the competition is always the interest of the dealers. To widen the market may frequently be agreeable enough to the interest of the public; but to narrow the competition must always be against it, and can serve only to enable the dealers, by raising their profits above what they naturally would be, to levy, for their own benefit, an absurd tax upon the rest of their fellow-citizens. The proposal of any new law or regulation of commerce which comes from this order, ought always to be listened to with great precaution, and ought never to be adopted till after having been long and carefully examined, not only with the most scrupulous, but with the most suspicious attention. It comes from an order of men, whose interest is never exactly the same with that of the public, who have generally an interest to deceive and even to oppress the public, and who accordingly have, upon many occasions, both deceived and oppressed it. (WN I.xi.p.10)

Resistance to such oppression requires eternal vigilance with no hope of permanent victory.

People of the same trade seldom meet together, even for merriment and diversion, but the conversation ends in a conspiracy against the public, or in some contrivance to raise prices. It is impossible indeed to prevent such meetings, by any law which either could be executed, or would be consistent with liberty and justice. But though the law cannot hinder people of the same trade from sometimes assembling together, it ought to do nothing to facilitate such assemblies; much less to render them necessary. (WN I.x.c.27)

Unfortunately, kings wanting to fight wars employing expensive mercenaries are driven to sell monopoly licenses to raise money. This is a singularly unhappy dynamic. It leads kings to adopt policies favoring merchants who have lost their economic edge, since inferior competitors are the ones eager to pay the king for protection from superior competitors. As Hume saw, easy transfer of external goods was both opportunity and risk (*Treatise*, 3.2.2.16). It enables crony capitalists to enlist the help of kings in bureaucratizing piracy and making it seem routine.

A second dimension of the threat to the city is that public servants can become "men of system": they treat fellow citizens as pawns to be patronized (or worse) and they in turn eventually become pawns of crony capitalists. As Fleischacker says, "the limitations Smith describes on what anyone can know about their society should give pause to those who are confident that governments can carry out even the task of protecting freedom successfully. Taken together with his scepticism about the judiciousness, decency, and impartiality of those who go into politics, this is what gives punch to the libertarian reading of Smith" (2004, 235, 233).[2] To Smith, a "man of system"

> is apt to be very wise in his own conceit. . . . He seems to imagine that he can arrange the different members of a great society with as much ease as the hand arranges the different pieces upon a chessboard. He does not consider that the pieces upon the chessboard have no other principle of motion besides that which the hand impresses upon them; but that, in the great chessboard of human society, every single piece has a principle of motion of its own, altogether different from that which the legislature might cause to impress upon it. (TMS VI.ii.2.17)

Men of system move "pawns" in pursuit of their goals, but the "pawns" respond as if they have minds of their own, which, after all, they do. They respond with a view to their own hopes and dreams, but also their own sense of what their society is about and where

---

[2] On fancying oneself fit to impose a central plan, see also WN IV.ii.10 and WN IV.ix.51.

it needs to go (TMS VI.ii.2.17).[3] So, public spirit leads people to respect traditions but also to want to see institutions perfected. In peaceful times the potential conflict between these two public-spirited impulses is no problem. But they come apart in times of strife, and, when they do, a "man of system" gripped by a vision of perfection can do real damage. Irritated by the pawns' contrarian response, men of system adjust, now seeking more to dominate pawns than to assist, and any virtue these would-be public servants initially brought to public office withers. Over time, an ordinary citizen's everyday dealings are less with equal trading partners and more with tyrannical bureaucrats. It is as if we reinvent feudalism and once again are at the mercy of lords. On one reading of Smith, the benevolent "man of public spirit" sees what a man of system misses: that representing one's personal vision as a consensus, then using that delusion to justify imposing it, is an act of violence.

Thus, there is a predictable if not inevitable disconnect between what truly benevolent people seek and what men of system deliver, as an office's logic aligns bureaucratic interests with those of "dealers" rather than the general public. To Smith, law cannot circumvent this logic, but law can at least avoid requiring dealers and bureaucratic men of system to be driven by it.

Smith was by no means extreme in his pessimism about the prospect of good governance. He was merely a realist. Above all, he saw the limits of a government's power to limit itself. He outlines a role for civil magistrates in upholding a commercial society's infrastructure of limited government (e.g., TMS II.ii.1.8), expressing hope, if not confidence, that magistrates will take to heart his message regarding their proper role. And they might; after all, they, too, have an expansive as well as a narrow self-love and, among other things, aim to earn self-esteem. Smith likewise reflects (e.g., TMS IV.1.11)

---

[3] My remarks here about the matrix of habit and tradition that thwarts best-laid plans are indebted to Jacob Levy (2015, chaps. 3 and 7). See also Vincent Ostrom's (1997) discussion of "habits of the heart" and shared meaning.

on what it would take to instruct people in the art of true public spirit. When he says this, he is self-consciously offering this very instruction to would-be public servants for whom he was writing.

13.3.2 Corrupting the Person
We discussed problems with crony capitalists and with bureaucratic men of system that divide a community against itself. A person's soul likewise can be divided against itself.

1. *First, after acquiring enough to meet genuine needs, workers tend to keep working.* Why? For one thing, they yearn to amass enough wealth to be more visible. Smith observes the "poor man's son" whose drive for visibility translates into a simplistic drive to *win* (TMS IV.1.8). The poor man's son is an embryonic form of both crony capitalist and man of system, the seed from which they grow. Tormented by untutored ambition, a son's quest for opulence comes to revolve around keeping up with the Joneses (or taking them down a peg) rather than around a meaningful life. And Smith sees poor man's sons everywhere. While success and wealth may "strike the imagination as something grand and beautiful and noble" (TMS IV.1.9), this useful illusion induces us to produce more than we need, selling our surplus to customers who have more use for it. Thus, Smith is glad people work as hard as they do for their customers but laments that people have so little regard for themselves.

One aspect of Smith's lament is that, in contributing to a community, we can lose our grip on the fact that it is our life. At the heart of liberalism is an idea that to respect persons as persons is to acknowledge that they have lives of their own. We show up for work as volunteers and normally retain a robust right to say no and walk away. If we lose our grip on this aspect of our sense of self, we are a short step from feeling alienated and oppressed.[4]

---

[4] I thank Jennifer Baker for the thought.

People working overtime for trinkets make our world a better place even while missing opportunities to enjoy their earnings in more self-fulfilling ways. Part of Smith's worry over the quest for trinkets is that it confuses the faux visibility that comes from conspicuous consumption with earning the true self-love that comes from conspicuous achievement.

We grow up aiming to be loved. *Adulthood* is the threshold we cross when our drive to be loved matures into the fully adult aim of being lovely. Baubles impress neighbors, but to impress ourselves, we need to stand for something.[5]

What makes market society unique, however, is not that it alienates but that it raises the frontier of human possibility. The fact that we achieve so much less than we could is partly a function of how much we have been liberated to achieve. Market society gives us free time to indulge such laments, but Smith's observing that we fail to hit the rising ceiling of our potential was a lament, not a damnation—not even a critique so much as a reflection on how much capitalism makes possible yet also how little it guarantees. In a free society, people accept (1) that they inhabit a world thick with possibilities (and responsibilities) and (2) that not all possibilities will be realized. We trust people to do their best. We accept that many won't.[6]

Rising productivity creates a new possibility: leisure time. Using leisure time well is a skill. Developing that skill is an achievement.[7] People and cultures both need practice to realize these new potentials. The surpassing compliment Smith wants to pay to commercial society is that workers, even in failing to be all they could be, make life better for their trading partners.

---

[5] This is essentially Adam Smith's idea, but I thank Mario Juarez for helpful discussion.

[6] Smith lamented that, for typical laborers, "their work through half the week is sufficient to maintain them, and through want of education they have no amusement for the other but riot and debauchery" (1982, 540).

[7] Smith makes the point implicitly, and only in TMS. It fell to Marx to press the point with unforgettable force.

2. *Second, specialization unlocks the benefits of human civilization*, but Marx would come to share Smith's worry that repetitive factory floor work would make minds drowsy. (Had Smith anticipated automation, of course, he would have worried less about drowsiness, since "drowsy" jobs are the ones that automation eliminates.) Smith's classic statement: One who spends a career on an assembly line has,

> . . . no occasion to exert his understanding or to exercise his invention in finding out expedients for removing difficulties which never occur. He naturally loses, therefore, the habit of such exertion, and generally becomes as stupid and ignorant as it is possible for a human creature to become. (WN V.i.f.50)

According to E. G. West, Smith feared that, without education, factory workers will have no idea what to fight for and will be dupes of (equally uneducated) populist revolutionaries (1975, 296). To West, "the root of alienation in Rousseau as in Marx—is economic interdependence and exchange based on private property" (West 1975, 297). To Smith, by contrast, "property, wealth, and commodity production are preconditions for the non-alienated state. And in this state individuals pursue refinement and art" (West 1975, 298). Thus, what may strike a Marxist as a dreary quest for marginal productivity increments becomes an art form, a healthy expression of a creative quest for excellence. Those who innovate experience commercial and technological breakthroughs as successive affirmations of their commitment to excellence, not as turns in a cosmic rat race.

3. *Marx anticipated, as did Smith, that alienation would not be confined to the factory floor* but eventually would be found even among well-paid white-collar workers. Alienation does not require dismal working conditions. It happens in posh offices to executives who no longer interact directly with tangible products and satisfied customers. It happens to investors, as investing starts to feel more like gambling than like helping creators turn ideas into embodied

excellence. Indeed, large organizations spawn legions of "Dilberts" whose main challenge every day is to cover their tracks in large bureaucracies where the ambition to deliver a great product is replaced by an ambition to secure a less vulnerable position in an office hierarchy.[8]

4. *Less obviously, and previewing* Chapter 14, *a different risk to our soul goes with the fact that one of life's great pleasures is finding kindred souls*—comrades with whom we reach a concurrence of sentiment (Otteson 2002, 207). Desire for concord runs deep. We tend not to notice how we adjust our attitudes to fit those of people around us. If we *notice* ourselves "going along to get along" then we can resist, or at least go along self-consciously. But if we do not even notice ourselves adjusting as needed to be agreeable company, it limits our ability to master this ever-present threat to our autonomy. The abdication is driven by self-preservation, yet also by a deficiency of self-love. It is only human to do whatever it takes to avoid being outcasts. So, when colleagues or teachers apply pressure, it is only human to voice no resistance and be willing to do *or believe* whatever it takes to qualify as team players. We then grasp at reasons to agree, however flimsy, to make the depth of our capitulation less humiliating (Haidt 2012). Pressure warps minds. To let oneself be corrupted by such pressure is to let oneself become a self that one cannot afford to examine too closely.

People thus corrupted are shallow and cannot afford to be anything other than shallow. As accurate self-perception becomes less affordable, a corrupt person *needs* to be less self-aware and less reflective. When one looks inward, there is not enough there to be worth being aware of. Cowardice under pressure is as corrupting as raw greed and, if anything, even more shattering.

---

[8] See https://dilbert.com, Scott Adams's comic strip depicting the disconcertingly familiar follies of an engineer lost in a corporate bureaucracy. I thank Eric Mack for making the connection.

Likewise from the perspective of a community: passively silent cowardice at one extreme can be more lethal to a community than active greed at the other. Yet, as James Otteson (2002, 298) observes, Smith also sees our sociality as a key to accurate self-perception. It drives us to take stock (Hanley 2009, 137).

> Were it possible that a human creature could grow up to man-hood in some solitary place, without any communication with his own species, he could no more think of his own character, of the propriety or demerit of his own sentiments and conduct, of the beauty or deformity of his own mind, than of the beauty or deformity of his own face. . . . Bring him into society, and he is immediately provided with the mirror which he wanted before. It is . . . here that he first views the propriety and impropriety of his own passions, the beauty and deformity of his own mind. (TMS III.1.3)

The image is haunting. *Human* life is *social* life. Humans are observant animals inescapably aware of being observed by other observant animals. Thus, the life of a trader who needs suppliers and customers but needs no particular trading partner is as in-dependent a life form as a rational agent wants. We may not have what it takes to be indifferent to whether we are visible to others, but we may have something more noble: an ability to distinguish between knowing we are esteemed and knowing we deserve es-teem. To Smith, wanting to be validated by others is healthy to a point because it can drive our maturation through a certain stage.[9]

---

[9] Smith treats the prior stage of socialization as a necessary stage through which maturing humans must pass in order to emerge as grown-up members of society. (It is tempting to read this as anticipating Nietzsche: the will to power drives a person to tran-scend the ideal types of unself-conscious "beast" on one hand and "ascetic priest" on the other, emerging from the process as a turned-inward exemplar of Stoic self-discipline.)

But soon enough we need to outgrow that impulse. Why? Because to care too much about validation is to be controlled by the hoped-for source of validation. Maturing children properly feel a need to insinuate themselves into socializing networks, but, for an adult, the liberating ideal is an ideal of being true to oneself. We must know ourselves well enough to know that sympathy for false facades is not what we want. It is our real core selves for which we want to make a place. It is hard to beat feeling like one belongs, but adulthood is knowing there is something better: having nothing to hide. My earlier remark about what a shame it can be to want too little was mainly about what a shame it can be to ask too little of oneself. We spend our lives writing a story, choosing as we go whether to be that story's hero. Heroes do not live forever, of course, but neither do cowards. What we choose is what to be along the way.

Our need for recognition leaves us open to disappointments. First, when a partner appeals directly to my benevolence rather than my interest, the relationship is all about recognizing my partner; its failure to sustain me materially translates into a failure to sustain me emotionally as well. I am being treated as a mere means, a resource. I am invisible.

Second, if I start to feel like a feudal serf, having no choice about with whom I do business or at what price—if I do not merely depend on others but have a sense of being at their *mercy*—then that is another way for relationships to become alienating rather than affirming. Moreover, this is true even if the feeling of being exploited is merely a feeling with no factual basis.

Third, if my way of making partners better off involves no special *alertness*—if I feel like a cog, endlessly repeating a mindless task of someone else's design—then I do not feel visible as an esteemed member of a community of estimable traders. That, too, leads me to stop caring about the excellence of my craft. I fail to realize my potential as a citizen of a commercial society and instead become the kind of creature that Marx and Dickens deplored. In sum, Smith's and Marx's concerns are related, albeit not identical. It is easy to see why Smith would have inspired Marx as he did.[10]

13.4 Self-Love

Smith's second book seems to treat self-interest as the fundamental motivation, while his first book privileges sympathy and a drive to earn esteem. Is this an inconsistency?[11] No. Here is the argument.

13.4.1 Is Self-Interest Fundamental?

To Smith, the so-called profit motive was not as fundamental a psychological foundation as typical readings of *Wealth of Nations* suggest. Strikingly, when Smith opens WN, Book I, chapter 2, his opening remark explains the emergence of a division of labor. His explanation refers not to a profit motive but to a propensity to truck and barter.

> This division of labour, from which so many advantages are de-
> rived, is not originally the effect of any human wisdom, which
> foresees and intends the general opulence to which it gives
> occasion. It is the necessary, though very slow and gradual

---

[10] I thank Dan Brudney (but don't hold him responsible) for the intriguing thought that "from each according to ability to each according to need" is not a principle of distribution but a description of how an economy ideally would work. People consume as necessary to sustain their best work. But communism is Marx's *ideal* theory; socialism is his nonideal theory. Idealist Marx does not care about the size of shares because, in an ideal post-capitalist world, goods are no longer scarce, so shares are immaterial. Rawls, by contrast, is all about distributing, and he aggressively denies that shares should track contribution. Circa 1844, realist Marx is like Rawls insofar as realist Marx treats justice as all about distribution, but unlike Rawls insofar as realist Marx was furious about workers getting less than they deserve. This ultimately is why Rawls's question of why workers should accept anything less than an equal *share* is not realist Marx's question. The question for realist Marx is why workers should accept the indignity of how their *productivity* is treated.

[11] See Otteson (2002, chap. 4). See also Leonidas Montes (2004, chap. 2).

consequence of a certain propensity in human nature which has in view no such extensive utility; the propensity to truck, barter, and exchange one thing for another. (WN, Book I, chap. 2)

This propensity, Smith says, is a necessary attribute of social beings whose ability to cooperate is mediated by faculties of reason and speech. To Smith, trucking and bartering is not grounded in a profit motive but is instead a primordial drive—our essence as social beings.[12] This is not what cartoon clichés of Smith as an apostle of profit would lead one to expect.

This drive to truck and barter is not about making money but about making *deals*. It is a drive to reciprocate favors, cultivate allies, and be part of a concord among trustworthy reciprocators who warrant esteem and whose good will is thus worth something. A merchant learns to show up with something that makes the community a better place for everyone with whom that merchant deals. The result may be no part of a merchant's intention, as Smith says in places, but neither is a successful merchant's intention simply a matter of self-absorbed acquisitiveness. A person of true benevolence puts herself in a customer's shoes not merely for the sake of predicting what customers will find irresistible but for the sake of anticipating how to make sure her partners are better off with her than without her. That is what enables a merchant to go home after working all day to be of service to strangers, look in the mirror, and like what she sees, having affirmed that she is good at what she does and that her community needed her to be good. When she dies, she will pass from this earth knowing that it is good she was here.[13]

By contrast, being tormented by raw ambition—a naked desire to be envied, undisciplined by a desire to be praise*worthy*—is a lamentable condition. Something is wrong with the poor man's son, and it may have no remedy. Worries about lack of authenticity

---

[12] I owe the point to Geoff Brennan (in conversation).
[13] See also Otteson 2002, ch. 3.

remain to haunt any reflective person, and there is no such thing as addressing it "once and for all." And yet we do have what it takes to worry about the possibility and at least to want to avoid being that kind of person. We spend a lot of time grooming. Some of that quiet time is for reflecting on what lies beneath the surface.

13.4.2 Is Benevolence Fundamental?

Second, it makes perfect sense for the author whose first book treated benevolence as primary to subsequently ask how to respond benevolently to trading partners. Why, as a benevolent person hoping to truck and barter with brewers and bakers, do you address their self-love? Answer: Because you want them to be better off for having come to you. Notice that Smith does not say bakers are motivated solely by self-love. He says we *address ourselves* not to their benevolence but to their self-love (WN, Book I, chap. 2). This is a reflection on our psychology, not theirs. He is offering insight not into the self-love of bakers but into what it takes to be benevolent in our dealings with them.

In sum, the author of *Moral Sentiments* gives center stage to virtue and benevolence, but, in elaborating what benevolence means, the author of *Wealth of Nations* belabors the obvious: namely, a man of true benevolence wants his partners to be better off with him than without him. The point of addressing other people's self-love is to give other people their due. That's what it's like to succeed in one's attempt to be sympathetic.

A harmony of interests among free people is not to be taken for granted yet is manifestly a real possibility. So long as people can see a way of building a community of partners who are better off with them than without them, and so long as they cherish the hope of carving out such a grand role for themselves, their skill in honoring each other's self-love will bring them together to form a free and thriving community.

Thus, we do not take magnanimity for granted. We encourage magnanimity by working to make it safe for people to believe in each other. We make our community robust by crafting institutions and a culture that do not depend unnecessarily on our magnanimity. What helps is people being free to decide for themselves whom to trust and being free to exit relationships where trust proves misplaced. That's when they can afford the risk of entering relationships in the first place.

Conclusion

Smith has a story about the wealth of nations: how wealth grows, liberating us in the process, but also how we fail to take full advantage of opportunities for liberation that wealth creates. Smith sees commercial society emerging, liberating people economically from shackles of destitution and culturally from vestiges of feudalism. He sees commercial society's potential to liberate us psychologically from the twin shackles of materialism and social pressure. So, market society teaches us how to create wealth. But will we teach ourselves what wealth is for? Will we teach ourselves that money can buy time?

So long as people are trading freely—that is, just in case their partners consent—they will be led as if by an invisible hand to do right by their trading partners. Yet they are *not* led as if by an invisible hand to do right by themselves. Practicing self-love in ways newly made possible by technological and commercial progress is life's greatest challenge. Markets throw down the challenge; nothing guarantees that we will rise to meet it.

14

The Political Economy of Corruption

THEME: *After Mill, academic theorizing about justice became an exercise in imagining how, ideally, to slice a pie. Could this be a bias? As an alternative to this blinding abstraction from the ongoing process of living together, what if our theorizing began with a truism that power corrupts? If power corrupts, then, ideally, how much power to slice the pie would there be?*

This chapter works toward an anatomy of corruption. After a remark on concentrated versus dispersed power, we canvass varieties of corruption. We observe that greed, the paradigmatically rotten motive, is but one among several corrupting vices, the subtle cost of which is a loss of self-awareness. We observe this loss of self-awareness afflicting organizations as well as individuals. The downfall of many an institution involves losing a sense of mission, such that an organization qua agent falls apart. Wanting to avoid this loss can motivate grasping for more concentrated power in a bid to unify corporate agency, but this often does more harm than good. It treats as spectators those agents on the ground who need to play—and play well—if a society is to prosper. We consider remedies for problems of concentrated power. Finally, we extend Chapter 3's contrast between justice and conflict resolution. We have reason to treat conflict resolution, not justice, as the first virtue of institutions. Otherwise, in the name of justice, we systematically confer more power on leaders than a society properly can afford.[1]

---

[1] This extends Chapter 13 on how cowardice corrupts, previews Chapter 15 on property and conflict resolution, and reflects many conversations with Mario Juarez.

Living Together. David Schmidtz, Oxford University Press. © Oxford University Press 2023.
DOI: 10.1093/oso/9780197658505.003.0014

14.1 Concentrated Power: The Cure That Is the Disease

Which social arrangements have a history of fostering progress and prosperity? One quick answer, falsely attributed to Adam Smith, holds that we are guided as if by an invisible hand to do what builds the wealth of nations. A more sober answer, closer to what Smith said and believed, is that *if* we have the right framework of rules—plus decent officiating—steering us away from seeking monopoly privileges and toward being of service to the people around us, we indeed will be part of the engine driving progress and a rising wealth of nations.

However, to have a rule of law framework within which commerce can grow a healthy nation, officials must exercise oversight. Officials not only enforce rules, but also interpret, amend, and so on. Smith saw this and perceived a further chronically tragic reality: this power to oversee markets is what crony capitalists are buying and selling.

Smith's observation changes everything. Imagine concentrated power in the hands of the worst ruler you can remember. Now, assume what you know to be true: concentrated power has a history of falling into hands like that. As a preliminary, then, when theorizing about what is politically ideal, we can ask two questions. (1) "Ideally, how much power would be wielded by people like *that*?" Or (2) "Ideally, how much power would be wielded by ideal rulers?"

Which of these two versions of ideal theory is a real question? Can political philosophy answer the one that truly needs answering?[2]

Why isn't it trying?

---

[2] To Woodrow Wilson, "the object of administrative study [is] to discover, first, what government can properly and successfully do, and, secondly how it can do these things with the utmost possible efficiency and the least possible cost" (1887, 197). Wilson's ideal was blind to the likelihood that power to impose an agenda with "utmost efficiency" would be weaponized. To Wilson, Napoleon's administration was an ideal (Wilson 1887, 205). He scorned English scholars for studying "the art of curbing executive power to the

14.2 Corruptions

Plato's *Republic* launched Western philosophy with a reflection on
the corruption of the soul and the city. An organization employs
officials to speak and make decisions on its behalf. *Corruption*
involves being entrusted by the public with discretionary power,
then using that power in service of a personal agenda.[3]

The paradigm of corruption consists of officials treating discretionary public authority as a service to buy and sell for personal
gain (Schwartz, 2004, 173). Officials may be tasked with making it
easier to transact with organizations they represent, but when corrupt officials regard authority as a service they are at liberty to *sell*,
they treat themselves as *licensed* to make it harder.

Yet paradigms are not definitions. Greed is one member of a
family of corrupting vices, but appointing your brother as Attorney
General may cross a line without being an example of greed. (There
is no rule against hiring the best candidate, but if you think the
best candidate is your brother, should you recuse yourself?) Or
politicians may ignore a leader's crimes out of party loyalty, which
is corrupt regardless of whether it is done for personal gain.

Other vices likewise need not involve greed but still look rotten.
Petty tyrants sometimes shrug and say, "rules are rules; what can
you do?" when in fact their job is to *get things done*, which includes
the latitude to grant exceptions as required by circumstances not
anticipated by those who made the rules. Pretending to lack discretionary power is a way of exercising discretionary power, which at
some point becomes an abuse.

constant neglect of the art of perfecting executive methods" (1887, 206). He saw ideals of
separated powers, even a constitution, as relics of a pre-scientific age (1887, 200–02). If
Robert Putnam had told Wilson, "Citizenship is not a spectator sport" (1990, 341), I imagine Wilson would have replied "Of course it is. Modern administration is an arena for
the best and brightest."

[3] I would not call this a sufficient condition. It may be necessary. I think it represents
how most readers expect to see the word used.

Sometimes a rotten motivation is hostile. Imagine county officials going the extra mile to make it gratuitously hard for minorities to register to vote. Petty tyrants, officiously withholding what isn't theirs to withhold, are not the same as those who sell what isn't theirs to sell. Yet both are abuses of power from rotten motive.[4]

Sometimes a vacuum of reason is more corrupting than spurious reason. Some officials are dead to the honor of being good at their jobs. They show up aiming to collect a paycheck or to kill time until retirement. They do not even aim to get the job done so much as to comply with job requirements and avoid being sued. They may bear no ill will, but they are useless.

A different corruption is manifested by junior colleagues treating every decision (to go to lunch, serve on a committee, help a student, *or profess a commitment to scholarship*) as a means to the end of getting tenure. Professors thus obsessed tend to fall apart upon receiving tenure. They aim to meet tenure requirements, but that is the wrong aim. When work has a scholarly component, then a prerequisite of deserving tenure is a driving scholarly ambition that will survive getting it.

In sum, using public office for private gain is a paradigm of corruption, not a definition. We naturally reason about paradigms, but philosophers are trained to reason about definitions. Be that as it may, when we aim to illuminate how the moral fiber of people in positions of responsibility can decay, we gain nothing by trying to define corruption so narrowly that we confuse the concept with its paradigm. Corruption can be a child of greed, to be sure, but also of other vices.

---

[4] What if the motive is not rotten? What if an official abuses power for reasons she finds morally compelling? Suppose someone in Personnel treats her conviction that abortion is murder as reason to sabotage applicants who had abortions: Not a paradigm of corruption, on my account. Still, even those who classify abortion as murder can see it as abuse.

14.3 Agency

An organization need not be vast to be corruptible. Expanding the parts of an organization from one to two, with the second part having a degree of power, responsibility, and discretion, is all it takes to create a possibility of corruption. To create a *principal–agent* relationship, and a consequent prospect of corruption, it takes only two: one principal and one agent.

More radically, where I say it takes only two, Plato says it only takes one! When Plato wrote about justice in the polis as a "writ large" model of justice in the soul, the paradigm of injustice to Plato was an individual soul divided against itself. Plato's discussion is archaic in some ways. Yet, I observe, people who speak of corruption presuppose that the motive is *rotten*, in a state of decomposition.[5] That seems natural from a Platonic perspective. To Plato, what makes a tyrant unjust is what makes a tyrant corrupt: the tyrant's soul is decomposing, falling apart, losing its unifying purposiveness. We need not entirely trust Plato's analogy. Yet note how it illuminates the political case. When an official accepts bribes under the table, the agency for which the official works becomes less transparent to itself. The agency is a soul out of touch with itself.

Needed regulations add new layers to an already complex regulatory ecosystem. Term-limited representatives are not around long enough to learn the system. So the only people who have a clue about how the system works or what would reform it are captains of industry who have spent their careers gaming the system. Thus we vest in captains of industry unrivaled power to stifle upstart competitors. Incredibly, *that* is our response to not trusting

---

[5] Mark Knights (2019, also personal communication) finds political cartoons in the mid-1600s beginning to depict soliciting bribes for timely performance as apt to make observers sick to their stomach, as if they had eaten something rotten (i.e., corrupted). Bureaucrats such as Samuel Pepys defended themselves by noting that they were serving the king (in Pepys case, handling the Navy payroll) as essentially unpaid volunteers, so receiving gifts and expressions of appreciation from clients was openly accepted standard practice.

captains of industry to regulate themselves. The loss of collective self-awareness is compromised agency. The left hand does not know what the right hand is doing, and the right hand wants it that way. As per Chapter 13, agency requires internal transparency, and corruption compromises transparency.

14.4 Agency Is an Achievement

I once heard an interview on National Public Radio. The guest was an expert in screening job candidates. Among the guest's survey questions: "If I had an opportunity to steal $20,000 from my company with no chance of being caught, I'd steal the money. True or false?"

NPR's perplexed interviewer said, why would you even ask? Every applicant says False, so why bother? The guest replied: on the contrary, about twenty percent of applicants admit they would steal. NPR's now-astounded interviewer asked why applicants would admit that. Paraphrasing from memory, the guest said, "All I know is, twenty percent say they would steal the money. My speculation is that applicants realize the survey is testing their honesty. Then they guess that the way to portray themselves as *relatively* honest is by admitting what seems obvious: like everyone else, they would steal."

I hear stories like this as indicating corruption's ultimate price. Warped by habits of corruption, you reach a point where you are so far from being honest that you no longer remember what honesty would be like. When you can't remember what honesty is like, you can't remember how to fake it either. You are falling apart. The self-awareness that comes with internal transparency is an achievement, not simply a decision.[6]

---

[6] In passing, we treat transparency as a policy instrument with which we fight corruption. But what if that mistakes correlation for causation? What if transparency is more an effect of corruption's defeat than a cause of it?

This undermining of agency can be a danger to organizations and individuals alike. Suppose your job involves balancing your unit's budget, and one of your tools involves collecting fees from other units within the organization. You may wake up one day to find that your job is to cannibalize other units. You need not be a monster to find yourself in such a position. It may happen as a consequence of supervisors restructuring your responsibilities. They need not be at fault either. They may be trying to impose fiscal accountability and discipline as part of an effort to *combat* corruption.

Some organizations are usefully seen as agents.[7] But as a corporation comes to lack both the appearance and reality of being on a mission, it stops resembling an agent. As with individuals, weakness of will—executive will—compromises the potential to be an agent with a unified purpose. Notice: where we lack reason to call x an agent, we also lack reason (linguistic habit aside) to call x an organization. In truth, x is a dysfunctional mess.

Finally, there are times when officials exercising discretionary power cannot simply follow rules for they have no uncontested interpretation of the law's letter or spirit. Suppose you are a compliance officer administering a grant, and a grantee asks you to look the other way while the grantee spends the money on an unauthorized but manifestly more effective way of serving the grant's purpose. Fill in the details to make the case as compelling as you like. The risk of emerging from that situation as more or less corrupt is real whichever way you decide—lazy and irresponsible if you go one way, a pompous bureaucrat if you go the other. Having fiduciary responsibility plus discretionary power and remaining uncorrupted over time is not easy.

---

[7] Philip Pettit believes in group agency. This is controversial, yet provides an intriguing vocabulary for talking about corruption of organizations. I thank Pettit for conversations over the years.

14.5 Who Are the Players?

As with sports, if the game inspires, it will be by virtue of what comes from letting the players play. The idea of giving officials the power to push our agenda is a fantasy because the power we give them to push our agenda is in fact power to push theirs. When officials push their agenda, other players are relegated to the sidelines waiting to see how it all plays out. (Schmidtz and Goodin 1998, chap. 1.4.3). Rich spectators tire of watching the madness from the sidelines and get into the legislative game in the only way they can: by buying and selling influence.

There is no use lamenting that valuable commodities are bought and sold or that power is a valuable commodity. What is disconcerting is that power's corrosiveness is proportionate to scale. More power commands a higher price, notwithstanding cosmetic tweaks to campaign finance laws. Why do candidates spend ever more on campaigns? Is it because regulators are more lax than ever? Or is it because the prize keeps getting bigger?

When political power is worth billions, billionaires will compete for it. It stands to reason that the process by which people gain political appointment would systematically, and *increasingly*, tend to select the wrong person for the job.

In sum, the truism that power corrupts implies that randomly selected officers would be corruptible. The more realistic worry, however, is worse. Namely, the process of selecting officers is not random. We *select* for corruption. It is the most ravenous fox, not a randomly selected fox, who tends to be willing to pay the most to win a contest for the right to oversee the henhouse.[8] Political debate then devolves into hens lobbying the fox to devour other hens first. Some candidates may be noble, but we won't be able to sort

---

[8] If anything, the most ravenous fox is also adept at convincing voters (for whom politics has become "infotainment") that they have nothing to lose by giving a charismatic leader more power. When a fox can make voters see politics as a team sport and the fox as the home team, voters seem to cheer even as the fox devours them.

them out. Like every other candidate, *bought* politicians denounce corruption and name names, but they pick names with a view to ruining the lives of rivals of their buyers.[9]

14.6 Is There an Alternative?

So, what else is there? Is any power not a license to treat subjects of that power like pawns? Is there any power that does not corrupt? I see one decent—although neither original nor fully satisfactory— answer. Powers defining liberal equal citizenship (a right to say no, a right to exit, constitutional limits on executive power) are as innocuous as power can be. These powers *limit* rather than extend the reach of those who would treat us as pawns. Arguably, these are powers worth endorsing. Such power as they embody is dispersed, not concentrated.[10]

The constitutional part of constitutional democracy is the part that enshrines these powers. So the constitutional part is the liberal part—when there is a liberal part. Democracy is premised on a core of individual rights not subject to the whim of a shifting majority. *We are a democracy only if some things are off the table.* Winning does not give the winning party a right to vote on whether a minority should lose its right to vote. In a liberal democracy, citizens can count on their status as equal citizens not being up for grabs every time someone can bring a motion to a vote.

You bind legislators because you don't want legislatures to be where the action is. Living in a free country involves letting rules

---

[9] I thank Majid Jafar for the observation that in developing nations, power buys money, and the most corrupt lives are studies in ostentatious opulence, whereas, in developed nations, money buys power, and corruption is more discreet.

[10] America's Framers aimed to create tools (including tools for fighting corruption) not easily weaponized by corrupt or overzealous officeholders. Seeing the problem, while seeing no real solution, the Framers strove to devise the most modest set of tools that would suffice to launch a viable nation and also to devise a set of tools such that any given tool of concentrated, corruptible power might counteract rather than amplify the power of other such tools (Juarez 2021).

settle down and become a matrix of mutual expectations around which real players make plans and within which real players make moves that lift their communities to the next level. By contrast, to the extent that legislators become the players, citizens become spectators regarding decisions that shape their lives. The right to say no to that logic is as liberal a right as there is.

Montesquieu and America's founders saw dispersed power as less corrupting than concentrated power. They sought to create a system of divided sovereignty, monitored by a free press, so that no ruler could rule with impunity simply by executive order. The idea was enough to blow the ceiling off the human condition as we knew it in the 1700s.

Yet there is a factual limit on how concentrated power can be. Why? Because concentrating power at the top entails delegating executive power to operatives on the ground. The result is a proliferation of corruptible middle managers and local politicians combined with decreasing ability to gather enough information to effectively monitor local conditions from a hierarchical top (Pennington, 2021). Legislators likewise delegate to regulatory agencies the task of making a bill of legislation work in practice when no one knows the bill in any detail, not even legislators themselves (Lawson, 2021).

This suggests an intriguing (if confusing) possibility: corruptibility is as much a function of power delegated as of power concentrated.[11] Still, it is where discretionary power is concentrated that we find the threat, regardless of whether power has been delegated. Nodes of discretionary power may exist by virtue of delegation, but, to people below, the danger posed by a node remains a function of power concentrated in that node. Thus, *delegated* power is not what Montesquieu and America's founders had in mind. They sought to institutionalize mutual accountability. They saw that a separation of powers can persist only as an ongoing hard-fought achievement,

[11] I owe this insight to Jacob Levy (in conversation).

not as a simple decision. They saw that it takes eternal vigilance to sustain experiments in democracy in moments of crisis. In any case, they aimed more for dispersal than for delegation. They might have seen the 20th-century regulatory state's consolidation of power in the executive branch as the capturing of American democracy by an unelected elite. (Chapter 16 extends discussion of the regulatory state.)

14.7 From Justice in Theory

Robert Frank once reported being baffled that I would reject modest redistribution from rich to poor.[12] Amartya Sen intervened at that moment and told Bob he needed to listen. Affluent scholars see a pie and see how they want to slice it, but Sen saw me starting in a different place—with the truism that power corrupts. Starting from that truism, what is baffling is that anyone could so cavalierly endorse concentrated power when we live in a world where concentrated power is so often used to redistribute not from rich to poor but from poor to rich. Sen went on to say that when it comes to inequality, the question is not whether we can find a statistic that gives credence to the resentment the richest scholars feel as the richest movie stars leave them behind, but which dimensions of rising inequality do poor people care about?

If we want to see evidence of progress, we look where evidence is. If we want to ignore progress, we look where evidence isn't. Diphtheria vaccine ended a disease that killed millions. My mother lost her oldest brother and her favorite aunt's entire family to diphtheria. Today we don't remember there even was such a disease. Yet many assume not only (1) income inequality is rising but also (2) rising income inequality is leading to famine or otherwise making poor people tangibly worse off. Is it? What would count as

---

[12] After my lecture on corruption at The Royal Society of London in 2014.

evidence? Which dimensions of rising inequality are causing life expectancies of poor people to crash?

In passing, I grew up on a small farm in Saskatchewan. My mother remembered waking up in the 1930s to floors crawling with locusts. I'm old enough to remember when we got indoor plumbing. (Water was too expensive to flush the toilet more than once a day, but it was better than the outhouse.) I drank powdered milk because bottled milk was too expensive. I remember my father being proud to work on the side as a janitor and part-time bartender. (I was a teenager: not old enough to get how a man could be proud of that, but I get it now.) So I remember where I'm from and I've never rejected modest transfers from rich to poor (of cash, that is—thanks, but no thanks, to the assumption that we don't know how to handle it). Still, as Sen understood, everyone should deplore power used to redistribute from those with less political power to those with more. We may want officials to have the power to win ultimate victory for our vision of justice in a world of rival visions, but, among corruptible human beings, the power to weaponize a vision of justice and impose it on a world of alternative visions is toxic.

14.8 To Justice in Practice

What should we infer from the premise that officials, given power, use it to pursue their agenda, not ours? The lesson I draw is that we should be skeptical of conceptions of justice that mislead us into thinking we have reason to invest enormous power in people who *crave* enormous power.[13] The truism that power corrupts bears on how much power we have reason to want there to be. When we ask

---

[13] As Mario Juarez puts it, rulers "weaponize" anticorruption policies. Juarez says power corrupts quite generally. Indeed, he documents how "even the power to purge the system of corruption is a power that corrupts" (2021, 10).

how much good we can imagine an ideal ruler doing with absolute power, it is as if we were resolving to ignore the fact that actions have consequences. We work on an idealized problem and end up gravitating toward endorsing as much power as it takes to realize our vision.

Given that there are limits to how much power we ideally would entrust to nonideal rulers, there is a reason why, anticipating Chapter 15, officials who make basic structures work must begin not with justice as a vision to be pursued no matter what, but rather with resolving and avoiding conflict. While theorists can treat justice as if it were more basic than conflict-resolving rules of practice, practitioners cannot.[14] Judges need to answer questions like, "Is flying over a ranch at a height of 10,000 feet a form of trespass or a way of minding your own business?" Many key questions of justice are more downstream than they appear; they have no answer until judges sort out what will help current and potential litigants to stay out of court and get on with their lives. After judges resolve a dispute, citizens go forward with validated expectations about what to count as their due. Judges get it right when they get actual closure—when they establish expectations we can live with, thereby minimizing the need for future intervention by corruptible public officials. Judges cannot settle for expressing their convictions about fairness or for otherwise pursuing their vision. They need to have higher standards than that because they have to resolve disputes.

While Rawls held that, "justice is the first virtue of institutions" (1971/1999, 3), Benjamin Barber marvels at how little *politics* he finds in Rawls. He says of Rawls's writing that "when political terms do occasionally appear, they appear in startlingly naïve and abstract ways" (1989, 310).[15] Robert Paul Wolff is equally harsh, seeing in

---

[14] Compare to Bernard Williams's point, as per Chapter 3, that how to secure peace is the first institutional question.

[15] Honig (1993) sees political theory losing touch with politics. Recall Rawls's remark that "We want to define the original position so that we get the desired solution" (1971/1999, 122). The wonder is how Rawls could think what he desires is *the* desire. Perhaps Rawls had a more political view by the time he wrote *Political Liberalism* (1993).

Rawls "no conception of the generation, deployment, limitations, or problems of political power" and notes that

> it would require very considerable political power to enforce the sorts of wage rates, tax policies, transfer payments, and job regulation called for by the difference principle. The men and women who apply the principle, make the calculations, and issue the redistribution orders will be the most powerful persons in the society, be they econometricians, elected representatives, or philosopher-kings. How are they to acquire this power? How will they protect and enlarge it once they have it? Whose interests will they serve?" (1977, 202)

It is indeed startling to see the work of the 20th century's most influential political philosopher described as "startlingly naïve."[16] Yet, upon reflection, it is amazing that contemporary philosophy has had so little to say about the idea that power corrupts.

An orientation toward conflict resolution could move a society in the direction of being less vulnerable to corruption. It weighs against creating power to ram through a thick conception of justice, which implies that when it comes to society's basic structure, no *thick* conception of justice is a *true* conception. When a theory of justice sets aside whether meeting its requirements would invite corruption, that is an idealization. Some idealizations need to be abandoned, not merely tinkered with later by regulators responsible for implementation.

If we settle for conflict resolution, for having our day in court, and for having a forum for airing grievances as they arise, we

---

[16] It would be wildly naïve to suppose fairness requires universities to distribute resources with a view to the greatest advantage of the least advantaged department. But my favorite Rawls essay (1955) observes that baseball's fairness requires umpires to uphold rules as practices, not to decide case by case how many strikes the least advantaged batter should get. So, if the DP applies only to basic structure—game-defining rules, not play-by-play events—then (as Jacob Barrett observed in my seminar) Rawls's view is less naïve than Barber and Wolff suppose.

remain vulnerable to corruption, but there is less scope for corruptible discretion. Judges have a mandate not to chase their dreams but to find out what litigants can live with. Judges are constrained by a need to converge on a result that leaves litigants—not theorists but real people whose futures hang in the balance—feeling like they had a say and were given terms of peace that let them carry on as equal citizens with lives of their own to live.

The least corrupt system minimizes reliance on powerful officials, thereby minimizing the concentrating of what corrupts (i.e., power) in corruptible officials. Even the power to purge the system of corruption can be a power that corrupts. Thus, a question for a legal system (Hasnas 2018) is: Does the rule of law as realized in this system minimize the need for ongoing tinkering? Can we live with problems that this rule of law cannot solve, while retaining a measure of dignity?

The power to tinker will be a supremely valuable commodity. Sooner or later those who possess that power will be corrupt. But our most widely dispersed, least corruptible power, when we have it, is our power as free and equal citizens to walk away from bad deals, to say no as individuals; that is, to *vote with our feet*. Being free to exit a relationship puts a limit on how corrupt your partner can be. The right to say no is hardly a panacea, but it separates equal citizens from mere subjects.

Conclusion

After playing high school football, I coached for four years, then served as a referee. Our task as referees was to interpret and apply the rules. With responsibility came power. With power came a measure of discretion. Our call could determine a game's outcome. Yet it was not our place to prefer a particular outcome. Favoring a team would have been corrupt.

Neither had we any right to prefer games ending in a tie. That would have been just as incompatible with the unobtrusive impartiality essential to successful refereeing. We had a duty not to aim for *any* outcome, not even an equal one. We had a duty to let the players play, and let their futures be of their own making.

POLITICAL ECONOMY AND MORAL SCIENCE II

15

Political Economy and
the Rule of Law

THEME: *Judges cannot do what philosophers do. They do not work in the space of ideal theory. Their task is to give flesh-and-blood litigants a way to get past a dispute and get on with their lives.*

This book began with a conjecture. Theorizing about how to live together might take its cue less from what we now call moral philosophy and more from what we once called political economy.

In turn, political economy might take its cue from the economic analysis of law, an area of research that tracks the evolution of law. It considers how evolving legal precedent may have shaped rules of engagement that help people to know what to expect from each other, get comfortable with what they are learning to expect from each other, and learn how to deserve to be esteemed as social beings.

Among our habitable ideals—principles we can live with—are those by which courts and citizens avoid and resolve conflict. As mentioned in Chapter 14, we have been taught to presume justice is more fundamental than conflict resolution. Yet philosophy done well is neither as autonomous as that nor as naïve. Hampshire goes so far as to say, "fairness in procedures for resolving conflicts is the fundamental kind of fairness" (2001, 4). Darwall says modern philosophy's break with scholasticism was rooted in a secular insight that harmony of interests is not guaranteed (1993, 416). Rather, such harmony as we observe is an achievement. Conflict is real.

Living Together. David Schmidtz, Oxford University Press. © Oxford University Press 2023.
DOI: 10.1093/oso/9780197658505.003.0015

Accordingly, the relationship between justice and conflict resolution is not a one-way relation of more to less fundamental. Instead, it is a dance of mutual specification anchored to evolving facts about what is helping people to manage traffic, settle disputes, feel at peace with settlements made, develop a liberating mutual understanding of what it means to mind their own business, and work toward making sure their neighbors are better off with them than without.

A rule of law that helps people resolve and avoid conflict will foster society as a cooperative venture for mutual advantage. To the extent that a society is such a venture, it is responding well enough to the human condition. People are learning to trust each other enough and adjust their expectations enough to constitute themselves as a kingdom of ends.

The work of judges can *yield* principles precisely by not *starting* with principles. Judges can start at the start by asking litigants what the fight is about. Cases close when people stop fighting. Ideally, cases culminate in verdicts that everyone is comfortable with, diverse though they may be. Adjudicated resolutions send litigants away with new information about what people going forward will expect from each other.[1] That goal—knowing what to expect—is at the heart of what it takes for social animals to be able to navigate in communities.

15.1　The Right to Say No

Working within a Lockean tradition, William Blackstone characterized property as the "sole and despotic dominion which

---

[1] In passing, imagine a judge hearing closing arguments and then asking the court, what would deontology say here? Or, what would utilitarianism say? Or, what would the theory behind door number three (the theory your professor prefers) say? If a judge were to ask such questions, those present at court might think, "Your Honor, this is serious. We're deciding how to go on living together, not how to dumb down homework problems for applied ethics courses."

one man claims and exercises over the external things of the world, in total exclusion of the right of any other individual in the universe" (1765, 2). In practice, though, Anglo-American property rights have always been hedged with restrictions. The dominion to which Blackstone refers has always been limited by easements, covenants, nuisance laws, zoning laws, and, more generally, by the public interest.[2]

Wesley Hohfeld (1913) distinguished mere liberties from full-blown rights: I am at *liberty* to use *p* just in case I have no duty to refrain from using *p*.

I have a *right* to *p* just in case (1) I am at liberty to use *p*, *plus* (2) I have the additional liberty of being able to forbid others from using *p*. A liberty, in this technical sense, is a nonexclusive right. What distinguishes a mere liberty from a proper right is that, with the latter, there is an owner who holds a right to exclude other would-be users.

Today, the term "property rights" generally is understood to refer to a bundle of rights that could include rights to sell, lend, bequeath, use as collateral, or even destroy. John Lewis (1888) called property rights a "bundle of sticks." Yet the core of any property right is a right to say no: a right to exclude non-owners. In other words, a right to exclude is not just one stick in a bundle. Instead, property is a tree. Other sticks are branches; the right to exclude is the trunk.

This is not merely a stipulation. Unless an owner has a right to say no, the other sticks are reduced to mere liberties rather than genuine rights. For example, I could be the owner of a bicycle in some meaningful sense even if for some reason I have no right to lend it to my friend. By contrast, if I have no right to forbid you to lend it to

---

[2] Thus, your authority within the bounds of your property may or may not include a right to build your fence at the edge of your parcel. It may or may not include a duty to leave an "easement" between your fence and the neighbor's fence sufficient to enable your neighbors to pass from their land to the marketplace. Making it harder for your community to facilitate commercial traffic will not fall within your purview.

your friend, then I am not the bicycle's owner in any normal sense. The tree would be missing its trunk, not merely a branch.[3]

This does not settle what, if anything, can justify our claiming a right to exclude, but it does clarify the topic. When we ask about owning a bicycle as distinct from merely being at liberty to use it, we are asking first and foremost about a right to exclude.

15.2 The Point of Property

When are we justified in claiming a right to exclude? There are legal questions, of course, but also moral questions about what the law ought to be. To claim a natural right is to say the case for claiming rights sometimes is grounded in what we know about the human condition rather than what we know about extant legislation. Some claims are claims about what our legal rights ought to be.

Dutch thinker Hugo Grotius (1625) secularized the idea of natural law. In his hands, natural law theory became a naturalistic question of what social arrangements were most conducive to the betterment of humankind, given fundamental facts about human nature. Grotius argued that there would be laws of nature, dictated by requirements of human nature, even if (perish the thought) there were no deity. Societies almost invariably create property as a legal category. Obviously, property rights are artifacts in that sense. Still, our propensity to create such artifacts is not itself an artifact. We are toolmakers by nature. As with other tools, we create rights for a purpose, and there will be an observable fact of the matter about how serviceable such tools are. Talk of rights may be cheap talk when someone is groundlessly demanding a

---

[3] Lest the metaphor be misunderstood, the point of calling the right to exclude the trunk is not that the right is indefeasible. The point is simply that the right to exclude does not presuppose the branches in the way that the branches presuppose the trunk. But see Lindsay (2018). On whether a right to say no can be pictured as the "trunk" of positive and negative rights alike, see Brinkmann (2022).

slice of the pie, but Grotius gave us a framework for making sober claims on verifiable grounds. What it takes to avoid and resolve conflict is part of it.

Following Grotius, John Locke (1690) argued that God gave the world to humankind in common for the betterment of humankind. God intended that we do what we need to do to put the earth to work. Furthermore, persons are self-owners; they may be God's property, but against other humans, individuals alone have the right to say yes or no regarding how their bodies are put to work.

As Locke might have observed, asserting self-ownership is controversial. Yet controversial though it may be to assert that Jane has a right to say no to a proposal to use her body in a given way, asserting she *doesn't* is far more so: less liberal, less respectful, more menacing.

This right to choose how to put our bodies to work would be useless in that original state, and God would be leaving us to starve unless we are at liberty to make a living by laboring upon otherwise unowned objects in the world. We typically are not at liberty to seize what already belongs to someone else. Why? Because seizing what belongs to someone else typically does not contribute to the betterment of humankind. By contrast, when a resource genuinely is unclaimed, we can come to own it by working on it in a way that renders it useful. We acquire a crop by being the ones who planted and harvested it. We acquire the land underneath insofar as our undisputed stewardship makes that land ten, a hundred, or a thousand times more productive than it had been in its unappropriated wild condition.

Locke argued that latecomers could afford to respect the claims of those who arrived first. This is putting it mildly. In fact, a Lockean today plainly can see that it is *better* to arrive late, after all the appropriating is done. Latecomers benefit from generations of people already having done the work of making a community thousands of times more productive than it was during the age of first appropriation, more than doubling life expectancy in the process (Schmidtz 2008).[4]

Locke thus extended the idea of self-ownership to include an external resource (land) that people could "incorporate" by mixing labor with it. While this extension may seem controversial, the subtle question concerns who has the least obstructed claim. Bob's claim to land that Bob has worked on and improved (cleared, planted, etc.) matters to anyone who cares about persons: Bob is the only one who can reap the fruits of land that Bob improved without having to seize the fruits of another person's labor. The idea is not that Bob has a deep and mystical connection to that parcel of land. The idea is simply that (1) Bob has *some* connection, and (2) no one else can establish even that much of a connection without disregarding Bob's prior claim. The first labor-mixing thus raises the bar on what can justify subsequent takings. There will be another owner some day, but legitimizing transfer and subsequent ownership typically will involve consent of a previous owner (rather than labor-mixing).

15.3 Good Fences

To Carol Rose (1994), a fence is a *statement*, one telling the world that you will defend what is inside and asking people to curb themselves so you won't need to, thereby saving everyone a lot of grief.

The whole point of a fence is to *get in the way*, which sounds hard to justify. But consider a different analogy: property rights are traffic

---

[4] Nozick (1974) launched a conversation about a "Lockean Proviso" according to which land's original appropriation can be legitimate if as much and as good is left for latecomers. Yet, Nozick observed, if the amount of land is fixed, then every appropriation necessarily leaves less for latecomers. Critics gleefully took Nozick's gambit, interpreting him as unwittingly conceding that private property (necessarily!) fails the Lockean test. It would fall to me to ask (in a 1994 essay reprinted in Schmidtz 2008): If first appropriators (necessarily!) left less for us, then why do we have so much more than they did?

lights. Traffic lights move traffic not so much by turning green as by turning red. Without traffic lights, we all in effect have a green light, which means gridlock. By contrast, a system where we take turns facing red and green lights is a system that keeps us moving. It makes us pause from time to time but ultimately enhances our ability to uneventfully get where we want to go. Red lights can frustrate, but the game they create is positive sum. We all get where we are going faster, safer, and more predictably by virtue of knowing what to expect from each other. As Locke might have argued, in a system of free-flowing *commercial* traffic, even "pedestrians" are better off because the trucking and bartering observably turns twenty-something have-nots into forty-something haves.[5]

We don't want *lots* of rights for the same reason that we wouldn't want to face red lights every fifty feet. Getting our traffic management system right is a matter of minimizing gridlock: getting the most compact set of lights that enables motorists to know what to expect from each other and thereby get from point A to point B with minimal delay.

Traffic lights hardly do anything. They sit there, blinking (as Jason Brennan puts it in Schmidtz and Brennan 2010). Yet, without them, we are less adept at knowing what to expect and thus less adept at getting where we need to go while staying out of each other's way. As with literal traffic management, so, too, with property conventions as managers of commercial traffic.

---

[5] Could the advantages of the rich be good for the poor, even imaginably? To make it look like the answer is no, we would model rich and poor as rigid classes. But what if reality is more fluid than that? Adam Smith could be indifferent to *some* dimensions of inequality because he was studying how societies alleviate misery. He denounced inequalities observable in stagnant economies where abject poverty is common, yet saw a world of difference between *impoverishing* inequalities versus dimensions of inequality characteristic of growing economies where every class is making progress over generations by metrics of life quality that poor people care about. Which societies are extending life expectancy? Which societies are the ones where poor people want to raise their children? Which are famine-proof?

15.4 How to Respect the Right to Say No

Exactly what protection the right to say no affords is a separable issue. Calabresi and Melamed (1972) describe three ways to protect property. In normal cases, property *p* is protected by a *property rule*, meaning no one may use it without the owner's permission. In other cases, *p* is protected by a *liability rule*, meaning no one may use it without compensating the owner. In a third case, *p* is protected by an *inalienability rule*, meaning no one may use *p* even with the owner's permission.

The rationale for liability rules is that sometimes it costs too much or is impossible to get consent, or sometimes the contemplated use is overwhelmingly important. Every time we pull out of a driveway, there is a risk that plans will go awry and we will accidentally damage someone's property. Is there a principled response? Yes. Imagine a rule: driving a car requires advance permission from everyone who might be put at risk of accidental trespass. Suppose we anticipate that, under such a rule, no one would be able to go anywhere, and much of what we call cooperation would never get off the ground. In that case, we can predict that advance permission will not be the operative requirement. The operative rule will be a liability rule, requiring that we compensate people after the fact if we accidentally damage their property. Why? Because people want to be able to live together. So they develop rules that reduce the cost of living together and of delivering goods and services to each other.[6]

An inalienability rule is different. One reason for inalienability is that, in some contexts, some forms of property are so fundamental that we would cease fully to be persons if we were to, for example, sell them. (Chapter 22 explores the history of this point.) We may say my kidney is my property, for example, even while denying that this implies any right to sell my kidney. In this case, we are treating my right to my kidney as inalienable.

---

[6] I thank Alex Schaefer for the thought.

The takings clause of the US Constitution's Fifth Amendment specifies that private property may not be taken for public use without just compensation. The clause does not explicitly affirm the public's right to seize property for public use, although that is the implication. We can see the takings clause as affirming that, even when a compelling public interest precludes treating a private property right as protected by a property rule, the public must still respect the right to the extent of treating it as protected by a liability rule.[7]

As a rule, the protection that liability rules afford is not good enough. Here is the problem. Suppose someone steals your car, then returns it undamaged with the gas tank full. Lack of damages notwithstanding, your rights were violated. For property rights to do what they are supposed to do, the right to exclude needs to have "teeth," which is to say it needs to be protected by property rules, not liability rules, and the penalty for *intentional* trespass must be real, not nominal. Thus, in 1997, Judge Bablitch of the Supreme Court of Wisconsin, in the case of *Jacque vs. Steenberg Homes*, reaffirmed the role of property rules in a functional system of property. In the case, Steenberg intentionally crossed Jacque's property to deliver a motor home to Jacque's neighbor, despite Jacque having denied Steenberg's request for entry. A lower court had awarded Jacque a single dollar in compensatory damages (because there had been

---

[7] *Spur Industries v. Del Webb,* 494 P.2d 700 (Ariz. 1972) is a notorious case in which developer Del Webb sued neighboring feedlot operator Spur Industries, alleging that Spur's feedlot was a nuisance. Spur was there first, though, and one principle of common law is that a party that moves to the nuisance, as Del Webb did, has no complaint. Yet the judge ruled that although Del Webb per se had no case, Del Webb's customers were "the public" and the public has a right to protection from nuisances. So the judge ruled for Del Webb, granting an injunction against Spur. Remarkably, the court held that the winner had to compensate the loser! The court judged that Spur's property claim was valid but that (because the feedlot was a public nuisance) Spur could be forced to move, with compensation. In effect, the verdict was that Spur's property was protected by liability rather than property rule. It was as if Del Webb accidentally damaged Spur's business by turning it into a public nuisance, with the damage consisting of Spur having to shut down. Then, as the price of victory, Del Webb had to make its victim whole by paying damages.

no significant damage) and had denied punitive damages on the ground that merely nominal damages could not sustain substantial punitive damages. Judge Bablitch ruled that this would have been the correct ruling in a case of *accidental* trespass, but in a case of *intentional* trespass, punitive damage awards can turn out to bear the sole burden of deterrence, so courts must have latitude to make punitive damages substantial enough to deter.

15.5 Common Law

Philosophy drives the evolution of Anglo-American conceptions of property to some extent, yet the history of property is not only a history of ideas. Philosopher David Hume (in his *History of England*) wrote that, so long as the property system was as precarious as it was in the Middle Ages, there could be little industry. To Hume, this was a "Dark Age" because people were not free to choose how to make a living. Moreover, they lacked secure title to the products of their labor.

What changed? To Hume, the rediscovery of Justinian's Pandects in Amalfi, Italy, in 1130 was pivotal (Hume, *History of England*, Book II, 520). The Pandects were a digest of state-of-the-art Roman civil law, commissioned by emperor Justinian and produced by the day's leading legal scholars (circa 530). Within ten years of its rediscovery, lectures on the Pandects were being given at (what would become) Oxford University. As law and legal thinking evolved, there emerged a class of independent jurists whose job was to apply known and settled laws. This is *common* law; that is, evolving judge-made law of the land. English King Henry II in the late 1100s extended this evolving body of judicial precedent, making its scope national rather than local. Much of the history of property law's evolution in the Anglo-American world is thus a history of judge-made legal precedent.

The remainder of this chapter discusses various legal cases that illustrate the sorts of principles that drive the evolution of the common law of property.

15.6 External Cost

Suppose I sell you a car. Are both of us better off? Not necessarily, given that we all make mistakes. Still, observing that our exchange is voluntary makes mutual benefit a reasonable expectation. The problem: a trade sometimes costs parties other than the buyer and seller. An *external* cost is a cost imposed on bystanders. Suppose you hire me to alter your muffler so that it makes a dreadful noise that wakes up neighbors when you go for a late-night drive. You and I may be happy with the work I did on your muffler, but if neighbors can't sleep because of it, then society as a whole may be losing.

Consider a second case. You don't alter your muffler but you do use your car as an airport limousine. Here, too, a neighbor may be worse off insofar as her services as a cab driver are no longer in demand. Yet, somehow, this case is okay. Why? In this case, customers are not the cab driver's property, so your "stealing" customers from her is not literally stealing; her customers were never hers by right. When you came to market with a better service at lower cost, your community no longer had a use for the cab driver's now-obsolete product. If she still wants to be of service to her community, and thereby earn a living, she needs to find another way.

Externalities that affect people's welfare only by affecting prices are called *pecuniary* externalities. From a community perspective, pecuniary externalities are nothing more than changing prices that tell you whether your community is losing interest in what you are trying to sell. And updating that base of information is a good thing, not a bad thing. It sends people a signal of genuine change in what it takes to be useful.

In 1707, the case of *Keeble v. Hickeringill* came before the Queen's Bench of England. Keeble was a farmer who had set up decoys to lure waterfowl into traps. He would then sell the captured birds. Out of spite, his neighbor, Hickeringill, began to fire guns into the air to frighten away the birds. Keeble filed suit. Judge Holt ruled in favor of Keeble, reasoning that Keeble was minding his own business and Hickeringill had no right to interfere. Holt refers to a somewhat analogous case where a defendant interfered with a neighbor's school *by starting a better school*. In that case, it was the defendant who won, because the students were not the plaintiff's property. The plaintiff had no right to protection from a defendant "stealing" students by offering students a better product. Holt next considered a hypothetical case where a defendant interferes with a neighbor's school by firing guns into the air and frightening students away. That would be an intentional trespass because the defendant would be sabotaging the plaintiff's product rather than offering the community a better product. Judge Holt distinguished between genuine and merely pecuniary externalities centuries before the vocabulary was coined, refining the property system so as to limit genuine externalities while leaving intact the liberty to compete for business, thereby making it easier for neighbors to live—and make a living—together.

Sometimes externalities are not worth eliminating. When people live miles apart, we don't bother to develop laws regulating the shooting of guns into the air. If no one is damaged or put at risk, no one sues. No case comes before the court, so no precedent is set. However, as population density rises, a cost becomes worth internalizing at some point. Again, driving has an external cost, but we don't want people to stop driving. So we aim to contain external cost, not reduce it to zero. It will always go with being a good neighbor to anticipate minor irritations. Good neighbors will always want to take reasonable steps to tread lightly on their neighbors' normal sensibilities. There is no perfect substitute for being considerate. No system of law is such that simply obeying the law is enough to make us good neighbors.

15.7 Possession

In *Armory v. Delamirie* (1722), a chimney sweep finds a ring, pockets it, then takes it to an appraiser. The appraiser pockets the jewel that had been in the ring. The chimney sweep sues the appraiser for the jewel's return.

The court rules that the question is not whether the plaintiff is the rightful owner, but whether there has been a wrongful transfer. The court determines that there has indeed been a wrongful transfer and rules that the wrongful transfer must be undone. This case was part of the history by which possession became a mark of presumptive ownership. Everyone understood that the chimney sweep was not necessarily the jewel's rightful owner. Even so, the court ruled that simple possession was enough to confer a right to maintain possession against a jeweler who takes it without consent.

A person must feel safe in going to the market and engaging a merchant's services. If an appraiser has a right to take your stuff—if your possession does not suffice to ground a (rebuttable) presumption that you are the owner—then you won't feel comfortable taking stuff to an appraiser. One purpose of law is to make people feel safe in going to market to truck and barter. If property rights are sufficiently secure, then one need not conceal one's valuables; on the contrary, one can *flaunt* their value, openly advertising what one has for sale, thereby making it easier for a community to trade. Indeed, one sign of a community becoming civilized is the emergence of laws against false advertising: far from needing to be secretive about one's possessions to avoid being robbed, traders come to need laws to curb incentives to *exaggerate* the quality of items available for sale.

15.8 Positive Sum Games

In 1880, in *Ghen v. Rich*, the court learns that Ghen fired a bomb lance into a fin-back whale. The dead whale sank, washed up on the coast of Massachusetts, and was found by Ellis. Ellis sold the carcass to Rich, who extracted oil from the blubber. Hearing rumors of this, Ghen filed a claim for the value of the oil extracted. Ghen's case rested on the whaling community's custom of treating the person who first harpoons a whale as establishing possession and thus ownership. Judge Nelson of the Massachusetts District Court ruled in favor of Ghen, acknowledging that whaling ports were close-knit communities that had worked out simple, transparent norms regarding how to establish possession and thus presumptive ownership and that these simple customs helped whalers to be of service to the larger community.

Specifically, where commercially valuable whales are slow and docile, the mark of possession is "fast fish, loose fish," meaning possession is established by fastening the whale to the boat (Ellickson 1991). In other communities where the most commercially valuable whales are too dangerous to consider attaching to one's boat, the operative rule is the less stringent "iron holds the whale," meaning that fatally harpooning a whale suffices to establish possession. This rule applied to the fin-back, which made the first possessor Ghen, not Ellis.

Carol Rose (1985) identifies two background principles. First, establishing possession should involve doing something unambiguous to notify the world of what one is claiming. Second, establishing possession should involve labor that adds to the value of what one is claiming.

15.9 Transaction Costs

In *Hinman vs. Pacific Air Transport* (1936), a landowner sued an airline for trespass, asserting a right to stop airlines from crossing over his property. The court's predicament: on one hand, a right to say no grounds a system of property that, in turn, grounds cooperation among self-owners. Therefore, the court had no choice but to uphold the right to say no. On the other hand, much of property's point is to facilitate commercial traffic. Yet this plaintiff's interpretation of our right to say no implied that landowners have a right to hold the air traffic industry for ransom. That kind of red light would gridlock traffic, not facilitate it, so the edges of our right to say no needed clarifying.

In *Hinman*, Judge Haney ruled that the right to say no extends not to the heavens but only so high as a landowner's actual use. Navigation easements quickly were interpreted as allowing federal governments to allocate airspace above five hundred feet for transportation purposes. This minimized the cost of airlines transacting with landowners for permission to pass overhead.

Common law judges need to formulate simple rules, in the spirit of equality before the law, that enable litigants to get on with their lives with a good idea of what to expect from each other and thereby avoid conflict. In *Hinman*, a property system suddenly was revealed to be inadequately specified for a newly emerging form of traffic. In a targeted way, Judge Haney made property law a better solution to the problem confronting his court. Judge Haney's verdict left us with an interpretation of our rights that we could *afford* to take seriously.

The right to say no is an institutional structure that facilitates community. It safeguards a right to come to market hoping to be of service. When people have a right to say no and to withdraw, that is when they can afford *not to withdraw*. They can afford to trust each other. That is, they can afford to live in proximity and to produce, trade, and prosper without fear.

For the same reason, the right to say no is not a weapon of mass destruction. It is a device whose purpose is to facilitate commerce, not prevent commerce, so it must not enable people to gridlock the system. The right to say no is a right to decline to be involved in a transaction, not a license to paralyze other people and prevent them from transacting with each other until they pay ransom.

15.10 Property and Justice

Property's purpose as a means of production (how the law must evolve to keep serving its purpose) has to condition the contours of justice, not the other way around. In other words, justice comes second, not first. Why see it that way? Because taking justice seriously presupposes seeing justice as something a society can afford to take seriously.

Facts, without entailing conclusions about justice, do reveal costs and benefits of seeing justice in one way rather than another. In the *Hinman* case, whether a court should recognize a right to say no that extends to heaven had everything to do with whether interpreting the right that way would facilitate the commercial traffic of a peaceful and productive community of sovereign, individual equals. In *Hinman*, it became clear that it would not. That told Judge Haney what he needed to know to decide the case.

Many of our most fundamental questions have no answers until judges sort out what will help current and potential litigants to stay out of court. After judges settle a dispute, citizens go forward not with personal visions of justice but with publicly validated mutual expectations about what to count as their due. Judges get it right when they settle it—when they establish mutual expectations that leave everyone with a basis for moving on.

Effective judges know this. To judges, having personal convictions about fairness is not enough. Judges aim higher. They aim to settle disputes in a way that philosophers and their theories hardly ever do. Philosophers spend their days imagining they have enough evidence for their view to excuse ignoring the evidence against. By contrast, judges spend their days giving litigants a way to get on with their lives. Our sense of justice takes shape in response.

Judges aim to treat like cases alike. They do this not only because they have an intuition that treating like cases alike is just; rather, judges seek to be guided by precedent because they want their verdicts to be what litigants should have seen coming. That is how judges help potential litigants stay out of court, and that is how judges enable a system of adjudication to be a predictable framework of mutual expectation. Judges aim to judge cases predictably, in line with how judges before them have judged. Judges play a role in enabling communities to climb, but climbing begins from where we are. It is natural but thoughtless to think a judge's job is to rebuild society from ground zero to make it match a personal vision.

Accordingly, if you buy a house in the United States, you do a title search. The question is not whether ideals of distributive justice single out your claim as the weightiest, but whether there is any active title dispute. If nothing turns up, we treat the deed as valid. No one needs reminding that there are no primordially clean land titles. Ascertaining that no one has disputed a title in forty years is not a way of giving up on justice; it is a way of getting on with the kind of justice that a society can afford.[8]

To philosophers, forty years is arbitrary. We have no axioms from which to deduce that forty years is the correct number. But the actual question is whether forty years is a limit that helps people to get on with living. We need to settle what to expect. When we see that settling on forty years *works*—when we see people knowing what to expect and getting on with living—then we are seeing what makes conventions as correct as conventions can be. Judges who find answers in common law history (or figure out how to extrapolate as predictably as they can when new cases require new answers)

---

[8] "Dwelling too much on the past is wrong for the same reason that ignoring the past altogether is wrong: excess in *either* direction reduces stability in transactions, thus making it harder to go forward in peace. A routine title search when buying a house (to verify that the seller's holding of the deed is in fact uncontested) is one thing; going back as many centuries as the land has been occupied is another" (Schmidtz 2006, 212). See also Zwolinski and Tomasi (2023, 99).

are doing what judges need to do to make their community a better place to live.

It would be a manner of speaking, at best, to say that the *Hinman* court, in coming to a verdict, was discovering a natural law. The court was trying to discover *something*, though, something closer to laws of nature than to legislation. That is, the court was discerning a logic of coordination—realizing that a rule of law's purpose is to enable people to prosper and that a prerequisite of people prospering is their being able to produce and trade. Moreover, it was becoming clear that air traffic was a revolutionary experiment in pushing the frontier of people's ability to produce and trade. The judge also realized that giving every landowner a right to treat air traffic as a trespass would throttle air traffic; the cost of transacting with every owner on the ground would be prohibitive.

At the time, there was no legal fact of the matter about whether landowners had a right to say "no trespassing" to people passing over their land at ten thousand feet. Before the advent of air travel, no legal dispute had brought the issue to a head. There had not been any debate needing to be settled one way or another. Once air travel emerged, though, and landowners filed suit against airplanes, judges had to decide what is entailed by an owner's right to say "no trespassing"—rather, what it *needs* to entail to be part of a system that helps people get on with living together.[9]

To be clear, it should be a rare event when judges step back to ask what property is for. Property is supposed to settle what is and

---

[9] Avner de-Shalit once asked me about hard cases. What often guides trial judges is a wish to avoid anything that looks creative. Trial judges aim to follow precedent, not establish it. They want their rulings to be what people had reason to expect. Only rarely do they welcome a verdict being overturned by an appellate court. A trial ruling may be suboptimal yet correct—more or less what litigants should have expected. Sometimes, however, a judge may say, "Who knows what the Court was thinking in 1896, but I need to reverse that error now, and pray that history forgives me for the whiff of lawlessness in my overturning established precedent on behalf of what I think the precedent needed to be." I thank David Poplar for helping me think this through.

what isn't within one's jurisdiction.[10] If p is your property, then you decide what p is for. At the end of our work day, you drive home in your car and I drive home in mine, period. When the law of property is working well, no discussion is needed. Judges need to step back to ask what property is for when and only when the institution is not working—when litigants run into a question that the institution has not yet evolved to answer.

15.11 Zoning

The case for zoning begins with a problem of internalizing externalities combined with a conjecture that a given externality problem can be unsolvable when the cost of transacting is too high. Neighborhood associations create covenants forbidding industrial development. Sometimes, though, there are holdouts whose interests lie in a different direction and who want to retain the option of selling their land to industrial concerns. Neighborhoods often seek to reserve to themselves a right to say no *as neighborhoods* to such sales. *Euclid vs. Ambler Realty* (1926) is the basis of all subsequent zoning in the United States. In 1922, the village of Euclid, a suburb of Cleveland, adopted a zoning plan. In the middle of this village, though, was a parcel owned by Ambler Realty. Ambler sued Euclid, alleging that the zoning plan robbed Ambler of the greatest value of Ambler's land because its parcel was next to a railroad that made it best suited for industrial than residential use.

A district judge found the zoning ordinance unconstitutional. The problem was that the Fourteenth Amendment says, in part, "No State shall make or enforce any law which shall abridge the

---

[10] A court's *jurisdiction* is a territory within which it exercises legal authority. Or an enforcement agency's jurisdiction can refer not to territory but to the kind of crime an agency is authorized to investigate. I use the term to mark a resemblance between these ideas and the limits of a landowner's right to say no. I thank David Poplar for his legal perspective.

privileges or immunities of citizens of the United States; nor shall any State deprive any person of life, liberty, or property, without due process of law; nor deny to any person within its jurisdiction the equal protection of the laws." In 1922, the US Supreme Court overturned the ruling. They acknowledged that zoning had a history of being used to exclude minorities, immigrants, renters, and low-income groups by creating single-family residential zones, minimum lot sizes, and so on. Still, the court saw no such concerns in play in *Euclid*. So, the court decided (with three dissenting votes) that their job was to rule on the merits of the case rather than on the general principle, acknowledging that zoning *could* be abused but holding that it was not being abused in the case at hand. If and when neighborhoods abuse the option of zoning, they could and would be sued, and future courts would then define and refine zoning's legitimate limits.

15.12 Equality Before the Law

And so it came to pass. Thirty of thirty-nine property owners in a St. Louis neighborhood signed a covenant in 1911 barring sales to non-whites. In 1945, an owner sold to Shelley, an African American family. Neighbors sued to stop Shelley from taking possession. Dodging the moral issue, the trial court dismissed the suit on technical grounds, ruling that the covenant was valid only when all neighborhood owners sign and not all had. The Supreme Court of Missouri reversed, arguing that those who signed the agreement had a right to do so, and exercising such right violated no provision of the Constitution. Shelley, by now occupying the property, counter-sued, saying the covenant did indeed violate the US Constitution's Fourteenth Amendment, which guarantees to each citizen "equal protection of the laws." So, the case went to the US Supreme Court, which ruled in 1948 that private racist covenants are constitutional, but *public enforcement* of such covenants is not. Private covenants need not involve or implicate the state, but public enforcement of such covenants must.

Shelley v. Kraemer terminated half a century of efforts to segregate via covenant. The idea of covenant is neutral in theory, but in practice overwhelmingly was used to exclude African Americans. *Shelley* signaled that courts would scrutinize actual patterns of discrimination, not mere formalities. The lawyer arguing Shelley's case was Thurgood Marshall, an African American and future justice of the US Supreme Court who would go on to argue, in *Brown v. Board of Education* (1954), that "separate but equal" is unconstitutional because there was precious little equality in segregation after *Plessy v. Ferguson* (1896).

We no longer care whether *Plessy v. Ferguson*'s "separate but equal" decision might conceivably have been well-intended. We know better than to ask whether the defect was in the people or the principle. We know better than to say the ideal of "separate but equal" may not work in practice, but it's beautiful in theory. We've seen enough.

What we are left with today is an enduring right to enter covenants, exchange easements, and so on. We can enter into private agreements; however, covenants meant to *run with the land* are not simply private agreements. Covenants meant to run with the land are attempts to shape the community of a future generation. Thus, being a racist is one thing; binding future owners to abide by a racist covenant is another. Idiosyncratic contractors can agree to whatever they want, but what they agree to among themselves does not bind future buyers of their property.

The court was willing to hear an argument that the covenant was not racist since, as written, it restricted sellers irrespective of race, but the court deemed the argument spurious. The seller's race was beside the point: what made the covenant racist is that it invoked public enforcement just in case the *buyer* was black. If the courts were to treat race-based exclusion as running with the land, that would amount to treating the enforcing of racist exclusion as legitimate business of the state—not necessarily, but as a contingent matter of observable historical fact. *That* is what the Fourteenth Amendment's "equal protection" clause forbids.

16

Cost-Benefit Analysis
as Moral Science

THEME: *Cost-benefit analysis is not a theory about what to do. It is not in that sense a moral theory, utilitarian or otherwise. Instead, it is a crude but serviceable tool of moral science, useful for (among other things) subjecting policies of the administrative state to public scrutiny.*

The rule of law is a product of negotiation and compromise, continuously evolving in ways only partly foreseen and only partly intended. As per Chapter 15, one source of law is a society's court system.

Another source of law, what we imagine to be *the* source, is a government's legislative branch. While we imagine that the law of the land is whatever the legislature decides, the truth is that legislators can only hope to influence how an accumulating body of law drifts as they compromise continuously with other legislators who see things differently and who are honor-bound to represent different constituencies. As per Chapter 14, once a bill's final shape is resolved, we may find that legislators have only a day to prepare to vote on a 12,000-page bill that no one in the world has read, not even the hundreds of legislative staffers and lobbyists who each wrote a few pages of it.

If different legislative branches pass different versions of a bill, reconciliation follows. Something gets treated as having passed, and then it falls not to the legislature but to regulatory agencies of the executive branch to make sense of what just became law. Subject

Living Together. David Schmidtz, Oxford University Press. © Oxford University Press 2023.
DOI: 10.1093/oso/9780197658505.003.0016

to judicial challenge, law-as-enforced will be law-as-interpreted by regulatory agencies of the executive branch.

So, regulatory agencies need to decide. When unsure, regulators may weigh pros and cons. Occasionally, regulators make the weighing explicit, listing pros and cons and assigning numerical weights. Courts of justice sometimes seem to do likewise. What could go wrong? In fact, things can go terribly wrong.

For example, let's add one more common law case to those considered in Chapter 15: *Peeveyhouse vs. Garland Coal.* Having completed a strip-mining operation on Peeveyhouse's property, Garland Coal refused to honor its contractual promise to Peeveyhouse to restore the land to its original condition. Garland estimated that restoring the land would cost $29,000 but would add only $300 to the land's value. Restoration therefore would not be cost-effective. So, Garland Coal conceded that it had damaged Peeveyhouse and proposed to pay damages, but argued that damages amounted to $300, not $29,000.

Incredibly, the Oklahoma court awarded Peeveyhouse only the $300, judging that Garland Coal could not be held liable for a restoration that would cost more than it was worth. The Court's verdict generally is regarded as mistaken (Morriss 2000, 144). One way to explain the mistake is to see it as applying cost–benefit analysis (henceforth CBA) in circumstances beyond CBA's legitimate scope.[1]

Shaking hands and signing a contract implies that something—a promise—can matter without easily fitting into categories of cost or benefit. Where does that leave CBA? This chapter considers what CBA can do and what it cannot.

---

[1] If we were to treat this as a case of property rather than contract, then we might liken it to *Jacque* as per Chapter 15, and call it wrong to treat Peeveyhouse's property as protected only by a liability rule.

16.1 What Is Cost-Benefit Analysis For?

Many critics of CBA seem driven by a gut feeling that CBA is heart-less. They think that, by denouncing CBA, they take a stand against heartlessness. In truth, weighing a proposal's costs and benefits does not make you a bad person. What makes you a bad person is *ignoring* costs—costs you impose on others. Problems arise not when regulators take costs and benefits into account, but when they neglect to do so.

As per Chapter 15, one issue is *external* cost—costs that decision makers ignore, leaving someone else to pick up the pieces. Ignoring external cost is all too natural. Every time you drive a car, you risk other people's lives and probably never feel guilty about it. (And, like you, industrial polluters defend themselves by saying, "Everybody does it!") It is only human.

The question is whether *any* form of CBA is defensible. Those with expertise in accounting draw fine-grained distinctions among variations on CBA's basic theme. *Full cost accounting*, for example, refers to CBA that takes all known costs, external as well as internal, into account. From here on, unless otherwise noted, when I speak of CBA, I mean CBA with full cost accounting.

When should we want regulators to employ CBA? Two answers come to mind: first, when one group pays a regulation's cost while another gets the benefit; second, and more generally, whenever regulators have an incentive not to take full costs into account. If benefits of political decisions are concentrated while costs are dispersed, we will see lobbyists pushing through policies even when dispersed costs exceed concentrated benefits. Requiring that policies be justified by the lights of a proper CBA, made available for public scrutiny, is one way of teaching regulators (in the face of otherwise blinding pressure from lobbyists) how to consider the full cost of what they do.

Proper CBA is not merely an accounting method but a way of holding people accountable. This makes CBA potentially a friend of the environment, yet environmental opinion tends to be anti-CBA. CBA may seem like a crudely quantitative way of deploying a moral theory—utilitarianism—that is controversial at best. This is a point of real contention. We will return to it. The first thing to say, how-ever, is that CBA is an analytical tool, no more, no less. Moreover, it is an analytical tool with limits. For example, imagine someone arguing that "By definition, everything we care about is either a cost or a benefit. Therefore, to say we should do CBA is simply to say we should take what we care about into account." There is a grain of truth here, but also two problems.

First, we can say everything we care about is a cost or a benefit but saying it does not make it so. To add costs and benefits is to add weights. Yet not everything is a weight.

This is one of the most tragically misunderstood points in moral philosophy. The truth: my saying no does not imply that you should put great weight on my refusal! What I'm saying is that it is not your call. My being the right-holder means that how much weight to put on my interests is my call, not yours. No means no. End of story.

A second problem with treating everything we care about as a weight is this: we are only human, and humans are wired to seek ev-idence that tells them what they want to believe. When we deal with weights, we aren't built to be impartial. We exaggerate what weighs in favor of what we want to believe, and we discount what weighs against. CBA's defenders do this. So do CBA's critics. It's a problem (Ballantyne 2015; Haidt 2012; LaFollette 2016). With that caveat, the following sections consider reasons (some cogent, some not) for distrusting CBA.

16.2 Is CBA Anthropocentric?

Is it only humanity's interest that CBA takes into account? Must CBA be anthropocentric? No. CBA as construed here is partly an accounting procedure and partly a way of organizing public debate.

In no way does it substitute for philosophical debate. Those who think, for example, that full costs must include pain suffered by animals must argue for the point in debate with philosophers who think differently (Shahar 2022). If CBA presupposed one or the other position, thereby falsely implying that there is no room for debate, that would be a real flaw.

16.3 Does CBA Presuppose Utilitarian Moral Theory?

Today's utilitarianism holds that x is right if and only if x maximizes utility, where maximizing utility is what produces the best balance of benefits over costs. Does CBA presuppose it? Chapter 5 explained why I reject utilitarianism as it came to be interpreted in the 20th century, but, in any case, the answer is no: CBA does not presuppose it. CBA is a framework for a public forum on what it takes to respect persons: not only persons present at a meeting but others as well, on whose behalf those present can speak (citizens of faraway countries, future generations, etc.). For that matter, people can speak not only on behalf of persons but on behalf of whatever they care about: animals, trees, canyons, historic sites, and so on. While CBA that ignores external cost would be endorsed by neither deontologists nor utilitarians, CBA with full cost accounting could be endorsed by either.

Note that utilitarian (including rule-utilitarian) moral theories are theories about what to do and what to choose. CBA is not a moral theory in that sense; neither does it presuppose a moral theory. I've said Hume and Smith theorized about what works, not what to do. CBA is analysis of how things work. It is a process of checking apparent costs and benefits, but CBA per se does not tell us to sum them in the way that a 20th-century utilitarian would. Neither does it tell us to use the sum in deciding what to do in the way that a 20th-century utilitarian would.

16.4 Does CBA Tell Us to Sacrifice the One
for the Sake of the Many?

We can imagine advocates of CBA assuming actions are justified
whenever benefits exceed costs. That would be a mistake. Suppose
a doctor, contemplating killing one patient to save five, performs
CBA and concludes that . . . five is more than one. So what? Does
that mean killing one is permitted? Required? No. CBA offers guid-
ance *if* our mandate is to promote the best balance of costs and
benefits, but not every situation is a mandate to maximize value.
Promoting is not always what morality calls for. Sometimes morality is a call not to maximize value but to respect it.

I argued that CBA does not presume the truth of utilitarianism.
Now I may appear to be arguing that CBA presumes utilitarianism
is false! Not so. Some institutions have utility precisely by taking
utilitarian calculation out of the hands of citizens. Hospitals, for example, cannot serve their purpose unless people can trust hospitals
to treat people as rights-bearers. As Chapter 8 observed, hospitals
save lives not by standing ready to sacrifice one patient whenever
that looks optimal but by instead enabling us to trust our surgeon
to be on our side when he or she picks up that scalpel. Therefore,
even a utilitarian should not try to justify killing one patient to save
five simply by saying five is more than one. Sometimes, numbers do
not count.

Think again about the case of *Peeveyhouse vs. Garland Coal*.
We expect companies like Garland Coal to honor their contracts,
as they normally do. Thus, we know where we stand. We do not
want to force our fellow citizens to spend their lives proving before
tribunals that strip-mining their land or killing them to save other
patients is inefficient. That is not a world we want to live in, if for
no other reason than that a society where people see efficiency that
way would be inefficient. What makes our society work is that we
have a right to say no. That simple right to say no enables us to live
with dignity in a community. It empowers us to decline to waste

resources on zero-sum games. In giving us moral space that we govern by right, laws limit how much energy we waste trying to influence regulators, fighting to keep what belongs to us and fighting to take what belongs to others.

Our having a right to say no teaches regulators along with everyone else to look for ways to get what they want in ways that benefit all. Utilitarianism at its crudest allows sacrificing the few for the sake of the many, but CBA is not a license to sacrifice the few. If we see CBA as indicating when takings are permissible, we will have a problem: breaking contracts or taking whenever the benefit of taking exceeds the cost is not a way of respecting people. However, if we instead treat CBA as a device for blocking inefficient takings rather than for licensing efficient ones, then it is not disrespectful. When we see winners gaining more than losers are losing, we conclude not that we have a license to take but only that the taking has passed one test. CBA so construed is a test that many takings fail and therefore is one tool for limiting the propensity to treat other people as mere means. CBA will *not* filter out every policy that ought to be filtered out, but it will filter out many of the more flagrantly disrespectful proposals, and that is its proper purpose.

16.5 Must CBA Treat All Values as Mere Commodities?

As Mark Sagoff notes, some believe, "neither worker safety nor environmental quality should be treated as a commodity to be traded at the margin for other commodities, but rather each should be valued for its own sake" (1981, 1288–9). Maybe so. But CBA is compatible with valuing worker safety and environmental quality for their own sake. Suppose a recycling process improves environmental quality but poses some risk to workers. Workers sometimes get into traffic accidents, and so on. Notice: if we treat both environmental quality and worker safety as ends in themselves, we still must weigh an operation's costs and benefits. Is the increment of environmental quality worth the risk? Simply reciting the slogan, "environmental quality is valued for its own sake" would be to ignore the question.

CBA would be needed even if environmental quality were the *sole* value at stake. Suppose recycling saves paper (and therefore trees), but only at a cost of all the water and electricity used in the process. Trucks use gasoline collecting paper from recycling bins. So, recycling has environmental costs as well as benefits. These are costs and benefits we need to know if environmental quality *matters.* "Recycling" is a politically correct word, but must we support any operation mentioning the word in its title, whatever the cost (and whatever the benefit)? Or should we stop to think? Those who are only posturing ignore such worries, but stopping to think is a way of showing respect.

In sum, we can find ourselves handling conflicting values. Critics of CBA sometimes seem to say, when values are important, that is when we should *not* think hard about the costs and benefits of resolving conflict one way rather than another. That seems backward.

Sagoff asserts that CBA "treats all value judgments other than those made on its behalf as nothing but statements of preference, attitude, or emotion" (1981, 1290–1). Many things are going on in this passage; I will mention two. First, Sagoff deems it a mistake to see all values as reducible to costs and benefits. I agree. On one hand, an economist's job is to go as far as possible in treating values as preferences, and this reductionist bias serves a purpose in economics narrowly construed. On the other hand, when we switch to philosophy, we cannot treat all values as mere preferences, as if valuing honesty were like valuing chocolate. What we take for granted in one discussion cannot be taken for granted in the other. Second, Sagoff is saying CBA treats all values as mere preferences. Perhaps, if Sagoff means to say CBA *typically* does so. But it would be incorrect to say CBA *necessarily* does so. CBA is about weighing costs and benefits. It does not presume everything is either a cost or a benefit. We must decide what to treat as mere preferences, costs, or benefits, and what to treat separately, as falling outside the scope of CBA. CBA itself does not decide for us.

To be clear, it is true by definition that to care about x is to have a preference regarding x. However, we can care about x—we can have a preference regarding x—without thinking x itself is merely a preference. *The only thing CBA assumes about the nature of values is that they can conflict.* CBA is for those days when we do, after all, need to choose.

16.6 Some Values Are Incommensurable. Some Are Qualitative. So What?

Steven Kelman says CBA presupposes the desirability of expressing all values as dollar values. As Kelman notes, converting values to dollars can distort the nature of the values at stake. On the other hand, it is incorrect to think that CBA requires regulators to represent all values as dollar values. If we care about elephants and do a CBA of alternative ways of protecting them, nothing in that process even suggests we have reduced the value of elephants to dollars.

More generally, we sometimes put a dollar value on x despite knowing that x's value to us is unlike the value of dollars. Philosophers distinguish instrumental and intrinsic value. The distinction matters here. An object's instrumental value is the value that it has as a tool. So, a paintbrush's instrumental value is a question of what I can use it for. I can paint with it. If I produce a painting, the painting may likewise have instrumental value. For example, if I can sell the painting, thereby using it as a tool for raising money, then the painting has instrumental value. Paintings, however, can have a second kind of value as well: intrinsic value. The value that a painting has to me in and of itself, simply by being beautiful, is its intrinsic value to me (Schmidtz 2015a).

Both values are real. Neither is necessarily huge. Having intrinsic value does not entail being priceless. Suppose I sell a painting.

Kelman says, "selling a thing for money demonstrates that it was valued only instrumentally" (1981, 39). Not so. Money I receive from the sale is the painting's instrumental value to me. But does deciding to sell imply that the painting lacks intrinsic value? No. I may love the painting, but if I need to quickly raise a large sum, selling the painting may be the best way to do it. The implication is not that the painting lacks intrinsic value but that the instrumental value of selling it can exceed the intrinsic value of keeping it.

Incommensurability of values is not an insurmountable obstacle to CBA. We can make up numbers when assessing the value of a library we could build on land that otherwise will remain a public park. Will the numbers mean anything? Maybe, maybe not. Even when we can predict a policy's costs and benefits, that does not entail that there will be any bottom line from which we simply read off what to do. When values are incommensurable—meaning they cannot be reduced to a number or to any other common measure without distortion—that makes it harder to know the bottom line. Often there is no unitary bottom line to be known. Often the only honest way to represent the bottom line is to say *this* precious thing is gained while *that* irreplaceable thing is lost (Bellamy 1999, 9). That does not mean we can't take costs and benefits into account. It just means we should not assume the bottom line will be simple.

In summary, there often is no point in trying to convert a qualitative balancing into something that looks like a precise quantitative tradeoff and thus looks scientific yet remains the same qualitative balancing, only now its qualitative nature is disguised by attaching toy numbers.

16.7 Some Things Are Priceless. So What?

Critics of CBA think they capture a moral high ground when they say some things are beyond price. They miss the point.

Choosing to call elephants priceless does not settle what to do about them. We still need to know whether our ways of protecting them are effective ways of spending whatever dollars we have available to spend on protection. We may also need to know whether we are saving them at a cost of sacrificing something equally priceless.

If baby Jessica has fallen into an abandoned well in Midland, Texas, and it will cost $9 million to rescue her, is it worth the cost? It seems wrong even to ask; after all, it's only money. But it is not wrong. If it would cost $9 million to save Jessica's life, what would the $9 million otherwise have purchased? Could it have supported peacekeeping forces in South Sudan that might have saved nine thousand lives? Is it obvious a decent person would not even *think* about the cost?

Critics like to say not all values are economic values. Yes. Indeed, no values are purely economic values. Even money itself is never only money. In a small town in Texas in 1987, money that took several lifetimes to produce was spent saving a baby's life. It was not only money. It saved a life. And, in the process, a small town in Texas inspired a planet. These are not trivial things. Neither are many other things on which they could have spent 9 million.

Some things are so valuable to us that we view them as beyond price. When we must make tradeoffs, should we ignore items we consider priceless or take them into account? The hard fact is, priceless values sometimes conflict. When that happens and we try to weigh our options, we in effect put a price on what is priceless. In that case, CBA is not the problem. It is a response to the problem. The world has handed us a painful choice.

Although critics of CBA often speak of incommensurable values, incommensurability is not strictly the issue. Consider the central dilemma of the novel *Sophie's Choice* (1979). Sophie's two children are about to be executed by a concentration camp warden, who offers to spare one child if Sophie picks which one to kill. Now, to Sophie, both children are beyond price. She does not value one more than the other. In some way, she values each more than anything. Nevertheless, she does in the end pick her daughter for execution, thereby saving her son. The point: although her values were incommensurate, she was still able to pick in a situation where failing to pick would have meant losing both. The values were incommensur*ate*, but not incommensur*able*. Sophie's children were beyond price, but when forced to put a price on them, she did.

Of course, as the sadistic warden foresaw, the process of ranking Sophie's previously incommensurate values would ruin Sophie's life. Commensuration is *always* possible, but there are times when something is lost (our innocence, perhaps) in the course of commensurating. That probably explains why some critics want to reject CBA; understandably, they deem it a mechanism for ranking values that should not be ranked (Holland 2002).

Elizabeth Anderson voices this concern when she says life and environmental quality are not "mere commodities. By regarding them only as commodity values, cost-benefit analysis fails to consider the proper roles they occupy in public life" (1995, 190). Yet Anderson would agree, if we blame Sophie for treating her children as commodities subject to tradeoffs, we blame the victim. Undeniably, Sophie treating her children in this way was a catastrophic failure to honor their value. Sophie knew it all too well. But Sophie's CBA was not causing the catastrophe so much as acknowledging and coping with it. Reducing values to mere commodities can be shattering, but the world sometimes forces tradeoffs that in a better world we would have been lucky enough to avoid. We can hope people like Sophie never need to rank their children and can go on thinking of each child as having infinite value. We can wish we never had to choose between worker safety and environmental quality, too, but we live in a world that sometimes forces tradeoffs. (See Chapter 19 for more on choices where something sacred is at stake.)

16.8 Does CBA Work?

Cass Sunstein observes that CBA often is defended on efficiency grounds and thinks CBA should instead be defended as a tool for correcting cognitive bias: "from thinking processes in which benefits are 'on screen' but costs are not, from ignoring systemic effects of one-shot interventions, from seeing cases in isolation, and from intense emotional reactions" (2000, 1059). As a way of correcting for bias, CBA is a tool, of course, not a miracle cure. Sunstein's endorsement of CBA is cautious, like mine.

When agencies engage in CBA, they sometimes ask how much they should be willing to pay. That is a legitimate question because they are, after all, constrained by their budget. Sometimes, though, legislators are asking how much to make *other people* pay. That is a problem. Situations where we are not accountable—where we have the option of not paying for our decisions—tend to bring out the worst in us. As with any accounting method, the quality of the output will reflect the quality of the inputs. Biased inputs generate biased outputs. CBA is potentially a smokescreen for the real action that takes place before numbers get added.

Can anything guarantee that CBA will not be subject to the same political piracy that CBA was supposed to limit? Probably not. I noted that the verdict in *Peeveyhouse* is widely regarded as mistaken. Here is what I did not mention. As Andrew Morriss notes, "Shortly after the *Peeveyhouse* decision, a corruption investigation uncovered more than thirty years of routine bribery of several of the court's members" (2000, 144). CBA per se does not correct for corrupted inputs. It is no miracle cure for political ills described in Chapter 14. However, if the process is public, with affected parties having a chance to protest when their interests are ignored, public scrutiny will have some tendency to correct for biased inputs. It may also encourage planners to supply inputs that can survive scrutiny in the first place. If the process is public, people can step forward not only to scrutinize valuations but also to suggest possibilities that planners overlooked.

Even if we know the costs and benefits of any particular factor, that does not guarantee that we have considered everything. Realistically, for any calculation we perform, it can turn out that we overlooked something. How do we avoid overlooking what will in retrospect be obvious? Although it is no guarantee, it is hard to beat opening the process to public scrutiny.

Kelman says CBA presumes we should spare no cost in enabling (or forcing) policymakers to use CBA in making decisions. It is fair enough for Kelman to mock the presumption; after all, CBA is itself an activity with costs and benefits. It can be a waste of time. Therefore, CBA on its own grounds should be able to identify limits to CBA's legitimate scope.

16.9 Must CBA Measure Valuations in Terms of Willingness to Pay?

CBA often is depicted as requiring us to measure a good's value by asking what people would pay for it. Problem: willingness to pay is a function not only of perceived values but also of resources available for bidding on those values. Poorer people show up as less willing to pay even if, in some other sense, they value the good as much.

Another problem: surveys designed to measure willingness to pay can fail to take willingness to pay seriously, asking subjects to declare not willingness to pay but *hypothetical* willingness. Surveys spuriously justify building waste treatment plants in poorer neighborhoods because we *judge* that poorer people would not pay as much as richer people would to have the plant built elsewhere. Critics call this *environmental racism* (because minorities tend to live in poorer neighborhoods).[2] Critics presume waste treatment

---

[2] See Hausman (2012); Salzman (2005); Bullard (1990); Shrader-Frechette (2002).

facilities will be sited by (possibly racist) politicians calculating how to minimize adverse effects on re-election bids.

What would be less corrupt? What if neighborhood waste treatment sites were chosen by random lottery? Suppose, by random luck, Beverly Hills is selected as the site of a new waste treatment plant. We then ask Beverly Hills's rich residents what they are willing to pay to site the plant elsewhere. Suppose they jointly offer $10 billion to locate the plant elsewhere. We then announce that the people of Beverly Hills are not just hypothetically but literally offering $10 billion to any neighborhood willing to serve as alternate host of that treatment facility. What if a poor neighborhood accepts the bid? Would that be respectful?

Alternatively, suppose no one accepts the offer and the plant is built in Beverly Hills. Then what? Is anything wrong with richer residents leaving, selling their houses to poorer people happy to live near a waste treatment plant if that means being able to afford a house like those in Beverly Hills? If siting a treatment plant drives down property values so that poorer people can afford Beverly Hills while rich people take their money elsewhere, is that bad? In what way?

The implication: even a random lottery would produce non-random results. No matter where waste treatment facilities are built, buyers who opt to move in, accepting the nuisance for the sake of having a nicer house at a lower price, will tend to be poorer than buyers who opt to pay higher prices to live farther from the nuisance.

One thing no one can change: waste treatment facilities will always be found in poorer neighborhoods. Not even putting them all in Beverly Hills could ever change that.

16.10 Must Future Generations Be Discounted?

In financial markets, a dollar acquired today is worth more than a dollar to be acquired in a year. Dollars acquired today can be put to work today. So, if you ask how much I would pay today to be given a dollar a year from now, I would not pay as much as a dollar. I might pay a few percent less, depending on available rates of return. Properly valued, then, future dollars sell at a discount. Therefore, borrowing to get a profitable project off the ground can be rational, even when the cost of borrowing a thousand now will be more than a thousand later.

Here is the catch. There is nothing wrong with taking out a loan so long as we pay it back. But there is something wrong with taking out a loan we have no intention of repaying. Discounting is one thing when the cost of raising capital is internalized and something else when we borrow against someone else's future. The problem here is not discounting; it is a problem of external cost. We have no right to discount the price that *others* will have to pay for our projects.

If we undertake a CBA to evaluate the merits of borrowing against our own futures, we decide how or whether to discount. CBA will not decide for us.

16.11 CBA As Political Compromise

I talked about CBA with full cost accounting, but no mechanical procedure is guaranteed to take all costs into account. For any mechanical procedure we devise, there will be situations where that procedure misses something crucial. This is not a problem with CBA per se, although it is reason to be wary of making decisions mechanically. At some point we draw the line, make a decision, and get on with our lives.

CBA is an important response to a real problem. However, it is not magic. There is a limit to what it can do. CBA organizes information. It can be a forum for eliciting further information. It can be a forum for correcting bias. It can be a forum for giving affected parties a voice in community decision-making, thereby leading to better mutual understanding and acceptance of tradeoffs involved in running a community. CBA can be all these things, but it is not necessarily so. CBA can limit a system's tendency to invite abuse, but CBA is prone to the same abuse that infects the system as a whole. It is an antidote to abuse that is itself subject to abuse. Biased inputs will tend to crank out biased outputs. However, although the method does not inherently correct for biased inputs, if the process is conducted publicly so that people can publicly challenge suppliers of biased inputs, there will be some tendency for the process to correct for biased inputs as well. We can hope there will be opportunities for those who see a bigger picture to challenge those who have tunnel vision and can't see anything beyond their narrow concerns, but we cannot guarantee it.

The most we can say: legislation or regulation that passes muster by the lights of CBA is *to that extent* morally defensible. Benefits exceed costs. This is a moral defense offered on the road to political compromise. It will not be conclusive. As per Chapter 11, we are moving toward political compromise when we realize that what we want is not what our fellow citizens want, but also that our fellow citizens are not enemies. We want fellow citizens to be partners in building communities that are resilient rather than fragile—by virtue of having a crowning liberal virtue of not depending on us to all want the same thing.

We want to send neighbors away with a compromise that may not give them all they want but that gives them something, leaves their dignity intact, and leaves them with a sense of being better off with us than without us.

If you must resort to a CBA, you are already in a situation where no one will get all they want, but if you can use CBA, you have a potential peacemaker: a way of deciding that is not inherently insulting. Specifically, if CBA is your basis for political compromise, then the fact that no one got all they wanted does not mean some of you are second-class citizens. Rather, it means what you wanted was on the table, but so was its price tag. It means that a CBA, done in public view, gave your democracy a fighting chance to operate as democracies are supposed to operate.

6

INVENTING THE SELF

17

The Reconciliation Project

THEME: *"Why be moral?"* needs answering when it is a question about a particular conflict.

Among the more damaging mistakes that philosophy has long made (not only since the siloing of social science): we tend to answer the "why be moral?" question in ways more clever than wise. Socrates sounds clever when he dismantles Thrasymachus, but wisdom emerges not when Socrates humiliates Thrasymachus but when he gives Glaucon something to think about. Reconciling morality and rationality starts there.

1. Before we ask, "Why be moral?" we do well to ask, "Why be rational?" Both questions are best seen as empirical, to be answered not by sophistry but by seeing how life goes for people who strive to be rational (or moral). What do we miss if we try and fail? What do we miss if we succeed? If what we *call* rationality would not survive self-inspection by the lights of a cost-benefit analysis, then we don't need to know whether morality can be reconciled with it. If reconciling morality and rationality has a point, the point is to show that morality lines up with something we have reason to be.

2. When we ask, "why be rational?" and begin to wonder how to interpret that question, we start to wonder whether being rational entails being a maximizer. Why would it? Better question: *When* would it? In passing, that people maximize is an assumption, not an observation. We postulate maximizing to

Living Together. David Schmidtz, Oxford University Press. © Oxford University Press 2023.
DOI: 10.1093/oso/9780197658505.003.0017

make our models tractable. Sometimes such models seem accurate enough, but not always.

3. As previewed in Chapters 4, 6, and 12, a life comprises
projects that need to make room for each other. We operate
under constraints, but constraints often are self-imposed. We
fabricate compartments out of self-imposed constraints and
thereby carve our world into spaces of tractable life.

4. We operate under two kinds of self-imposed constraint.

   a. We constrain resource *inputs*. Maximizing within a given
   project compartment is maximizing with respect to local
   input constraints; that is to say, within the limits of how
   much we can reasonably afford to spend on that particular
   project.

   b. We also constrain the *output* we seek within a compartment. Having solved an actual problem, and thus having
   hit a tangible target, self-appraisal often is a matter of
   acknowledging that we got what we came for. That can
   be what rationally signals us to close that life compartment and get on with other compartments in our lives—
   compartments defined by problems not yet solved.

   Then we put both constraints together. Imagine a two-
   dimensional Cartesian space.[1] For any given pursuit, let the x-
   axis measure how much we spend. Let the y-axis measure how
   much we achieve. Having defined the axes in that way, a hard
   input constraint would appear in the resulting space as a ver-
   tical line, a border somewhere out on the x-axis, while a hard
   limit on aspiration would appear as a horizontal line, a ceiling
   somewhere up on the y-axis. We terminate a pursuit and close a
   compartment either when (a) we hit a ceiling, having achieved
   what we set out to achieve, or when (b) we run up against the
   limit of how much we are willing to spend on that pursuit.

---

[1] To see these graphs, check the QR code under "Choosing Strategies" (Appendix,
Figure 2.3).

5. As Anthony Laden notes, reasoning can aim at choosing what to do, but also at choosing what to aim at (Laden 2000, 2012). We can decide how to decide.[2] Humanly rational choice embraces the challenge of identifying a constellation of targets, some chosen, that add up to a life worth living.

6. If we are open to having more to live for, then as our constellation of targets comes to include living for loved ones, communities, or causes, we make room for morality. Making *room* is not the same as making morality *necessary*. An honest reconciliation of rationality and morality will never be quite so tidy. Reconciling morality for Glaucon involves showing that morality is an *excellent* choice for Glaucon, not that morality is the *only* choice for Thrasymachus. To think philosophy needs to show the latter is to think philosophy needs to be clever rather than honest.

7. We must theorize about the morality we are trying to reconcile with rationality. Just as we need to conceive of rationality as something worth reconciling with morality, so we need to conceive of morality as something worth reconciling with rationality, and as consisting in part of mutual expectations out of which we build communities that command our respect.

8. There is no conflict between morality and rationality as *types*. As *types*, morality and rationality do not conflict necessarily, or even typically. On the contrary, a normal day is a series of opportunities to do the right thing that coincide nicely with what a self-loving social animal wants to do. Still, we do sometimes need to choose among contingently conflicting *tokens* of moral and rational agency.[3] In those moments of crisis, as

---

[2] Crucially, there is no all-purpose decision algorithm. Before we trust a formula for maximizing expected utility, for example, we need to learn the lesson of Newcomb's Problem: namely, we start by deciding when to see correlation as causation. Only then can we decide whether to treat possibilities as having independent probabilities (Schmidtz and Wright 2004). Decision theory, realistically, is never the place to start.

[3] BACKGROUND: In philosophy of language, there is an important distinction between a *type* (which is a general category) and a *token* (which is a particular instance of the

Socrates observed, we define ourselves. In those moments, the choice is in our hands whether to have lived a life to be proud of.

It may seem clever to argue that moments of crisis never really occur. But a wiser course is to see those moments coming and get ready for them so that, in the crunch, we won't forget that we aim not merely to survive but to live a life worth living. I want to consider what prepares ordinary people to be what they will want to have been when the time comes to make a stand.

Previous chapters treated the human condition as a question of how to live with others. This chapter reflects on how to live with oneself. In either case, the question of how to live becomes concrete enough to answer, even if honest answers tend to remain moving targets. Still, lives do culminate in something, even if not in ultimate answers. These final chapters pull together the threads of a career as well as a book.[4]

17.1 Selves and Reasons

I have supposed that, as self-aware social beings, we navigate both an internal terrain of integrity and self-esteem and an external terrain of political compromise and working to deserve each other's esteem. Moral science studies this twin challenge. As per Chapter 13, and as Adam Smith realized, self-love is not something to take for granted. We have selves. Selves take shape as outcomes of our habits and choices. We not only discover our self; we invent it.

type). For example, if Jill says "arguing is stupid," you may wonder whether she means to say "arguing is stupid in general" or "arguing is stupid in this particular instance."

[4] I drafted this in 1997 as a sequel to Schmidtz (1992, 1994, 1995). A reviewer described it as, at the time, "having no genre." But even if there was a grain of truth in that remark back then, see Bedke (2008), Blau (2021), Broome (2000), Callard (2018), Kolodny (2018), Paul (2015), Raz (2005), or Stegenga (2013).

Will we love the self we invent? Yes, hopefully, but it takes work. We are social beings who run a gauntlet of maturation. We are wired to grow up craving the esteem of others. As Smith observed, we never outgrow this craving, but adulthood complements the craving with a propensity to reflect on whether we are *worthy* of esteem. We come to want not only to be loved but to know that the love is not a case of mistaken identity. We want to love who we truly are.

Therein lies a measure of moral objectivity. We are creatures that observably need the love of others, but also need to nurture a sense of being worthy of love. Thus, the Holy Grail for fully mature *political* animals is being esteemed for playing an important role in making a community tick. It is what makes life feel right.

I say this to preface an argument that may superficially seem to go in the opposite direction. Namely, the bare fact of something being our end is some reason to pursue it. Or so I argue. It may sound as if my conclusion is subjectivist: that "there is no accounting for taste" and our ends are not subject to evaluation. My actual conclusion is the opposite. Precisely because our ends are that important—they are our reasons for action and our ultimate reasons to love (or not love) our selves—we need to get them right.[5]

17.2 On Being Overcome by Reason

Must we have reasons for everything? Must we have reasons for wanting what we want? Intuitively, the respectable answer is a table-thumping yes, but in this dogma lies insecurity and a lack of

---

[5] One factor pulling me toward such reflection is the challenge I posed to ideal theory. I have no problem with idealism. My problem is with wishing ideals were fact-insensitive—wishing to insulate ourselves from having to learn that what once seemed worth living and dying for has been tested and found unworthy. Kai Nielsen says "things we are interested in asserting or taking as rock bottom . . . are not, whether we like it or not, unrevisable or fact-insensitive" (2012, 224).

self-awareness. Part of the challenge of being as realistic as we can be is the challenge of understanding that there comes a time for being realistic about how far down reasons can go and for being realistic about how far down we have reason to want to go.

We think we can be overcome by passion. Is there such a thing as being overcome by reason? What would that be like? Chapter 16 offered a qualified defense of cost-benefit analysis, but what if the calculating becomes obsessive? What if calculating costs and benefits becomes an excuse for talking yourself out of following your heart?

Intriguingly, young children can go through a stage of asking "why" as a generic response to anything a parent says. At that stage, a child does not yet know why we ask why or what it would be like to have a point, which is why a child can fail to know when to stop. It is a form of immaturity.

How accountable would ideals (ideally) be? How far down do rationales and corroborations need to go to count as real? At what point is there insufficient reason to keep going? As per Chapter 2, it is not our natural task to deduce conclusions from indubitable axioms. Instead, our organic, evolving objective is to go until we see nothing to gain by going further—or, more realistically, to a point where we have more to gain by doing something else, such as sending this off to the publisher in time to figure out what to make for dinner.

We face a challenge. We want to see ourselves as having reasons for what we do. Yet having reasons for everything is a prerequisite neither of having reasons per se nor of being reasonable. Wanting reasons for everything may even be incompatible with being reasonable. It can be a form of childishness. Why, you ask? (Why *do* you ask?) Because there comes a point when nothing is achieved by being unwilling to just let it go and let a chain of reasoning come to an end. Past some point, a chain of reasoning becomes more neurotic than properly goal-directed. In sum, there is a problem with reasoning when there is no longer a *reason for reasoning*.

Philosophy can be illuminating in ways that are useful and agreeable to self and others. If philosophy were that much, it would be an extraordinary dimension of any ordinary life, but philosophy becomes a false promise if we insist on it being much more than that. How far down can our reasons and the consolations of philosophy go? These chapters reflect on the human condition as an organizational challenge that is both inter- and intra-personal.

18

Rational Choice Theory's Silence About Ends

> THEME: *Must we have reasons for everything? Must we have reasons for wanting what we want? Among the most fascinating aspects of the challenge of being as realistic as we can be is the challenge of being realistic about how far down reasons can go.*

This is a valid argument:

1. I know that *A* (an available course of action) would serve my end *E*.
2. Therefore, I have a reason to do *A*.

I will call this *The Argument*. To say this argument is valid is to say it preserves truth; if you construct a truth table, it will turn out that there are no cases where the premise is true yet the conclusion is false. In short, the Argument has no counterexamples. In what follows, I explain why the Argument is, semantically if not syntactically, valid.

Then I explain why it matters. I have spent my career stressing that purely instrumental rationality is awfully limited; it may not be worth reconciling with morality. I have made a career out of explaining why purely instrumental reasoners would come to have reason to want to get past being purely instrumental reasoners.

Barbara Herman says, "The ends of rational agents are adopted, not given" (1993, 228). She adds, "A being whose ultimate grounds

Living Together. David Schmidtz, Oxford University Press. © Oxford University Press 2023.
DOI: 10.1093/oso/9780197658505.003.0018

of action were given—who truly acted from desire—would not act for reasons all the way down. Its desires would be causes of its actions. Such a being would not, in the end, have a reason for acting one way rather than another" (Herman 1993, 228).

I want to agree with Herman, but I do not want my agreement to sound pious, self-righteous, or vacuous, and I do not want to beg the question. So, I need to pursue the matter. What is it like to act for reasons all the way down? I imagine a driver approaching a railway crossing. Does the driver have reason to look both ways? Must reasons be "deep" to be real? Why? When? Is there some deep reason to assume that simply wanting to avoid being hit by a train is "in the end" no reason to get off the tracks? Does wanting to avoid being hit work better as a reason to jump *off* the tracks than as a reason to jump *on*? Or does wanting to avoid being hit amount to nothing—no reason to act one way rather than another?

Although I doubt this is Herman's intent, I have observed her being interpreted as saying we have no reason unless we have reasons for the reason "all the way down." The implied regress threatens to leave us with no reasons at all. This is rational choice theory's repugnant conclusion. So, is it true? To have a reason for acting one way or another, must we act for reasons all the way down?

To be clear, we typically do manage to look both ways before crossing the tracks. Moreover, and tellingly, our reason to look both ways is obvious. No more needs to be said to make it *obvious* that we have reason to look.

18.1 Reasons All the Way Down

Again, I defend the Argument not because I have an allegiance to instrumentalism but because I aim to offer an observably realistic reason to get past instrumentalism. The Argument is a key to a non-standard defense not only of instrumental but *noninstrumental* reason. It can help us see that instrumental reason is not a ceiling but a launching pad. The status of noninstrumental reason, no less than that of instrumental reason, stands or falls with the Argument. There are two parts to the doctrine of instrumentalism:

1. Ends are reasons for the actions that serve them.
2. Means-end reason is all there is to practical reason. Practical reason concerns only the choice of means. There are no reasons for ends as such.

The second part will not do. The human condition is that we sometimes have doubts about our ends. *Insisting* on having nothing to say about our ends, as if that were a way of being hard-nosed and scientific, can undercut those very ends. Some people believe there is a realm of reason out there beyond mere means-end reasons. I am one of them. I aim to show that the realm of noninstrumental reason is real, using only premises that instrumentalists correctly accept.

These chapters address two audiences. I write for instrumentalists unsatisfied by instrumentalism who seek to retain instrumentalism's hard-nosed naturalism while identifying richer roles for human reason than instrumentalism has so far been able to see. I also write for noninstrumentalists unsatisfied by noninstrumentalism who seek an observation-based naturalistic account that explains rather than dogmatically insists upon the possibility of our having reasons for our ends.

Here, then, is one way to think of the challenge posed by these meditations. Suppose we began life as beings accurately described by instrumentalism. The question is, what would happen next? Would we remain beings accurately described by instrumentalism, or would we become something else? If we would (*and observably do*) develop into something else, would the process be merely a biological process with nothing to be said in favor of it, or would the process be such that we accurately could describe ourselves as developing into something more for good reason?

Rosalind Hursthouse notes that nonhuman animals seemingly have largely hard-wired, species-characteristic ends (1999, part III). Human ends often are not hard-wired. (For example, I was not programmed from birth to want to get the phrasing of this parenthetical remark exactly right.) Is this an obstacle to naturalistic analyses of ethics and rationality? Of course! Yet it is also a naturalist's key to a realm of noninstrumental reasons. This realm emerged in the natural world along with human (or near-human) psychology. There is no doubt that this happened; the question is how. The naturalistic story I wish to tell explains how it is in our nature to transcend our nature. It begins by noting that our corpus of ends is plastic—subject to growth, decay, and drift. Our plasticity is both asset and liability: *asset* because our plasticity is our key to a realm beyond instrumentalism, *liability* because our plasticity is why we need a key.

Because of our plasticity, we can have extra ends. And we do have an extra end: namely, an end of giving ourselves extra ends—giving shape and content to our plasticity. Nature built us to give ourselves ends beyond those given by nature. The story of how this happens not only explains but justifies us in having an evolving corpus of chosen ends. Our nature is such that it serves a purpose for us to give ourselves purposes.

I do not claim there is a reason for everything. Having reasons is a challenge, one we have an impressive yet limited capacity to meet. One aspect of the achievement in becoming a rational adult is making peace with our limits. We learn not to expect our reasons (or anyone else's) to go all the way down. However reflective we become, we remain somewhat opaque to ourselves. It would be unreflective to suppose otherwise. We become more than instrumental reasoners if all goes well but remain something less than beings who reason all the way down. The closest we ever get to being reasonable all the way down is to become aware of our limits, and serene about them.

18.2 An Intuitive Argument
for the Argument

Suppose Bob finds himself standing on a railroad track in the path of an oncoming train. Does Bob have reason to step off the track? What would we need to know?

We have not yet said whether Bob wants to live. Is that a relevant piece of information? Consider two cases. In one case, Bob wants to live. In the other, Bob wants to die. Does this difference make a difference? Is wanting to live a reason to step aside where wanting to die is not? If so, then ends can be reasons for actions that serve them.

Bob's ends give him reasons for action, and they do so independently of any further argument concerning whether Bob ought to have those ends. Therefore, we can know Bob has reasons for action without knowing whether Bob has reasons for reasons.

An end can be a reason without always being decisive because other ends (or moral constraints) also provide reasons for action that can compete with wanting to live. But if a skeptic asks why Bob is stepping aside and Bob says he wants to live, Bob answers the question. We get it. What Bob says is intelligible and not merely as a causal explanation. Rather, we hear Bob's stated reason as a reason. A skeptic may want to pursue the issue, but Bob's answer puts the ball in the skeptic's court.

18.3 Burden of Proof

If Bob says he is stepping aside because he wants to die, *that* would baffle us and would fail to shift the burden of proof. Why? Because the action (on its face) fails to connect to the end. Stepping aside to survive is intelligible because the action connects.

A skeptic may offer a different account of why wanting to die would call for further explanation, where wanting to live would not: "Yes, survival gives Bob reason for action, but that is because survival is survival, not because survival is an end. Survival is a reason because of its inherent reasonableness, not because of the bare fact that it is an end." A fair conjecture. Must we leave it at that—dueling intuitions? No. This conjecture is testable.

To see whether any work is being done by the simple fact that Bob *wants* to live as opposed to all the work being done by survival's inherent normativity, consider two variations. In the first variant, Bob does not step away. As the train hurtles toward him, we scream at him to get off the tracks. Bob does not move. He calmly says he wants to die. In that case, Bob has given us a reason for action, but not because we see wanting to die as inherently reasonable: we see no such thing.

In the second variant, Bob again does not step away. This time, Bob responds to our screams by saying he is standing on the tracks because he wants to live. In this case, Bob has given no reason at all for standing on the tracks. The inherent reasonableness of the end of survival does not help.

In the first variant, we would ask, "Bob, why do you want to die?" In the second, we would *not* ask the parallel question: "Bob, why do you want to live?" Instead, in the second variant, we say: "Bob, you're not making sense. What does wanting to live have to do with stepping in front of a train?" Observe: it is the second variant, *not the first*, where Bob's alleged reason is no reason at all.

Therefore, identifying an end's inherent reasonableness is neither necessary nor sufficient. What does the work is the instrumental connection between action and end.[1]

---

[1] Another example: an addict craves heroin. If the craving is a reason to inject heroin, the reason remains overridable. A friend can say, "You want to satisfy your craving, but long-term happiness lies in forcing your body to get over craving." Now, the friend has given the addict a real reason not to inject. Compare this to an addict who responds to a craving for heroin by swallowing the needle and choking to death. On its face, this response is unintelligible. The craving is not an overridden reason to swallow the needle; it is no reason at all, and what makes it "no reason at all" is the fact that the action does not connect to the end. The example is from Railton (1997, 67).

18.4 Ends and Reasons

The Argument's key terms need clarifying. First, as Michael
Bratman (1987, 20) says, intentions are distinctive states of mind,
on a par with desires and not reducible to them. Ends are not reducible to desires either. Clearly, an end is more than an urge. Ends are
the sort of thing on behalf of which we *resist* urges. Urges defy the
will; ends express it. If I intend to lose five pounds but feel an urge
to eat a doughnut, I have a conflict between an end and a mere urge.
An end is not the same thing as a plan, but there is a connection. An
end is that for the sake of which we plan.[2]

A paradigm case of an end, as I use the term, would be something
we not only wish for but fully intend to achieve. By "fully intend"
I do not mean we necessarily have reflected on it. We could fully
intend to turn left at the next intersection without having given
the matter much thought. All I mean is, we are not conflicted—not
acting against our better judgment. In a paradigm case, our end is
what we wholeheartedly plan to achieve by acting.

Having an end ordinarily is conjoined to the state of arousal
we call desire, but the conjunction is contingent. Thus, I may intend to achieve E while having only the hollowest of desires for E,
expecting no satisfaction, as when I review a book I unexpectedly
dislike only because I promised. Or I may desire D while having no
intention of trying to obtain D. Perhaps my desire for D is a mere
urge, or perhaps it is more like an intellectual recognition of D as
worthy of desire—something I might have wanted under different
circumstances.

The term "reason" likewise is used in various ways. We could define a reason as that for the sake of which we act by contrast with
what merely causes us to act. That would make reasons virtually
synonymous with ends as just described, which would be a problem

---

[2] I do not assume all action is end-directed in the same way. Sometimes we have reason
to distinguish between trying to promote a value and trying to respect or exemplify it.

because I do not want to win the Argument by turning it into a tautology. Whether ends are reasons is a question of whether an end as such is a reason for actions that serve it. So, let us begin with that: to offer a reason for A is to offer a consideration that speaks in favor of doing A. If we characterize the terms this way, then it becomes a real question whether ends as such are reasons. We are not settling the question by fiat.

While there is a connection between explaining and giving reasons, reason as it concerns us here is more than mere explanation. When we explain a behavior by citing Bob's reason, we explain the behavior not as a mechanical process but as a token of agency. We say E is Bob's reason for action without implying that Bob is a thoroughly rational agent, but we do count E toward making A rational for the agent that Bob is. Further, we can say E is Bob's reason for action without implying E is a reason for observers to approve of Bob's action. All we are saying is that if Bob intends to achieve E, then that counts toward explaining Bob's E-seeking behavior as a token of agency rather than as a mechanical process.

Second, we can separate reasons provided by facts from reasons provided by what we believe to be facts. "A *would* serve my end" implies what we may call an objective reason. "I *believe A* would serve my end" implies what we may call a subjective reason.[3] The premise that I *know A* serves my end E implies both the fact and the belief.[4]

Given this distinction, Pete can have reason of a kind to buy a lottery ticket even if the ticket turns out to be a loser. Pete likewise can have reason of a kind to drink petrol (Williams 1981, 102).

---

[3] Matt Bedke (2008, 110) says "Do I have reason to do what I believe I have reason to do?" is always a sensible question.

[4] The premise "I *believe A* would serve E" fails to entail an objective reason, whereas "A *would* serve E" fails to entail a subjective reason. Either failure might be misinterpreted as a counterexample to the thesis that ends imply reasons. That is why I cast the Argument in terms of knowing.

Saying Pete drank petrol because he thought it was gin has an explanatory aspect if it helps explain why events unfolded as they did. It also has a justificatory aspect if it explains how Pete's role in such a bizarre event could have been played by a rational agent. We do not defend "buying a losing ticket" or "drinking petrol" under that description. In each case, Pete had no objective reason for acting as he did. We explain what Pete objectively did in terms of Pete's subjective reasons when we appeal to what Pete thought or hoped he was doing. If I falsely believe A would serve my end, then my reason for A is merely subjective.[5] Conversely, I can have an objective reason without knowing it if I fail to notice that A would serve my end.[6]

Third, reasons can be inconclusive. A reason is a "pro" consideration that feeds into all-things-considered judgment. We sometimes use the term to refer to all-things-considered judgment itself, but not here. Ends are not stopping points in the sense of being points past which we need not remain "open to reason," but only in the sense that they meet or shift a certain burden of proof. That is, coming to know that E is my end, and that doing A would serve E, is coming to know that I have some reason to do A. (I may have other ends ill-served by A, or some other action might be a more effective means, so it is normal to have reason to remain open to reason.)

Faced with overwhelming reason not to do A, it would remain false to say this reason not to do A is so overwhelming that my reason to do A is no reason at all. On the contrary, something was there to be overwhelmed. There was a reason, one that ultimately

---

[5] I could have another kind of merely subjective reason if I know A would serve my end while falsely believing A is an available course of action. Thus, my desire for lasting fame could be reason for my trying to prove a theorem that, unknown to me, is not provable. (I thank Chris Maloney and John Pollock for the point.)

[6] A related point. *Believing* I have reason involves a self-awareness not implied merely by noticing a connection. When a dog grasps that the kitchen is where the food is, we can describe it as heading to the kitchen for a reason, without supposing that it self-identifies as an agent acting for a reason. See Darwall (1983, chap. 3).

was not good enough, as opposed to there having been no reason at all. To say E is overridable is to underscore that there is something to override, something that stands as a reason until overridden. If it counted for nothing in the first place, there would be nothing to override.

Thus, a further gloss on the Argument would be as follows:

1. I know that A (an available course of action) would serve my end E.
2. Therefore, I have reason for A. Moreover, E is sufficient reason for A, barring overriders.

In medieval times, the phenomenon of motion was thought to need explanation. (Why do objects remain in motion, absent any obvious force to sustain motion?) The Newtonian insight is that objects in motion have inertia. Objects carry on unless something (friction, say) stops them. What needs explaining is not motion but change. We make a mistake, analogous to the medieval one, if we assume we need an extra boost in favor of counting E as reason for A. To say Bob intends to survive and that stepping away from the train is safe but stepping forward will get him killed is to say enough to generate an asymmetry and a burden of proof: the action that cries out for a reason is stepping forward, not stepping back. No extra boost is needed to convert Bob's end into a reason to step back. Bob's end is sufficient reason to step back unless something (some analog of friction) stops it from being so.

Means-end reasons are overridable, but overridable reasons are reasons with bite. They stand as reasons until something overrides. That would not be true if they were not real reasons in the first place. To suppose a reason is real only if it *cannot* be overridden is to wish for practical reason to be something it never was and never needed to be.

18.5 More on Validity

While commenting on David Gauthier's "Reason's End" at the Jean Hampton Memorial Symposium in Tucson in 1997, Michael Bratman suggested (and Gauthier agreed) that to reach a conclusion that I ought to do *A* (where *A* is a means to *E*) we need a premise like "I ought to seek end *E*." Clearly, the Argument lacks the truth-preserving syntax that we look for when we do sentential logic.

Suppose we give the Argument a truth-preserving syntax by adding a premise:

If I know that *A* would serve my end *E*, then I have reason to do *A*.

Call this the Hypothetical Imperative, or simply the *Hypothetical*. Do we need the Hypothetical to ensure that the Argument is truth-preserving?

1. I know that *A* (an available course of action) would serve my end *E*.
2. *If* I know that *A* would serve my end *E*, *then* I have reason to do *A*.
3. Therefore, I have a reason to do *A*.

We want to say no here because the issue is not whether Line 2 would fix the syntax. Even bracketing Hume's skepticism about deduction (as per Chapter 2) and working within the confines of deductive logic, the fact remains that Line 2, the Hypothetical, does not do what premises do. It does not supply extra information upon which rules of inference can operate. Instead, what Line 2 says is that Line 1 is the only premise we need to warrant moving to Line 3.[7] In other words, when we deliberate, the Hypothetical

---

[7] The Argument, Brandom might say, is a materially, as opposed to logically, good inference (1994, 97–8 and 247).

enters our thought process not as a premise but as an inference rule.[8]

The force of means-end reasoning comes from ends, not from a suppressed premise that ends are reasons. I agree with Railton (1997, 68) that the reason-giving force of ends "does not presuppose a further, contingent desire on my part that I realize my ends." The Hypothetical itself implies as much. The Hypothetical does not say that the Hypothetical gives us reasons. The Hypothetical says that ends give us reasons. And that is where we started, because asking whether that is true is the same thing as asking whether the original Argument is truth-preserving.

---

[8] Peter Railton explains why, "one cannot treat rules of inference (such as modus ponens) as premises, on pain of regress" (1997, 76). See also Lewis Carroll's astounding 1895 article.

Following Quine (1951), we might wonder whether "Bob is a bachelor" suffices to entail "Bob is unmarried." Do we need a second premise that "Bachelors are unmarried" or is it enough to know what the words mean?

19

Reasons for Reasons

THEME: *A realist's story of how far down our reasons go,*
or can go, is a developmental story. Our original ends are
given, but our original ends are not enduring foundations so
much as launching pads. They are not something to build on
so much as something to leave behind.

Whether ends imply reasons is controversial. Simon Blackburn
(1995) worries about deducing "ought" from "is." Elijah Millgram
(1995) wonders whether ends might be reasons only under further
conditions. Jean Hampton (1996) worries that a merely contingent
end, not grounded in a Kantian noumenal self, might be no reason
at all. T. M. Scanlon (1998, 37) explicitly denies that desires are nor-
matively significant.[1] As noted, Barbara Herman believes that "A
being whose ultimate grounds of action were given—who truly
acted from desire . . . would not, in the end, have a reason for acting
one way rather than another" (1993, 229). Christine Korsgaard says
"the instrumental principle cannot stand alone. Unless there are
normative principles directing us to the adoption of certain ends,
there can be no requirement to take the means to our ends" (1997,
220). Perhaps along similar lines, Robert Nozick says, "If other
modes of rationality cannot justify themselves without circularity,
the same can be said of instrumental rationality" (1993, 134).

---

[1] When Scanlon says "desire," he is talking not about mere urges but about something
like what I call ends. Thus, he says that if I desire a new computer, my desire "involves a
tendency to judge that I have reason to buy a new computer" (Scanlon 1998, 43). See also
Warren Quinn (1995).

Living Together. David Schmidtz, Oxford University Press. © Oxford University Press 2023.
DOI: 10.1093/oso/9780197658505.003.0019

I am not saying we can summarize the complexity of these wonderfully complex thinkers in a paragraph. Moreover, my purpose is not to blame them for some mistake. Upon reflection they might repudiate what I will call the Regress:

E is a reason for A only if there are, in turn, reasons for E.

But we embrace the Regress when we refuse to acknowledge that, as we switch from justifying actions to justifying ends, one quest for reasons is over and a different quest begins.

Is there good reason to embrace the Regress? No. Before we look for reasons for reasons, we should ask: What cries out for reasons? Do reasons themselves cry out for reasons?

Suppose Bob says, "I want to have reasons for what I do."

The skeptic poses a challenge. "But why do you want to have reasons?"

Bob responds, "It's just a brute fact about me. I want to have reasons for what I do."

The skeptic pounces. "But then you're unreasonable. You want to have reasons, yet you have no reason for wanting *that*."

Bob is stumped, then pulls himself together. "You have a point. And I don't want to be unreasonable. Thus, I'll stop trying to have reasons, because merely wanting reasons is no reason for trying to have them."

What went wrong? If Bob simply wants to have reasons for what he does, is he being unreasonable? On the contrary, wanting reasons for what one does is a hallmark (if not a guarantee) of reasonableness. It is a parody rather than a paradigm of reason for Bob to repudiate his unexamined desire to have reasons. Bob's mistake lies in buying the premise that because he has no reason for his end, his end does not give him reason for action. He mistakenly accepts the Regress. As an antidote to this regress, consider the Anti-Regress Hypothesis.

"Why *E*?" is a good question when you have a purpose in asking and when asking serves that purpose.

The Anti-Regress is one way of taking seriously the idea that what we choose to do cries out for reasons, and seeking reasons is among the things we choose to do.[2] If I have no reason to seek reasons, then, well, end of story. To say otherwise is not a way of being reasonable. If we insist on seeking reasons when we have no reason to seek reasons, we are not being reasonable all the way down. Rather, by hypothesis, we are insisting on doing something *for no reason*.

Does this picture of the dialectical burden leave too much room for ends to be reasons, thereby leading us to endorse things by default that should not be endorsed? On the contrary, this picture properly identifies challenges as challenges rather than as preconditions of there existing anything to challenge. It leaves room for all the challenges to extant ends that noninstrumentalists rightly pose.

Thus, accepting the Anti-Regress stops the regress in its tracks and stops it without precluding *motivated* skeptical challenges. At any point, we determine how much longer a chain of reason-giving needs to be by asking what purpose is served by saying more. We go back as far as we have reason to go. Then, when we have no reason to keep going, we stop.[3]

---

[2] It is no mere tautology that seeking means to our ends helps us achieve our ends. When it helps is a complex empirical question. I have made this point before (1995, 19–26). I now see that Railton (1984, 143) was making a more specific version of the same point when he observed that the happiest life makes only so much room for hedonistic deliberation. I would have given him credit back then if I had seen the connection.

[3] So, as Deirdre McCloskey observes (in conversation), I might say I prefer vanilla. If you ask why, that may be an interesting question. I may have an interesting answer. But the fact that I prefer vanilla is already established. What could problematize my reason to choose vanilla is not doubt about whether I have a reason for the reason—that is, whether I have a reason to prefer vanilla—but doubt about whether I do in fact prefer it. Further point: suppose I discover that vanilla causes cancer, which then becomes my reason not to choose vanilla. What is happening to my preference? Does finding that vanilla causes cancer lead me to re-examine my reasons for preferring vanilla, or does it simply lead me not to prefer it? The former looks a bit like "one thought too many" but we could go either way.

19.1   Why It Matters: The Real Roots of Human Autonomy

It seems more or less an observable fact that Kantian autonomy is a hard-fought achievement. We do not have the option of starting with it. I would begin the story where humans begin, with means-end reasoning in service of a literally infantile corpus of biologically given ends. Instrumental reason can—and in real life does—drive a process by which beings become capable of rationally choosing ends. The process is called "growing up." Growing up must start somewhere. It does not start with Kantian autonomy. It starts in the only place it can. It is a fact of our developmental history that anyone who ever embraced categorical imperatives began with the phenomenal desires of a human infant. The long journey toward regarding imperatives as philosophers might grow up to regard them started from there.

Herman says, "even when we act for the sake of desire, desire is not the cause of our action. We act on such principles as desire satisfaction, or even this-desire satisfaction, is good. Our adoption of ends always has a principled basis" (1993, 229). Yet Herman would agree that given ends are, after all, what we start with.[4] So, *if* there is reason for a purely instrumental reasoner to become something more—if he or she has *reason* to transcend instrumental reason— then it must be an instrumental reason, engaging a maturing instrumental reasoner as he or she really is.

19.2   Leaving Foundations Behind

One might think a categorical imperative cannot have a developmental history lest it be tainted by its hypothetical foundations.

---

[4] Actually, Herman (1996, 45) says we do not start with desires, either, but with mechanical responses to physiological states of agitation. Desires come later. Herman might be right. I do not know.

Not so. That would overlook the fact that our history is a story not of mere causation but of transcending. Immature ends are a launching pad for adulthood, not an architectural foundation. We achieve adult moral autonomy not by being permanently rooted in childhood's hypothetical imperatives, but by being boosted into self-sustaining orbit by them, then leaving them behind.[5]

The element of instrumentalism in my story is thus not a foundation. It is merely historically prior. It is what there was to work with at a certain stage. Reasons we had at that stage propel us through that stage. Or they can. Evidently something does. As we get through that stage, we become beings with different kinds of reasons. Moreover, we can look back and see: although Kantian reasoners had to pass through a stage where they were not Kantian reasoners, it is possible to pass through that stage for a reason. The process need not be blind biology. It can be driven by reasons to embrace the Categorical Imperative that count as reasons for beings *who have yet to embrace it*.

Korsgaard says she is thinking of a being who must talk to herself and come up with reasons for acting and living that she can live with (1997, 251). This is why she says, "hypothetical imperatives cannot exist without categorical ones, or anyway without principles which direct us to the pursuit of certain ends, or anyway without something that gives normative status to our ends" (Korsgaard 1997, 250). Korsgaard is, of course, presupposing a sophisticated capacity for reflection. We cannot take for granted that human beings possess such capacity. Quite the contrary: we can take for granted that they do not—not when they are very young. For the very young, it is false to say hypothetical imperatives cannot exist without categorical ones.

Yet, for all that, Korsgaard is near enough to a crucial truth. As Korsgaard realizes, she is talking about a kind of being we may become as we mature. But becoming such a being is a challenge. It is

---

[5] See Jonathan Lear (1990, 76, also 156). I also thank Lije Millgram for helpful conversation.

a challenge to which we are driven as our maturing capacities interact with our given end of survival and present us with the challenge, over and over, of moving to the next level, as our corpus of ends comes to be inadequate motivation for the self-conscious being that we became.

Of course, the process need not culminate in a person growing up to be a Kantian. Growing up to be an Aristotelian would meet the same need for transformation. In any case, the point is to make room not for specifically Kantian reasoning so much as for noninstrumental reasoning in general.

19.3 Leaving Instrumentalism Behind

Ends (more specifically, final ends) stop regresses. Can final ends be justified? Yes, but the trick is to justify them without turning something final into something not-final. Suppose you embrace an end, incorporating it as a link in your justificatory chain, at a time when there is a further reason for embracing it. So far, it is justified, albeit as an instrumental end.[6] Next, suppose the chain breaks—the further ends are abandoned—leaving the newly embraced end as the *terminal* link in that chain. It has become a genuine final end, something you now pursue as an end in itself, for no further reason, even though the *embracing* of it was justified.

One more step: when the chain breaks, leaving the embraced end as a final end, the *breaking* might be no accident but might itself be instrumental because the embraced end serves its purpose *only* when the chain breaks and the new end becomes final. Now we are

---

[6] BACKGROUND: We have not yet needed to distinguish between instrumental and final ends. A merely *instrumental* end is pursued merely for the sake of some further end. A *final* end is pursued for reasons that do not depend on further ends its achievement might serve. When E is an end only because achieving E is instrumental to a further end, and when it turns out that E does not in fact serve the further end, then E is no reason for A—at least no objective reason. It may remain a subjective reason if the agent still believes E serves the further end.

talking about an end not only justified as a final end but justified *by virtue of becoming* final.

For example, suppose you have an end of making life less lonely. Avoiding loneliness may be an end in itself. Or it may be instrumental, as when you worry, in the depths of your pandemic isolation, that you will die unless you find relief from your loneliness. Either way, you suppose you could relieve your loneliness by joining a campaign to save the whales. At the same time, you also know that saving whales will relieve your loneliness only if you come to have a serious interest—a vibrant, shared passion—in uniting with fellow travelers to save whales. In other words, you see that you must abandon the idea of saving whales as a relief from aimless loneliness and must instead embrace whale-saving as an end in itself.[7] So that is what you do, if you can (and you've done it before).

Instrumentalists have not done what I've done here with the instrumentalist principle. But the instrumentalist principle has more potential than instrumentalists have realized. It has more potential—transformative potential—than noninstrumentalists have realized.[8]

19.4 How We Avoid Being Overcome by Reason

It is natural for philosophers to think an end is a reason only if reflected upon. But a lot has to happen before we succeed in developing that capacity to reflect. Long before developing her capacity for reflection, a child who puts her hand on a red-hot stove has a reason to move. She will not need to wait (for no reason) until she reflectively endorses her end. An agent could develop in such a way

---

[7] Harry Frankfurt (1992) says avoiding boredom is a fundamental human urge, which is one reason why having final ends is useful. He does not say how ends become final, but I expect he would find my account congenial.

[8] For the full account, check the QR code under "Choosing Ends."

that Korsgaard's view[9] eventually *becomes* close to the truth for that agent, but it is not close for a child whose hand is on a red-hot stove. The burn is the child's reason to move, not some endorsement of a principle that one ought to move when one judges that one's hand is burning.

Our experience of ourselves as agents is that we can deliberate about ends, not only means. Indeed, the normativity of ends makes ends matter and thereby makes it important to deliberate about them.[10] Once a person sees that her ends are her reasons for action, and thus that having them is consequential, she will have reason to take *E* seriously and thus to reflect on *E* in ways that further her development as an autonomous agent.

We could worry that to believe in the reason-giving force of ends as such is to abandon our philosophical responsibility for reflecting upon our aims in life. Not so. My maturational story explains rather than ignores our responsibility for reflecting on our corpus of ends. We can ask: If children are not rational all the way down, how do they ever become more reflectively rational? Would it just happen to them—an accident? If we aspire to explain how it can be rational to become more reflectively rational, that is where my argument comes in. A growing child's burgeoning capacity for reflection eventually leaves a childish corpus of hypothetical imperatives unable to sustain itself. At some point, the process creates a capacity for self-inspection. But as self-inspection becomes possible, passing self-inspection becomes important. For that evolving corpus to become durable, it must transcend itself.

I reject theories that say means-end reasoning is all there is, but a theory that says reasons have developmental origins in means-end

---

[9] Namely, that "it is the endorsement, not the explanations and arguments that provide the material for endorsement, that does the normative work" (Korsgaard 1996, 257).

[10] David Velleman (1989) speaks of a desire to make sense of ourselves. We can do that by seeing ourselves as goal-directed. If *E* makes sense of our actions, that gives us reason to want to make sense of *E* as well—a reason we will not have if *E* does not do that. That is, we have reason to ask about *E* when *E* answers questions about our actions.

reasoning does not say that. By considering how new reasons emerge in the course of means-end reasoning, my theory never assumes what it is supposed to be proving. It concedes instrumentalism for argument's sake, then still goes beyond it. In my theory, and in real life, instrumental reasoning by beings with a reflective and maturing human psychology can get past itself and leave us with rationally chosen final ends (Schmidtz, 2008, chap. 3).

In schematic terms, the kind of transcendence that occurs in real time works like this: something in our nature or environment somehow gives us a goal of rising above mere instrumentality. Then it turns out "somehow" that we have the means to achieve that goal. Then it turns out "somehow" that we implement such means successfully. In that case, we will have risen above mere instrumentality. By a process of instrumental reasoning, we will have bootstrapped ourselves into taking responsibility for reflecting upon and rationally choosing our ends.

Less schematically, how does all that "somehow" work? Like this: we begin life with an end of survival, then we grow up. As we grow up, it can serve our end of survival to embrace further final ends, projects that we pursue for their own sake and that give our lives adult meaning. Because embracing new ends effectively serves our temporally prior end of survival, these ends become part of our corpus of ends as not merely ends but rationally chosen ends. By taking on a life of their own and becoming final, they secure our commitment to surviving. They do so by converting survival from a biologically given final end into an end we rationally embrace as instrumental to our growing adult array of chosen final ends. We take care of ourselves because we want to be there for our loved ones. We take care of ourselves because we want to finish that book.

The unchosen end of mere biological survival evolves in the process, eventually dropping away to be replaced in our adult corpus of ends by an end of living a particular life. The loose end of the chain (the original reason for which there was no reason) is left behind. We carry on with a circle of rationally chosen ends. This is not only a story about choosing ends as a descriptive fact; it is a story about choosing ends for good reason: good for the instrumental reasoners we once were, then good for the more reflective reasoners we became.

If critical reflection on a desire leads to the desire's extinction, the reason for action collapses along with the ends that were grounded in the desire. When infantile desires are lost, any reasons solely grounded in them are lost along with them. But other ends, once grounded in infantile desires but now part of an adult edifice of reasons that have taken on a life of their own, can survive (and indeed can precipitate) the extinction of infantile desires.

I reject the view that there are no reasons without reasons for reasons. The truth is roughly the opposite: there are no reasons *for* reasons unless there are, first of all, reasons. Reason can go a long way down if instrumental reason, operating on given ends, is reason enough to get started. And it is enough. We start with a reason—namely, the end of survival—not with reasons for reasons. Then we come to have reasons for reasons in due course, so long as we can start out not *needing* reasons for reasons; that is, so long as the kind of ends we actually start with can launch the process.

20

Navigating the Terrain of Reasons

THEME: *There are reasons for doubting the Argument's validity.*

This chapter offers a range of test cases raising interesting doubts about the Argument's validity. In some cases, doubt is realistic and well-taken; in other cases, what may seem to be doubts about validity are actually doubts about the truth of the premise.

20.1 Immoral Ends

A may serve end *E*, but what if *E* is immoral? Does *E*'s immorality imply that my means-end reason for doing *A* is no reason at all, or merely that (from a moral perspective) it is not reason enough?

Here is why I need to say the latter. Consider a variation of the Argument:

1. I know *A* would serve my end *E*.
2. Therefore, I have a moral reason to do *A*.

Inserting the word "moral" does indeed make this variation on the Argument invalid. There were things Hitler thought would help him wipe out whole races. However, we do not say genocide is a moral reason that sometimes is not good enough. Instead, genocide is no *moral* reason at all.[1] This variation on the Argument does indeed have counterexamples.

[1] I thank Simon Blackburn for the example.

Living Together. David Schmidtz, Oxford University Press. © Oxford University Press 2023.
DOI: 10.1093/oso/9780197658505.003.0020

Yet "no moral reason at all" does not imply "no reason at all." Notice that "Hitler's reason was immoral" is not a contradiction. It is not paradoxical. Hitler had a kind of reason, notwithstanding the fact that it was not a kind that can even begin to morally justify his actions. That is why we can correctly say Hitler had no moral reason at all. Needless to say, we want to go farther and insist that Hitler was so evil that we should refuse to dignify his actions by recognizing them as tokens of agency. We want to say he was nothing but a rabid dog.

If we give in to that visceral urge, though, we are posturing and obscuring the actual problem with monsters like Hitler. Hitler's crime is not that his behavior was a random event that happened for no reason. Straightforward truth: Hitler had his reasons for doing what he did, and his reasons were evil.

I say this partly for the sake of realism and partly because I spent my career working within Western philosophy's oldest tradition, with roots in Plato's *Republic*. That tradition treats "why be moral?" as a real challenge. Embracing that challenge starts with recognizing morality and rationality as two things, not one. It starts with seeing real space between them, so that bridging the gap can be seen for what it is: not a clever trick, but an ongoing achievement that needs to rise above dogmatism and sophistry. On my view, a token of agency can qualify for the respect implicit in calling it rational yet fail to qualify for a different kind of respect implicit in calling it moral.[2] Seeing the contingency (yet also the robustness) of the connection between moral agency and rational choice is what vindicates Western philosophy as a timelessly worthy, daunting challenge.

---

[2] Compare this to a Kantian distinction between the foundation of dignity consisting of having a rational *capacity* for obeying universal law as opposed to obeying per se.

20.2 Ends That Seem Crazy

Suppose I ask my neighbor Jane what she is doing on her hands and knees peering at her lawn. She says she is counting blades of grass. If her end seems crazy, has she answered my question? Yes, she has. If I have a further question, it will be about something else: why she wants to count blades of grass, not why she is peering at her lawn.

If I ask, "Jane, why are you counting blades of grass?" it would be fine for Jane to respond with, "why do you ask?" But then I continue. "I ask because I believe you also intend to live a good life, and blade-counting has no evident place in that larger plan." Now I am offering a challenge. Now Jane needs a reason for her end of counting blades, not because I am asking, but because I gave her good reason (on purely instrumental grounds) to question her stated end. She needs to ask whether she intends to live a good life, whether blade-counting serves that end, and, if not, how to mend the fracture in her corpus of ends.

Conceivably, Jane could meet the challenge. A more complete description of Jane's end might reveal that, although blade-counting per se serves no purpose, meditation does, and achieving her desired meditative state requires occupying the surface of her mind with a repetitive, aimless task, like saying "Om" or counting blades of grass. But Jane has no occasion for defending her action in the absence of a real challenge—a real reason for wanting to have more to say. Properly locating the dialectical burden is crucial, for if ends stand as reasons until something knocks them down, then they stop regresses, too (until something knocks them down).

Suppose Jane says she is kneeling on her lawn because she is being monitored by the CIA and wants the spies to be so bored that they give up and leave her alone. That sounds crazy, but it could be worse. Suppose instead that Jane says she is kneeling on her lawn because she wants to confirm that those mangos she passed up in Mexico last winter were contaminated. The second answer adds a new dimension of unintelligibility. In the first case, Jane sounds crazy, but not unintelligible. The difference between the two answers shows that something is accomplished by connecting the action to the agent's end *even when the end is crazy.*

On my view, then, even when her ends are crazy, Jane doing *A* is more recognizably a token of agency if she cites a crazy end served by *A* than if she cites a crazy end *not* served by *A*.

No matter where we draw conceptual boundaries, we will have borderline cases. Philip Clark (2010, 234) describes a man who spray paints one of his shoes. Asked why, the man says the painted shoe will be slightly heavier. Upon being asked for a story—a *project* that makes sense of using paint to make one shoe heavier—the man says, "That's the whole story." We are baffled. Since the act has a cost, we want a story—a cost-benefit analysis, perhaps—that reveals some reason to bear the cost.

Paul Boswell describes "full-blooded" reasons as requiring an agent to have an answer to "why did you do that?" that is intelligible to the agent (2018, 2). Yet we see ourselves through each other's eyes, too. We test-drive reasons by "running them past" other people, so when others find our reasons unintelligible, it shakes us. As social beings, then, we want a better story about Clark's shoe-painter. Even if we agree that the ultimate test of a reason is whether it is intelligible to the agent, we still want to see for ourselves what makes him intelligible to himself. We want to take his word for it, but his words make no sense.

20.3 Overridden Ends

Suppose Stan's fraternity plays a game that involves chugging a glass of beer, then placing your hand on the pavement underneath a bowling ball held six feet high.[3] The objective is to pull your hand away after the ball is dropped but before it hits and breaks your

---

[3] I thank Mark LeBar for the example.

hand. Everyone takes a turn, chugs another beer, and the next round begins. The game continues until someone is too drunk to remove his hand in time. Stan wants to remain a member in good standing, which he cannot do if he does not play the game. Therefore, he has a reason to play.

The problem: Stan also wants to be a concert pianist, so he also has a reason not to play. Where does that leave Stan's reason to play? Presumably Stan's reason to play is not good enough, all things considered. Why? Is it because, in light of his other reasons, Stan's reason to play the game is no reason at all? Or is his reason to play overridden? I say the latter. There is nothing paradoxical about having a reason that is not good enough. And Stan *does* have a reason. He wanted to be a member of the fraternity. It is because Stan liked being in the fraternity that he feels a twinge of loss when he decides not to play.

We show that this E is not good enough as a reason for A by identifying reasons that override it. Showing that E is no reason at all is a different job. We do the latter by discovering reasons to think E is not really our end at all. It is something we mistakenly thought we wanted.

20.4 Underdescribed Ends

Ed and Clara hire an electrician to install a doorbell in their new home. After a day of shopping, they come home to find that the electrician has built a cat into the wall, its head sticking into the house and its tail sticking onto the front porch. The electrician explains how it works: visitors step on the cat's tail as they approach the front door, the cat shrieks, and that lets Ed and Clara know someone is at the door. The end is not crazy. Let us suppose the means is effective.[4]

---

[4] I owe the example to Dan Russell, who tells me he got it from Monty Python.

Yet Ed and Clara say "We had something else in mind." The electrician says, "You said you wanted a doorbell." Ed and Clara respond "If cats count as doorbells, then saying we asked for a doorbell turns out to have been a case of misleading underdescription. We were not asking for a cat."

The lesson: there is a difference between serving E and serving E under an incomplete description. ("Monkey's Paw" tales, where a malicious genie ruins lives by granting spoken wishes interpreted in perversely literal ways, illustrate how ends differ from descriptions thereof.)[5] A more complete description of E sometimes reveals that E is pursued not for its own sake but for the sake of a further end. For example, Bert sees he could secure a tenure-track job by lying about his publication record. If Bert embraces getting a tenure-track job because he thinks such a job would enable him to live an exemplary life, and if that further end remains operative, then Bert should say, "When I said I'd do anything for a tenure-track job, I didn't mean it literally." Bert has no reason to lie, even though lying would serve his nominal end under a misleadingly incomplete description.

"Overridden Ends," was a case of our having overwhelming reasons not to do A, leaving E as an overridden reason for A. "Underdescribed Ends" is a case where A does not truly serve E adequately described, leaving no reason at all to do A. If Bert knows that lying about his publications would help him get a job, he nevertheless has no reason to lie, for he also knows that getting a job is not his real end. It is a description of his end, a working verbalization rendered inadequate by the context.

Jonathan Dancy describes a scene where "I am stranded in the desert, desperate for an ice-cool beer; the Devil offers me a beer in exchange for my child. Do I have some reason to give my child to the Devil? I think not" (1993, 191). But Dancy's situation differs from Bert's. Bert has no reason to lie about his publications because doing so would get him a mere appearance of what he truly wants,

---

[5] I thank Holly Smith for the thought.

whereas if Dancy sells his child, he gets a beer he desperately wants. We lose nothing by acknowledging a difference between having no interest in cold beer at that price and having no interest in cold beer at all. To make Dancy's case an example of "no reason at all," like Bert's, imagine Dancy desperately wishing for a cold drink, then being offered petrol. *That* is what having no reason at all is like. Once Dancy sees he has been offered petrol, not beer, his response changes from "I'm not interested in beer at that price" to "I'm not interested in drinking petrol at all."[6]

If I fully intend to achieve E, then I have reason to act in ways that serve E, but there are times when E is not what I thought it was, in which case my reason for A is not what I thought it was either. There is a sense in which E was my end, so I had reason for A, but there is another sense in which it turns out I had no reason for A because it turns out E is not what I wanted.

I acknowledge that this story can be a deadly oversimplification. In the heat of the moment, we can be misled by simple working descriptions of our end. Thus, I may be tempted to lie because the lie *seems* to serve my end, but, given a minute to reflect, I realize I have no reason to lie and I stop feeling tempted.

Further complication: if I do succumb to temptation and lie in the heat of the moment, I thereby create a pressure to justify myself to myself. I may respond to that pressure by reconceiving my end so as to make my lie look more instrumentally rational than it was. In so doing, I pressure my ends to evolve toward becoming the ends of a liar.

---

[6] To be clear, this is not a case of me winning an argument against Dancy. This is sorting out issues of common interest. Imagine Dancy saying, "Dave, as a reason to sacrifice my son, cold beer is not merely outweighed. It's literally nothing." I reply, "You need not claim that where one value is sacred, other values are nothing. Suppose your case is more like Sophie's Choice (Chapter 16): the Devil offers to save your daughter (and he'll even throw in a cold beer) if you sacrifice your son. You want to say sacrificing your son is unthinkable. Fine. Say it. But you can say that without having to say your daughter is literally nothing.

20.5 Mistaken Beliefs

A counterexample to the Argument would show that I could know A would serve my end E even while having no reason to do A. If I merely *think* A would serve my end, but do not know that it would, then the case is not a counterexample. Rather, it is a case in which the Argument's premise is false. Nevertheless, such a case can be instructive. If I walk to the library to get a book and the library turns out not to have it, it would be intelligible for me to say, "I went to the library for no reason!" In this case, though, to say "I had no reason" is to say I had no reason of an objective kind. It is not to deny that I had a subjective reason. My walk to the library was fruitless rather than aimless. I had a reason of a kind, but not the simultaneously subjective and objective kind at work in the Argument.

Sometimes beliefs about means-end relations are not merely mistaken but crazy. Bill believes he has inherited the fortune of a foreign prince he never heard of; all he needs to do is to give his credit card information to an internet stranger. Does Bill have a reason to give a stranger access to his credit card? Objectively, no. Subjectively, yes. By explaining his belief, Bill connects his action to his end, thus explaining why he gave away his credit card. You wonder how Bill could believe the scam, just as you wonder how Jane could have an end of counting blades of grass. But although you may doubt a rational person would believe what Bill believed, you see how someone might act as Bill acted *given* Bill's belief.

20.6 Better Means Available

Suppose I know A would serve my end E and also that some alternative would serve E in a better way. I need a book from the library. I could drive. I could walk. It is a beautiful evening. If I thought about it, I would realize that I'd rather walk. But if I drive to the library, saying I have better reason to walk is not to say I have no reason to drive. My end of getting a library book is a reason for the drive. If we say I had no reason to drive, we mean not that I drove aimlessly but that I had no good reason to drive rather than walk. My end of getting to the library was a reason for action, even given that I had no reason to choose a less effective means over a more effective one.

I could avoid the issue of alternative means by starting the Argument from a premise "I know *only* A would serve my end *E*." But that would simplify the issue and clinch my argument at a cost of ignoring the real-world uncertainty that makes rational choice interesting. When *A* is a type of action, more than one token of which would serve *E*, then we may neither have nor need reasons for picking one token rather than another (Schmidtz 1992).

7
THE POSSIBILITY
OF CIVILIZATION

21

Ecological Justice

THEME: *General principles of ecological reasoning are grounded in ideas about competition, scarcity, consequences predictable, and consequences unintended. Such principles would (testably) describe the logic of how systems respond to attempts to manipulate them.*

Not many animals think about justice (and perhaps plants never think about anything), but humans do. Why? One thing we know: whatever else justice may be, when people speak of justice, they are talking about something that matters to them. We also observe from linguistic practice that to speak of justice is to speak of what we should be able to expect from each other and specifically what we should regard as a person's due.

How would we know whether people are *warranted* in seeing one thing rather than another as their due? What can I *realistically* expect others to see as my due?

One mark of adulthood is getting past thinking of oneself as the center of the universe. An adult conception of justice will be a conception of our place and our due, alongside a conception of what other people are due within a community that has a logic of its own. That logic will be described by economics (among other social sciences) and by ecology. Realistic possibilities are implications of those logics. Mature perspectives on ethics and justice are disciplined by those logics.

Living Together. David Schmidtz, Oxford University Press. © Oxford University Press 2023.
DOI: 10.1093/oso/9780197658505.003.0021

That puts a different spin on what I can realistically expect others to regard as my due. If I ask people to give me my due, I am after all asking for something. When I speak of justice, I speak of treating like cases alike, which is to ask the same of myself as of everyone else. That rudimentary egalitarian mutual respect is built into the basic concept of justice. Indeed, that rudimentary egalitarian respect is built into the concept of a mature adult.

That can give us a handle on how to separate mature conceptions of justice from the sort of ideas that siblings develop in early childhood when they imagine that *their* feelings—feelings about their *share*—are the feelings that count. Which expectations have a history of leading people to behave in ways that people find useful or agreeable in actual practice?

21.1 Justice as an Enduring, Evolving Response to the Human Condition

We are social and political animals, and justice is a human adaptation to an ecological niche. Here are several further ideas that can make a conception of justice more ecological.

FIRST, *justice manages conflict*. Our sense of justice—as a community and as individuals—emerges from our experience with conflict. Litigants go to courts of justice hoping that a judge will resolve their conflict. Suppose an emerging community of expectations does indeed help people to resolve or avoid conflict and get on with their lives. That would go some way, if not all the way, toward everyone involved having reason to call those expectations just.[1]

SECOND, *justice manages traffic*. Freedom of religion may be humanity's most liberating achievement, but it had nothing to do with reaching consensus on which religion is correct. Our grand

---

[1] Hampshire (2001) and Darwall (1993) reflect on the priority of conflict resolution, as per Chapter 15.

political achievement consists not in reaching consensus but in making consensus unnecessary.

We learned that we need to manage traffic and that traffic management in large communities starts with not even trying to dictate destinations. Judges and legislators cannot decide what to do as "America" any more than judges and legislators can decide what to do as the animal kingdom. Yet they can give people a basis for knowing what to expect from each other.[2]

Humanity lives in a sea of politics as fish live in water. Our ecological niche is inherently political. That people decide for themselves (and therefore, that cooperating with them will require negotiation) is a political fact of life. It is an observable regularity that people share an interest in avoiding collision, but otherwise have destinations of their own. Justice, even as an ideal, is never about pretending otherwise.

The truth for political animals is that since we began to settle in large communities, being of one mind has not been an option. Being on the same page is not an option. Even our diverse ideas about how to resolve conflict are a source of conflict. And, disturbing though it may be for a theorist to admit it, theories do not help. It is a political fact that we live among people who have theories of their own, who do not find each other's theories compelling, and who are perfectly aware that there is no reason why they should.

THIRD, *justice is an adaptation.* Ecological justice is a response to reality. This is not a platitude but a consequential working hypothesis. Mutual expectations are validated as evolving and contingently useful and agreeable responses to real conflict and real

---

[2] The so-called Public Choice school of thought often is interpreted as reuniting political theory with economics by positing that the game's referees are as self-interested as the players. But to me, Public Choice's true insight is that social and political animals must behave strategically to achieve anything, and this does not change when they are tasked with governing. Governors do not *decide* how to govern; they *negotiate* how to govern. The task of governing all the trucking and bartering is its own exercise in trucking and bartering (that is, with fellow legislators). I do not consider myself a member of the Public Choice (or any other) school, but I have learned to see it as deserving credit for this insight.

constraints. Norms of ecological justice need not be ideals. They may be imperfect, retaining vestiges of adaptations to ancient problems long forgotten, yet they sometimes apply well enough to new circumstances, coordinating expectations and thus enabling people to live together.

FOURTH, *justice pertains to process.* For justice to be an adaptation, it must be an evolving solution to an evolving problem. To articulate principles of justice we can afford to take seriously, we start with an understanding of which institutional frameworks are enabling us to thrive in communities and which are not. Starting this way lets us sort out alleged principles of justice by asking which mutual expectations promote our thriving and which do not.

We fell into thinking of justice as a question of how to slice the pie. Of course, that sometimes is the question. Still, "pie" is a theoretical construct that, at best, represents reality as a snapshot does. A snapshot of a system of green and red lights will make reality look zero-sum. Observers of snapshots see the rich getting richer and imagine this entails that the poor are getting poorer, but the snapshot hides what matters in the long run: traffic management is a process, not an outcome.

No system of property can look fair to those who see it as a snapshot. It is not possible. In a healthy economy, twenty-somethings tend to be poorer than forty-somethings. And, as a society gets richer, progress inevitably manifests as forty-year-olds pulling ever farther ahead of where they were twenty years earlier when they started with next to nothing, and also ever farther ahead of what is currently the society's statistical bottom rung: young people, new immigrants, or anyone starting with next to nothing. But statistical appearances hide this fact: As bottom-rung people start ever farther behind increasingly wealthy forty-year-olds, bottom-rung people are seeing their own prospects and their own futures, not only the present situation of current forty-year-olds, pulling ahead. Today's wave of penniless twenty-year-old newcomers will some day earn more as forty-year-olds than current forty-year-olds who misleadingly appear to be leaving them behind in the statistical snapshot.[3]

Unless we arrive simultaneously, we cannot even answer *descriptive* questions about what to count as, say, an equal share. Suppose twenty-year-old Smith is hired at half the wage of his forty-year-old colleague Jones but at twice the real wage Jones was paid when Jones was hired twenty years ago. Does one have less than an equal share? Which one? Consider that so long as Smith and Jones are born on different days, they might agree on equal shares without ever agreeing on what to count as an observably equal share.

Is it okay for skilled fifty-year-olds to have incomes that even out over a lifetime but which dwarf what unskilled teenagers are making *at that moment*? Answers come not from philosophical analysis so much as from contingencies of ongoing adjustment of expectations within communities (Lindblom 1959). It is not something one learns by surveying intuitions.

Snapshots hide dynamics. Meanwhile, the serious question will always be what a given society makes possible over a lifetime. It matters whether everyone gets a chance to seek their own destination; what matters not at all is whether everyone's light turns green simultaneously.

How did we get past starvation, violence, and plague being so normal that average life expectancy was under forty years? Can moral science ask what we did right—how we got to where poverty is wondering "Can you afford a second car?" versus a few centuries ago when poverty was wondering, "Can you afford to bury your five-year-old son in his shirt, or do you need to pass on his possibly plague-infested shirt to his younger brother?"

---

[3] In 2020, 48% of minimum wage workers were sixteen to twenty-four years old. Another perspective: "The percentage of hourly paid workers earning the prevailing federal minimum wage or less declined from 1.9 percent in 2019 to 1.5 percent in 2020. This remains far below the 13.4 percent recorded in 1979 when data were first collected on a regular basis."

Source: https://www.bls.gov/opub/reports/minimum-wage/2020/home.htm.

Evolutionary selection processes aim at no particular outcome. So, too, I'd say, with justice. As per Chapter 1, ecological justice is less about how to *distribute* what bakers bring to the table and more about how to *respect* what they bring. Respecting what bakers bring to the table is an ongoing process.

Of course, a realistic perspective on these processes must acknowledge that there has been injustice—crimes against humanity that we must not repeat. Moreover, in the spirit of not repeating mistakes, there is much to rectify. But aiming to undo wrongs is not aiming to engineer an ideal outcome. For example, if a wallet has been stolen, a court's job is to return the wallet to the person from whom it was stolen, not to give it to the person who would have it in our ideal theory. Trying to twist the world into the shape of our vision, at other people's expense, leaves other people wanting revenge, and visions have a way of being lethally oblivious to other people's reasons for feeling that way.[4] Our vision may be as warped as visions of the past whose damage we are trying to undo, but we won't see it.

One aspect of the human condition is our pervasive tendency to see someone else as having fired the first shot. Everyone has grievances, so putting ours aside and just listening is a feat, as is growing up enough to understand that rectification done well is not about giving the "other" a taste of what it feels like to lose, thereby creating new threats and new enemies.[5]

---

[4] It is human nature for us to deem mutual expectations just when we find them useful and agreeable. One trick is to notice when not everyone finds them useful and agreeable, and thus not everyone deems them just. Grown-up trick #2 is to avoid feeling offended, which we do by seeing that if we were in their position, we would feel the same way. Grown-up trick #3 is to explore opportunities to negotiate ways forward with people whose visions are different. Problems will never stop evolving, so solutions will never be final, but that is life.

[5] Michael Walzer once asked where I stand on rectificatory justice. How to respond to histories of expropriation that we find everywhere? Without claiming expertise, I observe that if and when it is too late to make victims whole, then rectificatory justice must concern something else, such as enabling people to repair broken relationships, reconcile, forgive, and understand where their culture was and where it must never be again. Walzer was correctly interpreting my view (Schmidtz 2006) that needing to move forward informs how we can afford to interpret principles of rectification.

FIFTH, *justice is not contractarian.* Ecological justice is not premised on a thought experiment that has us all arriving at the same time, as adults, to a bargaining table with no history, and to a task of dividing a pie with no history. Instead, if there is a bargaining table at all, we are born to it one at a time. As Chapter 3 put it, we each arrive to a world knee-deep in the baggage of bargaining, compromise, and lifetimes of service and sacrifice. Thus, to people who got there first, there will be only so much we latecomers can insist they owe us while still plausibly claiming to have come in peace.

SIXTH, *justice is somewhat particular and local.* Mutual understandings about how to avoid or resolve conflict will be as universal as the conflicts themselves. If a problem is found in all human societies and if x is the only solution, then that will explain all societies converging on seeing x as just. But if problems differ, or if there are many solutions so that a given society needs only to hit upon one or another to solve the problem, then people with different histories predictably will have—and be warranted in having—conceptions of justice that are not identical.

I say "somewhat local" but that is itself an evolving variable. If we see new problems—climate change in particular—expanding beyond borders of more local problems that developed economies have a history of solving, we may need new solution concepts. Meanwhile, if (as we currently think) populations most vulnerable to climate change are those of developing countries, that mandates working to invent green technologies that can profitably be deployed at scale *in developing economies* so that developing countries continue to develop and thereby become less vulnerable.

This merely gestures, of course, at what may turn out to be humanity's greatest ecological challenge. The point, though, is that even when the problem matters—especially when it matters—responding justly will involve responding to the whole challenge, the whole ecological logic, not only the part that enrages us and makes us demonize those who see what we may be missing.

SEVENTH, *justice is somewhat testable*. Ideals are not mere intuitions. When the world tests our ideals and finds them unworthy, we need to rethink.[6] Common law is not a theoretical response to a classroom homework problem. It is a situated, ongoing attempt to enable political animals to form useful and agreeable mutual expectations. When we articulate our ideals, we will be heard as saying we want to put them into practice. We imply that our principles are consistent with sound practice. We imply that we have done our homework. If we have not—if we never went beyond blackboard cartoons to undertake the hard work of observing elements of sound practice—then when practitioners ignore us, they are doing the right thing.

These seven features do not define ecological justice, and do not exhaust it, but they indicate whether a conception of justice is more or less ecological. I have no settled view about how ecological a theory ought to be, or whether trying to theorize in ways that exhibit these features has much to do with winning philosophical arguments. Yet the features listed seem worth wanting.

Again, our most fundamental way to think about how to live involves thinking about how to live together. We may want a measure of independence. We may want to be able to decide for ourselves and may want to be treated as having both a right and a responsibility to mind our own business. Yet it is because we are social animals that we want a measure of independence. Questions about how to live are still questions about living together.[7]

---

[6] In philosophy today, we tend to defend our intuitions by picking three rival theories, identifying counterintuitive implications, then declaring that, by process of elimination, our preferred theory is the one left standing. Waldron (1999, chap. 2) discusses the phenomenon in a nonjudgmental way.

[7] Again, postponing "how to live *together*" until we settle "how to live" amounts to postponing political theory until we settle on moral theory. To Rossi and Argenton (2021), the assumption that moral theory is more fundamental is what Bernard Williams was criticizing when Williams coined the term "political moralism." Maynard and Worsnip (2018) doubt that political reasons are distinct from moral reasons, but seem not to have anticipated my distinction between morality as deciding how to live and politics as *negotiating* how to live together.

22

A Brief History of the
Human Condition

By David Schmidtz and Jason Brennan[1]

> THEME: *A social animal survives by cooperating. Humans
> are a kind of social animal that is also a political animal,
> which is to say that learning to negotiate, trade, and be of
> service is part of what made us human.*

To simplify a crucial idea about the problem to which ecological
justice is a response: nature does not obey us. Nature has no mind
of its own, yet it has its own logic. We can work with or against that
logic. While we may learn how to nurture, there is a limit, as any
gardener knows, to what we can decide. Even dictators cannot dictate how things are going to go, any more than exterminators can
dictate whether insects will evolve resistance to a pesticide. Every
action has more than one effect and more than its intended effect.
As poet Robert Burns observed, even best-laid plans go awry. We
plan, but to plan is to focus. To focus is to ignore what is in our pe-
ripheral vision. And some day, what we ignore will matter.

---

[1] This chapter revises Chapter 1 of Schmidtz and Brennan (2010).

Living Together. David Schmidtz, Oxford University Press. © Oxford University Press 2023.
DOI: 10.1093/oso/9780197658505.003.0022

22.1 Neanderthals

Is *Homo sapiens* truly the wisest of primates? Maybe, but when modern humans emerged as a species 40,000 years ago, Neanderthals had been around for a half million years, and they had larger brains. Yet it was Neanderthals who went extinct. Why? Were humans smarter?

The pivotal difference may have been more specific. We often conceive a species in terms of what we see as its characteristic survival mechanism. When we think about birds, we think flight. When we think about chameleons, we think camouflage. When we think about cheetahs, we think speed. What about *Homo sapiens*? What is humanity's superpower?

Charles Darwin revolutionized how we view the seemingly miraculous "Descent of Man." We know Darwin was influenced by Enlightenment political economy and by Smith in particular.[2] Thus, to Darwin, humans have sentiments and sympathies, but capacities for moral sentiment are products of natural selection. Hominid species in particular and simian primates in general tend to be social animals, but modern humans are not merely social animals. We are *political* animals. We not only cooperate. We negotiate terms of cooperation. We talk about what we have to offer each other. We talk about how we might be of service. In the process, we arrive at mutual expectations that make us more predictable and consequently more useful to each other.

If there is a unique capability that enabled *H. sapiens* to thrive even as *H. neanderthalensis* went extinct, it seems to have been our capacity to make deals with strangers—a capacity not possessed by Neanderthals, to judge from available anthropological evidence.[3]

---

[2] Greg Priest (2017) concludes that the only direct influence of Smith on Darwin was *Theory of Moral Sentiments*, not *Wealth of Nations*. Thanks to Scott Scheall for the reference.

[3] Horan, Bulte, and Shogren (2005, 2).

That is humanity's superpower. It is arguably more astonishing than the speed of a cheetah or the wings of an eagle.

We negotiate cooperative arrangements that will play out over weeks or years, over generations and across continents. We negotiate durably agreeable terms of a cooperation from which arises both our ability and our need to reflect on what to regard as a person's due. We can ask what is worth negotiating for and, more philosophically, what is worth wanting at all.

Expanding beyond face-to-face bands of hunter-gatherers, people began to build far-flung trading networks from which everything we now call civilization arose. As we spread, humanity's closest cousins went extinct. Why? Neanderthals were an amazing form of life and had a long run. Yet *Homo sapiens* had something that *Homo neanderthalensis* lacked. Consider this: 500,000 years ago, Neanderthals formed communal hunter-gatherer groups of about two dozen. 40,000 years ago, Neanderthals were still isolated groups of two dozen communal hunter-gatherers. It would be science fiction to imagine a human society remaining so static for half a million days, let alone almost half a million years. The implied reason why Neanderthals (their way of life if not their genes) disappeared and modern humans flourished is that, among Neanderthals, there is little evidence of a tireless search for new ways of being of service.

Ian Tattersall (2012) speculates that modern social and economic behaviors express an underlying capacity, recently acquired, which Neanderthals did not have. There is no evidence of major technological progress in Neanderthal societies. Neither is there evidence of trade between groups. Cultural cross-fertilization did not happen. Neanderthals did not experiment much and did not learn much from each other's experiments. By contrast, modern humans evidently practiced division of labor from the start, trading services within and between groups. Horan, Bulte, and Shogren (2005, 5) explain Neanderthals disappearing even as modern humans flourished by saying the former were not entrepreneurs. Cultural cross-fertilization did not occur. So, the ascent of *H. sapiens* may have been less about developing weapons and more about something relatively mundane: an evolving propensity to truck and barter. Humans innovate. Humans invent and reinvent their ecosystems.

Why? Why did Neanderthals not learn as humans learned, expanding networks of cooperation as humans did? George Grantham speculates that what separated humans from Neanderthals "was not their respective cranial volumes, which overlap, but modern man's capacity to articulate consonants and vowels required to sound an extensive vocabulary of distinct words" (2022, 267). Human adaptations for speech—such as a descended larynx that increased risks of choking and a flattening of the "snout" that increased the airway's curvature and reduced aerobic efficiency—were costly, so the benefits of speech had to be substantial. And of course they were. Horan, Bulte, and Shogren (2008, 3) explain the benefits of speech in terms of incremental gains in ability to make intentions known (and be of service) in an environment where cooperation was life and death.

As the faculty of speech evolved, so could complex trading relationships built on a mutual understanding of such variables as the time and place of one's next meeting, the exact nature of what was to be delivered, contingency plans, and so on. Grantham notes that

> Adam Smith was the first and long the only economist to observe that the ability to communicate is a precondition for voluntary exchange. That capacity is tightly linked to the faculty of speech. For although conceptual information is mostly stored in nonlinguistic neural networks, contingent agreements involving temporally and spatially separated actions are all but impossible to achieve in the absence of linguistic reference to immediately unobservable events.[4]

---

[4] Grantham (2022, 266). What Adam Smith says on the matter:

Nobody ever saw a dog make a fair and deliberate exchange of one bone for another with another dog. Nobody ever saw one animal by its gestures and

As benefits of trade mushroomed, selection pressures favored being able to convey detailed thoughts and intentions. To sustain expanding networks, people had to develop written language, accounting tools, and an increasingly elaborate sense, mediated by manners, of what to expect from each other.

22.2 Humans

As trading networks grew, cooperation became a matter of communicating and working with strangers. People needed to develop the concept of a legitimate expectation. Thus, a capacity and need for gossip evolved, and with it the possibility of having a reputation. People needed to relay information about who can be trusted. From there developed concepts of law and morality. To have business partners a hundred miles away, potentially serving thousands of customers, people had to develop the idea of a schedule, the idea of a contract, and the closely related moral idea of a promise.

As the possibility of relying on a partner's reputation evolves, so does the possibility of vast trading networks. At human (but not Neanderthal) sites, archeologists find tools made hundreds of miles away. Trade goods traveled, contributing massively to the spread of ideas. To see how other groups do things is to see different and sometimes better ways of doing things. This very

natural cries signify to another, this is mine, that yours; I am willing to give this for that. . . . A spaniel endeavours by a thousand attractions to engage the attention of its master who is at dinner, when it wants to be fed by him. Man sometimes uses the same arts with his brethren. . . . [But] in civilized society he stands at all times in need of the cooperation and assistance of great multitudes, while his whole life is scarce sufficient to gain the friendship of a few persons. In almost every other race of animals each individual, when it is grown up to maturity, is entirely independent, and in its natural state has occasion for the assistance of no other living creature. But man has almost constant occasion for the help of his brethren, and it is in vain for him to expect it from their benevolence only. (WN, I.ii.2)

idea—there may be better ideas out there!—may have been the most inspiring of all.

Herbert Muller says,

> The range in choice was widened by trade; for if the Neolithic village was basically or potentially self-sufficient, it chose not to remain so. The earliest villages have yielded materials (such as obsidian) the nearest source of which was hundreds of miles away; and trade grew ever brisker as Neolithic culture developed. (1961, 17)

Nevertheless, to move trade goods over long distances, people had to be able to count on partners being willing to deal on consensual terms. They needed a rudimentary rule of law and a rule of property in particular—you had to be able to grasp, and respect the difference between, what you brought to the table and what someone else brought—or trade would never get off the ground.

Trade gets off the ground as people begin to feel so secure in their possessions that they begin to count on having a right to say no. They spend less time defending what they produce and more time producing it. People no longer see themselves as needing to conceal any valuables they possess. As per Chapter 15, the phenomenon of people advertising (*advertising!*) the fruit of their productivity heralds revolutionary progress in achieving a security that enables a commercial society.

We tend to imagine nomadic tribes settling down as they begin to develop crops, then coalescing into villages and finally into cities. To Jane Jacobs, though, cities must have come first, for "agriculture is not even tolerably productive unless it incorporates many goods and services produced in cities or transplanted from cities. The most thoroughly rural countries exhibit the most unproductive agriculture. The most thoroughly urbanized countries, on the other hand, are precisely those that produce food most abundantly" (1970, 7).[5]

---

[5] See also James Scott (2017).

Paul Seabright remarks that

> Citizens of the industrialized market economies have lost their sense of wonder at the fact that they can decide spontaneously to go out in search of food, clothing, furniture, and thousands of other useful, attractive, frivolous, or life-saving items, and that when they do, somebody will have anticipated their actions and thoughtfully made such items available for them to buy. For our ancestors who wandered the plains in search of game or scratched the earth to grow grain under a capricious sky, such a future would have seemed truly miraculous, and the possibility that it might come about without the intervention of any overall controlling intelligence would have seemed incredible. Even when adventurous travelers opened up the first trade routes and the citizens of Europe and Asia first had the chance to sample each other's luxuries, their safe arrival was still so much subject to chance and nature as to make it a source of drama and excitement as late as Shakespeare's day. (2004, 15)

But the emerging class of merchants who made it their business to develop commercially viable grains and domesticate livestock were sitting ducks, even more vulnerable than relatively mobile traders had been. Farmers had to count on a rule of law to an even greater extent.

However, peace was not easy to find. Steven Pinker says that,

> many intellectuals have embraced the image of peaceable, egalitarian, and ecology-loving natives. But in the past two decades anthropologists have gathered data on life and death in pre-state societies rather than accepting the warm and fuzzy stereotypes. What did they find? In a nutshell: Hobbes was right, Rousseau was wrong. (2002, 57)

Pinker means that hunter-gatherers tend also to be warriors and raiders. As civilizations grow, the propensity to make war against neighbors does not disappear. States can and do organize warfare on a more massive scale, while technology enables warriors to be more lethal. Even so, wars have (by some measures) become less destructive. Lawrence Keeley and other archeologists note that, in hunter-gatherer tribes today (our best approximation of our past), the percentage of males dying in war can approach 60 percent as compared to just a few percent among 20th-century Europeans despite two world wars (Pinker 2002, 57). Why? One explanation is that civilized societies find occupations for adult males other than hunting and fighting. Soldiering becomes a specialized vocation. Most adult males belong to classes of non-combatants. When people turn to agriculture and begin to make a living in ways that render them sitting ducks to raiders, it become more imperative to develop a rule of law to protect more settled ways of life. In the process, advancing societies make a life of peaceful trade ever more interesting, more secure, and more rewarding.

Trade became common perhaps 40,000 years ago, farming perhaps 10,000 years ago. New possibilities arose with written language. Language in general, written or spoken, is an unimaginably elaborate, delicate, rapidly evolving form of cooperation, and its evolution is typically spontaneous: that is, it is law-like and rule-governed yet not a product of any legislature. Muller describes Sumeria as the earliest Near East civilization (1961, 29). Samuel Kramer describes how Sumerians invented a large-scale drainage system, a large-scale bureaucratic government, formal laws, standard weights and measures to facilitate markets, a medium of exchange, institutions of credit, and devices for keeping time.[6] They

---

[6] Wittfogel (1957) claims that large-scale irrigation required a bureaucracy capable of overseeing the irrigation system, from which emerged powerful states with absolute monarchs. Thanks to Joshua Weinstein for this.

developed cuneiform writing around 3000 BCE. They invented schools around 2500 BCE (Kramer 1981, 3).

In the late 1870s, a set of stone tablets of Sumerian provenance was dated back to 2350 BCE. Some of them record complaints about a rising tax burden (Kramer 1981, 45–50). One word from these tablets, rendered as *amagi*, is the first known written reference to a concept of freedom. *Amagi* translates literally as "return to the mother." How was this a word for freedom? J. N. Postgate notes that the word was used to denote the freeing of persons enslaved for debt. People would speak of a man freed from debt servitude as having been returned to his family or returned to his mother (1992, 195).

Muller also reflects on the ups and downs of Sumer's invention of the city.

> The inevitable constraints imposed by the more complex life of civilization may likewise obscure the positive gains in freedom. . . . whereas education in the village trained the child to do and to be just like his father, education in Sumer might train him to do something different or to become something better. . . . The always crowded, restless, noisy, wicked city would in time be deplored by many writers, denounced by many more preachers; and it would always remain the mecca of bright, ambitious young men from the countryside. (1961, 33)

Mycenaean Greece, a cluster of small states consisting of rural populations dominated by fortified palaces (Patterson 1991, 48), had its heyday from around 1400 to 1200 BCE. As it collapsed, the eastern Mediterranean regressed to tribalism. Why it collapsed is unknown, but Lewis Mumford suggests that culture was a problem: Mycenaeans glorified war and piracy and had an aristocratic contempt for work and trade. Mumford says, "the Mycenaean ascendancy seems never to have developed the permanent urban forces essential to further growth: the code of written law, the bureaucratic controls, the system of taxation, that would have ensured its continuity for even a millennium. Power, dependent chiefly on personal force, soon crumbled" (1961, 123–4). From 1200 to around 900 BCE, literacy, trade, architecture—urban life in general—disintegrated along with the rule of law.

One benefit of this collapse: the disappearance of cuneiform writing set the stage for the emergence and triumph of the alphabet, developed and spread by Phoenician traders (Grantham 2022, 296). Cuneiform writing survived in various cultures, but the symbols were clumsy and hard to learn. Merchants or anyone aspiring to be literate "naturally preferred the much more economical and efficient alphabet. Common men could now easily learn to read and write" (Muller 1961, 94). Literacy had long been the trademark of a particular profession: scribes. But scribes were becoming numerous, laying foundations for literacy as a general phenomenon.

Toward the end of this period, long-distance shipping was encouraged by advances in hull construction and rigging that permitted sails to be furled or unfurled, thus allowing larger ships to cope with changing wind conditions (Wachsmann 1998).

Muller says the Bronze Age was one where metal was largely the preserve of the ruling class owing to the scarcity of the basic ingredients: copper and tin. Ordinary peasants continued to use tools made of stone. The Iron Age began in the Near East and Greece in the 12th century BCE, and it was revolutionary. While copper and tin are scarce, iron is common. A smith needs higher temperatures and greater expertise to smelt iron, but foundries had to figure out how to do it as the collapse of Mycenaean trading networks made tin much harder to acquire.

Iron tools were cheap.

An unprecedented number of new tools were fashioned, among them spades, tongs, shears, and planes, while oxen were made to work corn mills and olive crushers. . . . Above all, iron was a boon to the little man. Able to possess his own metal tools, he might now become an independent farmer or artisan, thereby providing more opportunities for small merchants too. (Muller 1961, 93–4)

In short, as rich people were switching to iron from *bronze* tools, poor people were switching to iron from *stone* tools. Iron thus was both an equalizer and a liberator. For people unable to afford bronze, iron was their ticket out of the stone age.

As coinage emerged in the 7th century, in Lydia, the frontier of possibilities for production and trade expanded yet again (Patterson 1991, 56). As Muller says,

> The Greeks, who most fully exploited the democratic potentialities of the alphabet, were also quick to exploit the invention of coinage, about 600 BC, which they credited to the Lydians, founders of a new kingdom in Asia Minor. Replacing bars of metal, standardized coins facilitated trade and encouraged industry, but the more revolutionary innovation was *small change*. Early coins, of silver and gold, had been in denominations too high for the daily transactions of the poor; with small change the little man could buy and sell things, in small quantities. (1961, 94)

Reflecting on inventions such as coined money and a written alphabet, Mumford says, "refinements of number and writing were prime tools of the mind, though they first developed as essential notations in long-distance trading and commercial accountancy" (1961, 191). Mumford adds: "The transposition of the village into the polis, the place where people come together, not just by birth or habit, but consciously, in pursuit of a better life, takes place before our eyes in Greece" (1961, 131).

As both Patterson and Muller note, however, inequality began to grow in the aftermath of the monetization of the marketplace. Financial institutions reached a stage where borrowers could offer their *person* as collateral. Much as a house used as collateral can be seized and sold during foreclosure, a borrower in default could be held in bondage. According to Patterson, toward the end of the 7th century the situation worsened and a new phenomenon emerged: not only debt servitude but the selling of Greek debtors into slavery, including selling them abroad. In any case, Athenians were defaulting and freemen were being turned into slaves and put to work on monocrop plantations that emerged with booming Mediterranean trade. Slaves being bought and sold on international markets suggests that this was full-blown slavery as we understand it today. The advent of slavery in this horrific form, whose victims included unlucky neighbors and not only "barbarians" from non-Greek lands, may have sharpened awareness of what it means to be free (Patterson 1991, 53).[7]

In the 7th-century BCE, the rule of law needed to catch up with the commerce for which it was a supposed framework. Money's emergence enabled people to share expectations about rates of exchange. Prices gave prospective providers timely and reliable information about where services were in demand. But in its inception in Lydia, money seemingly was not a win-win game. Compare this to the subprime mortgage lending scare earlier this century. On one hand, mortgage lending is a massively liberating institution. Without it, ordinary people could not afford modern housing. On the other hand, credit has always been a dangerous servant and terrible master.

Many societies experimented with debt servitude. Should people be free to risk giving their liberty away by using it as collateral to secure a loan? Or should the status of free citizen be seen as an *inalienable* right (as per Chapter 15)? The question is fundamental and 7th-century BCE Greeks had not yet come to grips with it. The

---

[7] Slavery in general is far older than this, and debt serfdom may be older as well. Another reasonable doubt about this story is that, according to Kramer, there was a currency—shekels—circulating in Sumer in 2350 BCE. Muller and Patterson may simply have been, at the time of writing, unaware of this earlier history of coinage.

market had run ahead of the rule of law. Eventually, though, Solon introduced Greek legal reforms that forbade citizens from using their freedom as collateral to secure loans, thus establishing the first inalienable right. Apparently the experiment was repeated in Rome with the same result: a prohibition was passed against debt-bondage (Raaflaub 2004, 268). Western societies opted for inalienable rights, refusing to enforce unconscionable contracts, thus repudiating the right of citizens to sell their freedom or even to put it at risk by offering it as collateral.

In Solon's time, populations were rising, which meant rising demands for wood (for construction), land, and agricultural products. This implied rising pressure not to become agriculturally self-sufficient but precisely the opposite. That is, pressure to find better ways to feed a growing population was pressure to use land to produce whatever crop could be used to *purchase* the most food. There was no hope of growing enough domestically to feed everyone. Greeks had to develop an economy with resources to import food, which meant Greece needed to have goods to sell. The more their goods could command in exchange for foreign agriculture, the better. Thus, increasing demand for foreign trade led Greeks to turn their agricultural land over to producing grapes and olives for export (Patterson 1991, 69). A rising need for grain drove Greeks to find a better use for land than growing grain.

Conclusion

Humans thus evolved capacities for cooperation, unique in degree if not kind. But along with other aspects of consciousness, we evolved a capacity for self-awareness.[8]

---

[8] It is astounding to think self-awareness could arise via natural selection, but so far as we can see, that is what did in fact happen. A likely untestable speculation: What evolved first may have been processes by which neurons physically maintain themselves. Neural

We have become so powerful that we can afford to care about the consequences of using our power in one way rather than another. We can afford to care not only about surviving but about whether our way of life is praiseworthy. We learn to be a kind of person whose partners can read in our eyes whether we are anxious to avoid letting them down. Alternatively, we learn to be a person whose eyes cannot be read, in hope of being able to cheat without consequence. But one lesson of adulthood is that it's the person who learns to have nothing to hide whose life is worth living.

Plato and his student Aristotle helped launch Western philosophy when they observed that we choose not only how to survive but how to make life worth living. Two millennia later, Scottish studies of the human condition were the chrysalis from which all of today's social sciences emerged.

Eons ago, as our communities and cultures evolved, the human condition took shape. People responded to the need to manage scarcity by learning what to expect from each other. They learned what to expect by inventing justice: recognizing what people needed to be able to expect and needed to be able to regard as each other's due.

---

self-maintenance involves re-storing memories and re-processing sensations; that is, dreaming. Once we started dreaming, we had to develop an awareness of the difference between dreams and genuine incoming information. We had to become sufficiently self-aware to avoid fatal confusion. That is to say, what got selected for next was an ability to wake up. I gleaned the germ of the idea from Walker (2017). See also Ismael (2009).

A further thought about the nature of realism: philosophers who work on free will have a history of worrying that modern physics cannot explain free will, or consciousness for that matter. That is often seen as a reason to be skeptical about free will or consciousness rather than a reason to be skeptical about physics. (Realistically, though, why would anyone imagine that physics should be able to explain free will?) Nevertheless, there manifestly is a realistic reason to be skeptical about free will, and realists are right to worry about it. Namely, it is an observable fact that we don't always say what we wanted to say or do what we wanted to do. We are limited beings. We often are not smart enough and don't have enough time in the heat of the moment to will ourselves to take a stand, seeing that what we can *stand for* matters in a way that what we can *get* doesn't. We often cave in to social pressure. As per Chapter 16 (and as per the chapter on psychological freedom in Schmidtz & Brennan 2010) it can get even worse than that if we start making excuses for caving in rather than simply resolving to do better. Self-deception can make it hard indeed to know who we are and who we want to be. Realistically, this is the actual free will problem.

We can go to market knowing what to expect from others—and more profoundly, knowing what to *want* from others—even as we get better at anticipating what we can offer them in return. We learn how to make people glad to have us around. This is humanity's way of surviving and ultimately prospering. Our working together to make our world a better place does not end here, but here is where it starts.

23

Toward a Realist Morality

THEME: *To Locke, one feature of civilized society is, if all else fails, being able to turn to impartial judges to settle disputes. To excel at delivering the service of impartial judgment is one among many valuable specializations.*

Plato had a conception of justice somewhat unlike ours. To Plato, while justice was about what people are due, it also was a properly functional relation of parts to a whole. Justice within a person was a matter of parts of a soul staying in their proper place. Justice within a polis was a matter of citizens who compose a community minding their own business and tending to their proper roles within society. This conception may seem archaic now, yet it retains some resonance. We can recognize his conception of a person's due as an ancestor of ours.[1]

No one is justly tasked with doing everything worth doing. Instead, in a thriving society, people develop specialties: plumbers have a job, teachers have a job, and the rest of us depend on them to internalize role-specific standards of excellence and integrity. In any case, for Plato, justice is a matter of people staying in their lanes.

This truth about the justice of staying in one's lane is equally true for governors as for anyone else. It is equally true for judges. As described in Chapter 15, the purpose of a court is to resolve whatever conflicts come before a judge's bench. Judges do not get

---

[1] Fred Miller (1997) revolutionized our understanding of Aristotle by tracing the development in Aristotle's *Politics* of a strikingly modern conception of rights. I've also been influenced by Miller's discussion of Aristotle's view that politics can be and should be scientifically studied.

Living Together. David Schmidtz, Oxford University Press. © Oxford University Press 2023.
DOI: 10.1093/oso/9780197658505.003.0023

to truck in imaginary cases. They do not get to set aside inconvenient details. Neither are judges tasked with resolving all conceivable conflicts. Instead, judges aim to enable flesh-and-blood litigants before their bench to get on with their lives with stable mutual expectations. Derivatively, judges also need to keep an eye on settling a dispute in such a way as to avoid the same dispute arising repeatedly. Judges aim to settle a *type* of dispute as well as a particular instance of it, thereby enabling people in general to understand how to stay out of each other's way, stay out of trouble, and stay out of court in the first place.

23.1 Moral Ideals and Political Compromise

Moral compromise is a concession, a departure from high standards. *Political* compromise, by contrast, is an ideal. Philosophers, unlike judges, can spend their days envisioning more perfect worlds, where "more perfect" means not needing to negotiate with those who have a different vision. We imagine that, in a monochrome ideal world, we would not need to justify imposing our standards on those with different visions because there would not be different visions. But there is nothing realistic about ideals so conceived.

The highest political standards are *not* the ones we personally find most appealing. Rather, truly having reason to embrace anything as a political ideal starts by observing that conflict resolution is an exercise in the art of compromise. A politically ideal community is habitable partly because no one's moral ideal ever sweeps the field. High standards are ones that, when met in practice, leave us with opportunities to muddle through that everyone in the community can live with, dignity intact. Personal ideals do not win, but neither are they second-class.

As Rawls properly acknowledged, that which works to the greatest benefit of the least advantaged as a class is not guaranteed to work to the benefit of any particular disadvantaged person.

We can hope everyone will have a reasonable chance to compete in some arena of their choosing. However, as Rawls admitted, we cannot reasonably hope that everyone will win. We do not want people to even imagine that the world owes them a guarantee, but we do want people to be able to see that the game is not rigged. The deck is not stacked against them. They have real opportunity. We also want people to see that they can afford to take a chance. Indeed, it is their life, so, within limits, they have a right to take a chance. If they take a chance and make a mistake, the world is not infinitely forgiving, yet it is somewhat forgiving. In a civilized community, our situation is not that we need to beat the competition or else literally starve (or be reduced to debt servitude). On the contrary, in a civilized community, another chance is probably just around the corner.

While we should not pretend that failure does not hurt, we should be able to make it a reliable fact about our community that failure is not a death sentence so much as an invitation to learn and come back stronger. Failure is real, even in the best societies we can realistically imagine. Still, there is a relevant ideal. In an ideal society, failure is something a person will have a chance to look back on as if it were a speed bump—jarring rather than crippling.[2]

Political realism is not an *alternative* to believing in moral truth. It is a *way* of believing in moral truth and a way of taking moral reality seriously. Sometimes, political compromise is not a way of giving up but is instead a diverse community's way of reaching for excellence. We might suppose we should strive to track the moral truth and never compromise. But suppose moral truth is not out there in such a way that it can be observably tracked. Rather, it must to some extent be negotiated. It must be political before it can be moral. In that case, when we hammer out a political compromise,

---

[2] This is one reason why a commercial society realistically needs a legal convention of limited liability: so that you can invest in a share of corporate stock without risk of being sued for everything you own.

the compromise *becomes* the moral truth that we become able to see well enough to track. The compromise becomes part of morality's interpersonal strand—what we can point to as warranting people in expecting one thing rather than another. Those warranted expectations, owing to their agreeable usefulness, become what we observably, verifiably, objectively (even if only contingently) share a reason to respect.

There are times for attending not only to our values but to other people's, too, even if we do not share those other values and, indeed, find them alien. Why? Because other people's values are integral parts of ecosystems about which we claim to care. We do not decide how people will act any more than we decide how elephants or viruses will act. People decide for themselves. If we aim to respond to them, we need to ask: Under what conditions do people with *their* values and *their* priorities act in ways we can live with? If we go to the table with an agenda, we must understand this: if we are to make a politically effective stand, our opponents must go home feeling like they got something better than mere truce out of the deal; it was not only they who made concessions. Politically, aiming for "win-win" goes with being serious about a *moral* ideal.[3]

Conclusion

Justice has its sociological origin in the need for cooperation among social and political animals who developed a capacity and consequently a need for self-inspection and who survive by negotiating mutually acceptable terms of engagement, then standing by those terms with enough integrity that they can afford to trust each other.

---

[3] Of course, being a realistic idealist involves acknowledging that there is only so much we can do. People who embrace violence or otherwise do all they can to avoid deserving to win will always be a problem.

Yet we cannot thrive except by continuously adapting to the sum of moving parts, always shifting, that make up our ecological niche.

Alexander Rosenberg (2016) asks us to imagine the terrain of justice as a rubbery surface, bouncing us around as we dance toward what looks like higher ground. Actual progress not only puts us in a different place but transforms the space of realistic possibility. What looks like Mount Everest may some day look like the bottom of an ocean of emerging alternatives, especially when our sensibilities are changing along with everything else. (A life expectancy of fifty years that might have looked like Mount Everest in 1850 may look like a pit of despair today.) Progress shifts the terrain while also shifting our map as knowledge and experience changes what we count as higher ground. Moreover, the terrain's shape at any given moment will in part be a *response* to our trying to make a place for ourselves in it. The human condition does not evolve rapidly enough for justice's basic content to change much, and no change could ever make it just to punish people for being innocent. So, Rosenberg's metaphor implies not that justice is wildly unstable, but only that in some respects it is not timeless. It evolves when that is what it takes for it to continue to be a framework that helps us become and remain what the people around us need us to be. A crucial contingency: while our ecological niche is not static, it has a history of being stable enough that some adaptations have so far proved durably better than others.

Further, humanity's adaptability is more phenotypic than genetic. Insects and viruses adapt, but their ability to adapt is genotypic. By contrast, humanity does not wait for mutations to appear in its gene pool, randomly affecting genetic fitness for better or worse, then letting natural selection sort things out over eons. Natural selection operates on our ideas, not only our genes. Our front-line survival mechanism lies in our ability to adapt on the fly to rapid shifts, inventing niches as we go: buggy whip manufacturer, key punch operator, "app" developer, Lasik surgeon (Millgram 2015).

Before we rush to apply a theory—about what justice would be in what we were trained to treat as paradigm circumstances—we must be cautious about extending any theory beyond the subject matter that defines its natural niche. So, if I ask what Sue is due, context matters. If Sue is an infant, you may suppose her "due" is a matter of what Sue needs. By contrast, if Sue is an athlete who just finished first, you'd be treating Sue like a child rather than a champion if you asked whether Sue *needs* a gold medal. The question in context is what Sue accomplished. A further contrast: if Sue is a colleague standing for promotion, it matters what Sue accomplished, yet you also need a sense of Sue's career trajectory because promotion is not only or even mainly a reward for past performance. Rather, a promotion is an opportunity. If Sue deserves an opportunity, it is partly in virtue of what she will do with it (Schmidtz 2006). We all have biases regarding criteria by which we would like to be evaluated. But justice does not cater to us in that way. Instead, it enables us, in all our modes of being fellow travelers (i.e., within niches where we serve as partners, competitors, caregivers, friends, neighbors, or citizens) to live in ways that makes our community a better place.

Perhaps we can go beyond treating environmental justice as an attempt to apply traditional theorizing to dynamic ecological problems. Can we start over? Can we imagine theorizing about justice as theorizing about what works in response to the human condition as an ecological problem?

Epilogue

I have been thinking about this for a long time, yet it remains a work in progress. I often wonder how much more I should say and how much I should leave to readers. We routinely come away from philosophical conversations with an acute awareness of differences between (1) what we were trying to say, (2) what we actually said, and (3) what we wish we had been trying to say; that is, what we would have been trying to say had we known then what we know now.

As Nathan Ballantyne notes in a recent issue of *Social Philosophy & Policy* (2022), our published arguments are actually argument *sketches*. As we sketch, we "meta-reason" about how we might construct more filled-in arguments, always constrained by an imperative to expedite getting to our conclusion without bogging down. An argument sketch is an "I Owe You." Readers can demand "payment" in the form of an expanded argument. But uncharitable critical responses disappoint. We lament that a critic fails to see how we invited readers to fill in what the critic identifies as a gap. If we see ourselves as virtuosos who have earned a right that our argument sketches be filled in charitably, we run afoul of critics who in turn imagine they are the virtuosos and their argument sketches are the ones entitled to the benefit of the doubt.

I have used Kantian and Rawlsian terminology as that seemed appropriate, along with the language of game theory, formal logic, philosophy of language, and so on. Filling in the "sketch" is easy and fun in conversation, but not so easy in a book. The printed text includes "Background" footnotes that gesture at further information that might help a nonspecialist reader. But there comes a time to let the text go to press and hope for further discussion.

Living Together. David Schmidtz, Oxford University Press. © Oxford University Press 2023. DOI: 10.1093/oso/9780197658505.003.0024

To facilitate discussion and further filling in of presumed background knowledge, here is an idea. Scan the QR codes. You will be taken to a web site that invites you to join the conversation. If you need background that isn't there, let us know. Someone will supply it. Or perhaps you will supply it. Post a question, identify a gap, ask other readers about alternative ways of filling it in, update statistical reports, alert readers to relevant literature as it appears—or whatever seems like an opportunity to help fill in the blanks of this work in progress. The site will evolve as topics become well-defined.

Thanks in advance.

References

Anderson, Elizabeth. *Value in Ethics and Economics*. Boston: Harvard University Press, 1995.

Axelrod, Robert. *The Evolution of Cooperation*. New York: Basic Books, 1984.

Badhwar, Neera. "Justice Within the Limits of Human Nature Alone." *Social Philosophy & Policy* 33 (2016): 193–213.

Ballantyne, Nathan. "Debunking Biased Thinkers (Including Ourselves)." *Journal of the APA* 1 (2015): 141–62.

Ballantyne, Nathan. "The Fog of Debate." *Social Philosophy & Policy* 38 (2022): 91–110.

Barber, Benjamin. *The Conquest of Politics*. Princeton: Princeton University Press, 1989.

Bedke, Matthew S. "Practical Reasons, Practical Rationality, Practical Wisdom." *Ethical Theory & Moral Practice* 11 (2008): 85–111.

Bellamy, Richard. *Liberalism and Pluralism: Toward a Politics of Compromise*. New York: Routledge, 1999.

Bentham, Jeremy. *Principles of Morals and Legislation*. Oxford: Clarendon Press, 1823.

Bilgrami, Akeel. "The Wider Significance of Naturalism: A Genealogical Essay." In *Naturalism and Normativity*, edited by Mario De Caro and David Macarthur, 23–54. New York: Columbia University Press, 2010.

Blackburn, Simon. "Practical Tortoise Raising." *Mind* 104 (1995): 695–711.

Blackstone, William. *Commentaries on the Laws of England*. Chicago: University of Chicago Press, 1979 [1765].

Blau, Adrian. "Defending Instrumental Rationality Against Critical Theorists." *Political Research Quarterly* 74 (2021): 1067–80.

Blau, Adrian, ed. *Methods in Analytical Political Theory*. Cambridge: Cambridge University Press, 2017.

Boettke, Peter. "Where Did Economics Go Wrong? Modern Economics as a Flight from Reality." *Critical Review* 11 (1997): 11–64.

Boettke, Peter, and Peter Leeson. "Liberalism, Socialism, and Robust Political Economy." *Journal of Markets & Morality* 7 (2004): 99–111.

Boswell, Paul. "Intelligibility and the Guise of the Good." *Journal of Ethics and Social Philosophy* 13 (2018): 1–31.

Brandom, Robert. *Making It Explicit*. Cambridge: Harvard University Press, 1994.

Bratman, Michael. *Intention, Plans, and Practical Reason*. Cambridge: Harvard University Press, 1987.

Brennan, Jason. *The Ethics of Voting*. Princeton: Princeton University Press, 2011.

Brennan, Jason. *Why Not Capitalism?* New York: Routledge, 2014.

Brinkmann, Matthias. "Freedom to Roam." *Journal of Ethics & Social Philosophy* 22 (2022): 209–33.

Broome, John. "Instrumental Reasoning." In *Rationality, Rules, and Structure*, edited by Julian Nida-Rumelin and Wolfgang Spohn, 195–207. Dordrecht: Kluwer, 2000.

Bullard, Robert. *Dumping in Dixie: Race, Class, and Environmental Quality*. Boulder: Westview, 1990.

Calabresi, Guido, and A. Douglas Melamed. "Property Rules, Liability Rules and Inalienability: One View of the Cathedral." *Harvard Law Review* 85 (1972): 1089–128.

Callard, Agnes. *Aspiration: The Agency of Becoming*. New York: Oxford University Press, 2018.

Carens, Joseph. *Equality, Moral Incentives, and the Market*. Chicago: University of Chicago Press, 1981.

Carroll, Lewis. "What the Tortoise Said to Achilles." *Mind* 4 (1895): 278–80.

Chappell, Sophie Grace. *Knowing What to Do*. New York: Oxford University Press, 2014.

Clark, Philip. "Aspects, Guises, and Knowing Something to Be Good." In *Desire, Practical Reason, and the Good*, edited by S. Tenenbaum, 234–44. New York: Oxford University Press, 2010.

Cohen, G. A. "Facts and Principles." *Philosophy and Public Affairs* 31 (2003): 211–45.

Cohen, G. A. *If You're an Egalitarian, How Come You're So Rich?* Cambridge: Harvard Press, 2000.

Cohen, G. A. *Rescuing Justice and Equality*. Cambridge: Harvard University Press, 2008.

Cohen, I. Bernard. "Faraday and Franklin's Newborn Baby." *Proceedings of the American Philosophical Society* 131 (1987): 177–82.

Congleton, Roger D. "A Short History of Constitutional Liberalism in America." *Constitutional Political Economy* 29 (2018): 137–70.

Cowen, Tyler. *In Praise of Commercial Culture*. Cambridge: Harvard University Press, 1998.

Dancy, Jonathan. *Moral Reasons*. Oxford: Blackwell Publishers, 1993.

Darwall, Stephen L. *Impartial Reason*. Ithaca: Cornell University Press, 1983.

Darwall, Stephen L. "Motive and Obligation in Hume's Ethics." *Noûs* 27 (1993): 415–48.

Demsetz, Harold. "Toward a Theory of Property Rights." *American Economic Review* (Papers and Proceedings) 57 (1967): 347–59.

Den Uyl, Douglas, and Douglas Rasmussen. *The Perfectionist Turn*. Edinburgh: University of Edinburgh Press, 2017.

De Waal, Alex. "The End of Famine? Prospects for the Elimination of Mass Starvation by Political Action." *Political Geography* 62 (2018): 184–95.

Ellickson, Robert C. *Order Without Law: How Neighbors Settle Disputes*. Cambridge: Harvard University Press, 1991.

Ellickson, Robert C. "Property in Land." *Yale Law Journal* 102 (1993), 1315–1400.

Estlund, David. *Democratic Authority*. Princeton: Princeton University Press, 2009.

Estlund, David. "Human Nature and the Limits (If Any) of Political Philosophy." *Philosophy & Public Affairs* 39 (2011): 207–37.

Estlund, David. "Prime Justice." In *Political Utopias*, edited by K. Vallier and M. Weber, 35–55. New York: Oxford University Press, 2017.

Estlund, David. "Utopophobia." *Philosophy & Public Affairs* 42 (2014): 113–34.

Estlund, David. *Utopophobia*. Princeton: Princeton University Press, 2020.

Farrelly, Colin. "Justice in Ideal Theory: A Refutation." *Political Studies* 55 (2007): 844–64.

Farrelly, Colin. "The Focusing Illusion of Rawlsian Ideal Theory." In *John Rawls: Debating the Major Questions*, edited by Jon Mandle and Sarah Roberts-Cady, 61–72. New York: Oxford University Press, 2020.

Finlayson, Lorna. "With Radicals Like These, Who Needs Conservatives? Doom, Gloom, and Realism in Political Theory." *European Journal of Political Theory* 16 (2015): 264–82.

Fleischacker, Samuel. *On Adam Smith's Wealth of Nations*. Princeton: Princeton University Press, 2004.

Foot, Philippa. *Virtues and Vices and Other Essays*. Berkeley: University of California Press, 1978.

Fossen, Thomas. "Modus Vivendi Beyond the Social Contract." In *The Political Theory of Modus Vivendi*, edited by John Horton, Manon Westphal, and Ulrich Willems, 111–27. Dordrecht: Springer, 2019.

Forcehimes, Andrew, and Robert Talisse. "Clarifying Cohen: A Response to Jubb and Hall." *Res Publica* 19 (2013): 371–9.

Frankfurt, Harry. "On the Usefulness of Final Ends." *Iyyun* 41 (1992): 3–19.

Freiman, Christopher. "Goodness and Moral Twin Earth." *Erkenntnis* 79 (2014): 445–60.

Galston, William. "Realism in Political Theory." *European Journal of Political Theory* 9 (2010): 385–411.

Gardiner, Stephen, and Allen Thompson, eds. (2017). *Oxford Handbook of Environmental Ethics*. New York: Oxford University Press.

Gaus, Gerald. "The Commonwealth of Bees: On the Impossibility of Justice-Through-Ethos." *Social Philosophy & Policy* 33 (2016a): 96–121.

Gaus, Gerald. *The Tyranny of the Ideal*. Princeton: Princeton University Press, 2016b.

Geuss, Raymond. *Philosophy and Real Politics*. Princeton: Princeton University Press, 2008.

Gheaus, Anca. "The Feasibility Constraint on the Concept of Justice." *Philosophical Quarterly* 63 (2013): 445–64.

Gilabert, Pablo. "Justice and Feasibility: A Dynamic Approach." In *Political Utopias*, edited by Kevin Vallier and Michael Weber, 95–126. New York: Oxford University Press, 2017.

Godfrey-Smith, Peter. "Abstractions, Idealizations, and Evolutionary Biology." In *Mapping the Future of Biology*, edited by Gerald Gaus, 47–56. Dordrecht: Springer, 2009.

Goldman, Alvin I. "A Causal Theory of Knowing." *Journal of Philosophy* 64 (1967): 357–72.

Grantham, George. "The Prehistoric Origins of European Economic Integration." *Social Philosophy & Policy* 38 (2022): 261–306.

Grotius, Hugo. *Rights of War and Peace*. London: Elibron, 2005 [1625].

Haidt, Jonathan. *The Righteous Mind*. New York: Pantheon, 2012.

Hall, Edward. "Political Realism and Fact-Sensitivity." *Res Publica* 19 (2013): 173–81.

Hall, Edward. "Skepticism About Unconstrained Utopianism." *Social Philosophy & Policy* 33 (2016): 76–95.

Hall, Edward. *Value, Conflict, and Order: Berlin, Hampshire, Williams, and the Realist Revival in Political Theory*. Chicago: University of Chicago Press, 2020.

Hamlin, Alan. "Positive Political Theory." In *Methods in Analytical Political Theory*, edited by Adrian Blau, 192–216. Cambridge: Cambridge University Press, 2017.

Hamlin, Alan, and Zofia Stemplowska. "Theory, Ideal Theory, and the Theory of Ideals." *Political Studies* 10 (2012): 48–62.

Hampshire, Stuart. *Justice Is Conflict*. Princeton: Princeton University Press, 2001.

Hampton, Jean. "On Instrumental Rationality." In *Essays in Honor of Kurt Baier*, edited by Jerome Schneewind, 84–116. La Salle: Open Court, 1996.

Hanley, Ryan Patrick. *Adam Smith and the Character of Virtue*. New York: Cambridge University Press, 2009.

Hanley, Ryan Patrick. "Justice and Politics in the *Enquiry*." In *Hume's Enquiry Concerning the Principles of Morals: A Critical Guide*, edited by Esther Kroeker and Willem Lemmens, 53–71. New York: Cambridge University Press, 2021.

Hanley, Ryan Patrick, ed. *Adam Smith: His Life, Thought, and Legacy*. Princeton: Princeton University Press, 2016.

Hargreaves Heap, Shaun. "Two Accounts of the Relation Between Political Economy and Economics, and Why It Matters Which Is Better." *Social Philosophy & Policy* 36 (2020): 103–17.

Hasnas, John. "The Corruption of the Rule of Law." *Social Philosophy & Policy* 35 (2018): 12–30.

Hausman, Jerry. "Contingent Valuation: From Dubious to Hopeless." *Journal of Economic Perspectives* 26 (2012): 43–56.

Henrich, Joseph. *The Weirdest People in the World: How the West Became Psychologically Peculiar and Particularly Prosperous.* New York: Farrar, Straus, and Giroux, 2020.

Herman, Arthur. *How the Scots Invented the Modern World.* New York: Three Rivers Press, 2001.

Herman, Barbara. "Leaving Deontology Behind." In *The Practice of Moral Judgment,* 208–40. Cambridge: Harvard University Press, 1993.

Herman, Barbara. "Making Room for Character." In *Aristotle, Kant, and the Stoics,* edited by Stephen Engstrom and Jennifer Whiting, 36–60. Cambridge: Cambridge University Press, 1996.

Hirose, Iwao, and Jonas Olson, eds. *Oxford Handbook of Value Theory.* New York: Oxford University Press, 2015.

Hohfeld, W. *Fundamental Legal Conceptions.* New Haven: Yale University Press, 1964 [1913 and 1917].

Holland, Alan. "Are Choices Trade-Offs?" In *Economics, Ethics, and Environmental Policy: Contested Choices,* edited by D. Bromley, D. Paavola, and J. Paavola, 17–34. Oxford: Blackwell, 2002.

Honig, Bonnie. *Political Theory and the Displacement of Politics.* Ithaca: Cornell University Press, 1993.

Hope, Simon. "Idealization, Justice, and the Form of Practical Reason." *Social Philosophy & Policy* 33 (2016): 372–92.

Hope, Simon. "The Circumstances of Justice." *Hume Studies* 36 (2010): 125–48.

Horan, Richard, Erwin Bulte, and Jason Shogren. "Coevolution of Human Speech and Trade." *Journal of Economic Growth* 13 (2008): 293–313.

Horan, Richard, Erwin Bulte, and Jason Shogren. "How Trade Saved Humanity from Biological Exclusion: An Economic Theory of Neanderthal Extinction." *Journal of Economic Behavior and Organization* 58 (2005), 1–29.

Hume, David. *Enquiry Concerning the Principles of Morals.* Indianapolis: Hackett Publishing, 1983b [1751].

Hume, David. *Enquiry Concerning Human Understanding.* Indianapolis: Hackett Publishing, 1993 [1748].

Hume, David. *History of England.* Indianapolis: Liberty Fund Press, 1983a [1762].

Hume, David. *Treatise of Human Nature.* Oxford: Oxford University Press, 2000 [1739].

Hurley, Paul E. "Does Consequentialism Make Too Many Demands or None At All?" *Ethics* 116 (2006): 680–706.

Hursthouse, Rosalind. *On Virtue Ethics*. Oxford: Oxford University Press, 1999.

Ismael, J. T. "A Philosopher of Science Looks at Idealization in Political Theory." *Social Philosophy & Policy* 33 (2016): 11–31.

Ismael, J. T. *The Situated Self*. New York: Oxford University Press, 2009.

Jacobs, Jane. *The Economy of Cities*. London: Vintage Publishers, 1970.

Juarez-Garcia, Mario. *Essays in Political Corruption*. Tucson: University of Arizona dissertation, 2021.

Jubb, Robert. "Tragedies of Non-Ideal Theory." *European Journal of Political Theory* 11 (2012): 229–46.

Kagan, Shelly. *The Limits of Morality*. New York; Oxford University Press, 1989.

Kamm, Frances Myrna. *Morality, Mortality, Volume I*. New York: Oxford University Press, 1993.

Kelman, Steven. "Cost-Benefit Analysis: An Ethical Critique." *Regulation* 5 (1981): 33–40.

Klosko, George, ed. *Oxford Handbook of the History of Political Philosophy*. Oxford: Oxford University Press, 2011.

Knights, Mark. "Corruption in Pre-Modern Britain." *Social Philosophy & Policy* 35 (2019): 94–117.

Kolodny, Nico. "Instrumental Reasons." In *Oxford Handbook of Reasons and Normativity*, edited by Daniel Star, 731–63. Oxford: Oxford University Press, 2018.

Korsgaard, Christine. *Sources of Normativity*. Cambridge: Cambridge University Press, 1996.

Korsgaard, Christine M. "The Normativity of Instrumental Reason." In *Ethics and Practical Reason*, edited by G. Cullity and B. Gaut, 215–54. Oxford: Oxford University Press, 1997.

Kramer, Samuel N. *History Begins at Sumer*. Philadelphia: University of Pennsylvania Press, 1981.

Laden, Anthony. "Outline of a Theory of Reasonable Deliberation." *Canadian Journal of Philosophy* 30 (2000): 551–79.

Laden, Anthony. *Reasoning: A Social Picture*, Oxford: Oxford University Press, 2012.

Lafollette, Hugh. "The Greatest Vice?" *Journal of Practical Ethics* 4 (2016), 1: 1–24.

Larmore, Charles. "What Is Political Philosophy?" *Journal of Moral Philosophy* 10 (2013): 276–306.

Lawson, Gary. "The Fiduciary Social Contract." *Social Philosophy & Policy* 38 (2021): 25–51.

Lear, Jonathan. *Love and Its Place in Nature*. New York: Farrar, Straus, & Giroux, 1990.

Levy, Jacob. *Rationalism, Pluralism, and Freedom*. New York: Oxford University Press, 2015.

Levy, Jacob. "There Is No Such Thing as Ideal Theory." *Social Philosophy & Policy* 33 (2016): 312–33.

Lewis, David. "Causation." *Journal of Philosophy* 70 (1973): 556–67.

Lewis, John. *Law of Eminent Domain*. Chicago: Callaghan and Co., 1970 [1888].

Lindblom, Charles. "The Science of Muddling Through." *Public Administration Review* 19 (1959):79–88.

Lindsay, Peter. "Re-envisioning Property." *Contemporary Political Theory* 17 (2018): 187–206.

Locke, John. *Second Treatise of Government*. P. Laslett (ed.). Cambridge: Cambridge University Press, 1960 [1690].

MacIntyre, A. C. "Hume on 'Is' and 'Ought.'" *The Philosophical Review* 68 (1959): 451–68.

Mandeville, Bernard. *Fable of the Bees, or Private Vices, Publick Benefits*. Indianapolis: Liberty Fund, 1988 [1714].

Marchetti, G., and S. Marchetti. *Facts and Values: The Ethics and Metaphysics of Normativity*. New York: Routledge, 2017.

Mason, Andrew. "Just Constraints." *British Journal of Political Science* 34 (2004): 251–68.

Mason, Andrew. "Justice, Feasibility, and Ideal Theory: A Pluralist Approach." *Social Philosophy & Policy* 33 (2016): 32–54.

Mason, Andrew. "Rawlsian Theory and the Circumstances of Politics." *Political Theory* 38 (2010): 658–83.

Mason, Andrew. "What Is the Point of Justice?" *Utilitas* 24 (2012): 525–47.

Massing, Michael. "Does Democracy Avert Famine?" *New York Times* March 1, 2003. Accessed January 3, 2021. https://www.nytimes.com/2003/03/01/arts/does-democracy-avert-famine.html.

Maynard, Jonathan L., and Alex Worsnip. "Is There a Distinctively Political Normativity?" *Ethics* 128 (2018):756–87.

McCloskey, Deirdre N. *Bourgeois Dignity: Why Economics Can't Explain the Modern World*. Chicago: University of Chicago Press, 2010.

McCloskey, Deirdre N. *Bourgeois Equality: How Ideas, Not Capital or Institutions, Enriched the World*. Chicago: University of Chicago Press, 2016.

McCloskey, Deirdre N. *Bourgeois Virtue: Ethics for an Age of Commerce*. Chicago: University of Chicago Press, 2006.

McCloskey, Deirdre N., and Art Carden. *Leave Me Alone and I'll Make You Rich*. Chicago: University of Chicago Press, 2020.

McQueen, Alison. *Political Realism in Apocalyptic Times* (Roundtable). 2019. https://issforum.org/roundtables/PDF/Roundtable-XXI-7.pdf.

Merrill, Thomas, and Henry Smith. *Property*. New York: Foundation Press, 2007.

Mill, John Stuart. *Principles of Political Economy*. London: John W. Parker, 1848.

Miller, David. *Justice for Earthlings*. Cambridge: Cambridge University Press, 2013.

Miller, Fred D. Jr. *Nature, Justice, and Rights in Aristotle's Politics*. Oxford: Oxford University Press, 1997.

Miller, Richard W. *Globalizing Justice*. New York: Oxford University Press, 2010.

Millgram, Elijah. *The Great Endarkenment*. New York: Oxford University Press, 2015.

Millgram, Elijah. "Was Hume a Humean?" *Hume Studies* 21 (1995): 75–93.

Montes, Leonidas. *Adam Smith in Context*. New York: Cambridge University Press, 2004.

Moore, G. E. *Principia Ethica*. Cambridge: Cambridge University Press, 1968 [1903].

Morriss, Andrew. "Lessons for Environmental Law from the American Codification Debate." In *The Common Law and the Environment*, edited by Roger Meiners and A. Morriss, 130–57. Lanham: Rowman & Littlefield, 2000.

Muller, Herbert. *Freedom in the Ancient World*. New York: Harper, 1961.

Mumford, Lewis. *The City in History*. New York: Harcourt, Brace, and World, 1961.

Murdoch, Iris. *The Sovereignty of the Good*. New York: Routledge and Kegan Paul, 1970.

Nielson, Kai. "Rescuing Political Theory from Fact-Insensitivity." *Socialist Studies* 8 (2012): 216–45.

Nozick, Robert. *Anarchy, State, and Utopia*. New York: Basic Books, 1974.

Nozick, Robert. *The Nature of Rationality*. Princeton: Princeton University Press, 1993.

O'Neill, Onora. "Abstraction, Idealization, and Ideology in Ethics." In *Moral Philosophy and Contemporary Problems*, edited by J. D. Evans, 55–69. Cambridge: Cambridge University Press, 1987.

Orr, Susan, and James Johnson. "What's a Political Theorist to Do?" *Theoria* 65 (2018): 1–23.

Östbring, Björn. *David Hume and Contemporary Realism in Political Theory*. Lund University Working Paper, 2012.

Ostrom, Elinor. *Governing the Commons*. New York: Cambridge University Press, 1990.

Ostrom, Vincent. *The Meaning of Democracy and the Vulnerability of Democracies: A Response to Tocqueville's Challenge*. Ann Arbor: University of Michigan Press, 1997.

Otteson, James R. *Adam Smith's Marketplace of Life*. New York: Cambridge University Press, 2002.

Patterson, Orlando. *Freedom: Freedom in the Making of Western Culture.* New York: Basic Books, 1991.

Paul, Laurie. *Transformative Experience.* New York: Oxford, 2015.

Pennington, Mark. "Hayek on Complexity, Uncertainty, and Pandemic Response." *Review of Austrian Economics* 34 (2021): 203–20.

Pennington, Mark. *Robust Political Economy.* Cheltenham: Edward Elgar, 2011.

Pettit, Philip, and Robert Sugden. "The Backward Induction Paradox." *Journal of Philosophy* 86 (1989): 169–82.

Pinker, Steven. *The Blank Slate.* New York: Penguin, 2002.

Pogge, Thomas. "Poverty and Innovation." *Social Philosophy & Policy* 40 (2023): in press.

Popper, Karl. *Conjectures and Refutations.* New York: Routledge and Kegan Paul, 1963.

Postgate, J. N. Early *Mesopotamia: Society and Economy at the Dawn of History.* New York: Routledge, 1992.

Priest, Greg. "Charles Darwin's Theory of Moral Sentiments: What Darwin's Ethics Really Owes to Adam Smith." *Journal of the History of Ideas* 78 (2017): 571–93.

Prinz, Janosch, and Enzo Rossi. "Political Realism as Ideology Critique." *Critical Review of International Social & Political Philosophy* 20 (2017): 334–48.

Putnam, Robert. *Bowling Alone.* New York: Simon & Schuster, 1990.

Quine, W. V. O. "Two Dogmas of Empiricism." *Philosophical Review* 60 (1951): 20–43.

Quinn, Warren. "Putting Rationality in its Place." In *Virtues and Reasons: Philippa Foot and Moral Theory,* edited by Rosalind Hursthouse, Gavin Lawrence, and Warren Quinn, 181–208. Oxford: Oxford University Press, 1995.

Raaflaub, Kurt. *The Discovery of Freedom in Ancient Greece.* Chicago: University of Chicago Press, 2004.

Railton, Peter. "Alienation, Consequentialism, and the Demands of Morality." *Philosophy & Public Affairs* 13 (1984): 134–71.

Railton, Peter. "On the Hypothetical and Non-Hypothetical in Reasoning About Action." In *Ethics and Practical Reason,* edited by Garrett Cullity and Berys Gaut, 53–80. New York: Oxford University Press, 1997.

Rangan, Subramanian (ed.). *Performance and Progress.* Oxford: Oxford University Press, 2015.

Rawls, John. *A Theory of Justice.* Cambridge: Harvard University Press, 1971 (revised 1999).

Rawls, John. *Collected Papers,* edited by S. Freeman. Cambridge, MA: Harvard University Press, 1999b.

Rawls, John. *Justice As Fairness: A Restatement,* edited by E. Kelly. Cambridge, MA: Harvard University Press, 2001.

Rawls, John. *Law of Peoples.* Cambridge: Harvard University Press, 1999a.

Rawls, John. *Political Liberalism*. New York: Columbia University Press, 1993.

Rawls, John. "Two Concepts of Rules." *Philosophical Review* 64 (1955): 3–32.

Raz, Joseph. "The Myth of Instrumental Rationality." *Journal of Ethics & Social Philosophy* 1 (2005): 1–28.

Ronzoni, Miriam. "Life Is Not a Camping Trip: On the Desirability of Cohenite Socialism." *Philosophy, Politics, and Economics* 11 (2012): 171–85.

Rose, Carol. "Possession as the Origin of Property." *University of Chicago Law Review* 52 (1985): 73–88.

Rose, Carol. *Property and Persuasion*. Boulder: Westview, 1994.

Rosenberg, Alexander. "On The Very Idea of Ideal Theory in Political Philosophy." *Social Philosophy & Policy* 33 (2016): 55–75.

Ross, W. D. *The Right and the Good*. Oxford: Clarendon, 1930.

Rossi, Enzo. "Being Realistic and Demanding the Impossible." *Constellations* 26 (2019a): 638–52.

Rossi, Enzo. "On Glen Newey's Prescient Political Realism." *Biblioteca della Libertà* 54 (2019b): 137–46.

Rossi, Enzo, and Carlo Argenton. "Property, Legitimacy, and Ideology: A Reality Check." *Journal of Politics* 83 (2021): 1046–59.

Rousseau, Jean Jacques. *The Social Contract*. [1762] translation by G. Cole. London: J. M. Dent, 1913.

Sabl, Andrew. "Realist Liberalism: An Agenda." *Critical Review of International Social & Political Philosophy* 20 (2017): 349–64.

Sabl, Andrew. "Review of Sleat." *Perspectives on Politics* 13 (2015): 1141–3.

Sagoff, Mark. "At the Shrine of Our Lady of Fatima, or Why Political Questions Are Not All Economic." *Arizona Law Review* 23 (1981): 1283–98.

Salzman, Jim. "The Promise and Perils of Payments for Ecosystem Services." *International Journal of Innovation and Sustainable Development* 1 (2005): 5–20.

Sandler, Ronald, and Phaedra Pezzullo. *Environmental Justice and Environmentalism*. Cambridge, MA: MIT Press, 2007.

Sayre-McCord, Geoffrey. "On Why Hume's General Point of View Isn't Ideal, and Shouldn't Be." *Social Philosophy & Policy* 11 (1994): 202–28.

Scanlon, T. M. *What We Owe To Each Other*. Cambridge: Belknap Press, 1998.

Scheffler, Samuel. *The Rejection of Consequentialism*. New York: Oxford University Press, 1982.

Schmidtz, David. "A Place for Cost-Benefit Analysis." *Philosophical Issues* 11 (2001): 148–71.

Schmidtz, David. "A Realistic Political Ideal." *Social Philosophy & Policy* 33 (2016d): 1–10.

Schmidtz, David. "Adam Smith on Freedom." In *Adam Smith: His Life, Thought, and Legacy*, edited by Ryan Hanley, 208–27. Princeton: Princeton University Press, 2016c.

Schmidtz, David. "After Solipsism." *Oxford Studies in Normative Ethics* 6 (2016a): 145–65.

Schmidtz, David. "Choosing Ends." *Ethics* 104 (1994): 226–51.

Schmidtz, David. "Corruption." In *Performance and Progress: Essays on Capitalism, Business, and Society*, edited by Subramanian Rangan, 49–64. Oxford: Oxford University Press, 2015b.

Schmidtz, David. "Ecological Justice." In *MacMillan Handbook of Environmental Ethics*, edited by David Schmidtz, 221–42. Boston: Cengage Learning, 2016b.

Schmidtz, David. *Elements of Justice*. New York: Cambridge University Press, 2006.

Schmidtz, David. "Environmental Conflict." In *Oxford Handbook of Environmental Ethics*, edited by Stephen Gardiner and Allen Thompson, 517–27. New York: Oxford University Press, 2017a.

Schmidtz, David. "Natural Enemies: An Anatomy of Environmental Conflict." *Environmental Ethics* 22 (2000): 397–408.

Schmidtz, David. "Nonideal Theory: What It Is and What It Needs to Be." *Ethics* 121 (2011a): 772–96.

Schmidtz, David. "Origins of Political Economy." *Social Philosophy & Policy* 36 (2020): 1–9.

Schmidtz, David. *Person, Polis, Planet: Essays in Applied Philosophy*. New York: Oxford University Press, 2008.

Schmidtz, David. "Property." In *Oxford Handbook of the History of Political Philosophy*, edited by George Klosko, 599–610. Oxford: Oxford University Press, 2011.

Schmidtz, David. "Public Choice as Political Philosophy." *Review of Austrian Economics* 31 (2018): 169–76.

Schmidtz, David. *Rational Choice and Moral Agency*. Princeton: Princeton University Press, 1995. (2015 revised edition, including Kindle, available at amazon.com.)

Schmidtz, David. "Rationality Within Reason." *Journal of Philosophy* 89 (1992): 445–62.

Schmidtz, David. "Realistic Idealism." In *Methods in Analytical Political Theory*, edited by Adrian Blau, 131–52. Cambridge: Cambridge University Press, 2017b.

Schmidtz, David. "Value in Nature." In *Oxford Handbook of Value Theory*, edited by I. Hirose and J. Olson, 381–98. Oxford: Oxford University Press, 2015a.

Schmidtz, David, and Jason Brennan. *A Brief History of Liberty*. New York: Blackwell, 2010.

Schmidtz, David, and Robert Goodin. *Social Welfare and Individual Responsibility*. New York: Cambridge University Press, 1998.

Schmidtz, David, and Sarah Wright. "What Nozick Did for Decision Theory." *Midwest Studies in Philosophy* 28 (2004): 282–94.

Schwartz, Adina. "A Market in Liberty: Corruption, Cooperation, and the Federal Criminal Justice System." In *Private and Public Corruption*, edited by W. Heffernan and J. Kleinig, 173–223. Lanham, MD: Rowman & Littlefield, 2004.

Scott, James C. *Against the Grain*. New Haven: Yale University Press, 2017.

Seabright, Paul. *The Company of Strangers*. Princeton: Princeton University Press, 2004.

Sen, Amartya. *Development as Freedom*. New York: Anchor Books, 1999.

Sen, Amartya. *The Idea of Justice*. Cambridge: Harvard University Press, 2010.

Shahar, Dan. *Why It's OK to Eat Meat*. New York: Routledge, 2022.

Shklar, Judith. "The Liberalism of Fear." In *Political Thought and Political Thinkers*, edited by Stanley Hoffman, 3–12. Chicago: University of Chicago Press, 1998.

Shrader-Frechette, Kristin. *Environmental Justice: Creating Equality, Reclaiming Democracy*. New York: Oxford, 2002.

Sidgwick, Henry. *Methods of Ethics*. Bristol: Thoemmes Press, 1996 [1874].

Simmons, A. John. "Ideal and Nonideal Theory." *Philosophy & Public Affairs* 38 (2010): 5–36.

Singer, Peter. "Famine, Affluence, and Morality." *Philosophy & Public Affairs* 1 (1972): 229–43.

Sleat, Matt. *Liberal Realism: A Realist Theory of Liberal Politics*. Manchester: Manchester University Press, 2013.

Sleat, Matt. "Realism, Liberalism, and Non-Ideal Theory." *Political Studies* 64 (2014): 27–41.

Smith, Adam. *Theory of Moral Sentiments*. Indianapolis: Liberty Fund, 1984 [1759].

Smith, Adam. *Wealth of Nations*. Indianapolis: Liberty Fund, 1981 [1776].

Stegenga, Jacob. "Probabilizing the End." *Philosophical Studies* 165 (2013): 95–112.

Stemplowska, Zofia, and Adam Swift. "Ideal and Nonideal Theory." In *The Oxford Handbook of Political Philosophy*, edited by David Estlund, 373–90. Oxford: Oxford University Press, 2012.

Stevenson, Charles L. *Ethics and Language*. New Haven: Yale University Press, 1944.

Styron, William. *Sophie's Choice*. New York: Random House, 1979.

Sunstein, Cass R. "Cognition and Cost-Benefit Analysis." *Journal of Legal Studies* 29 (2000): 1059–103.

Swift, Adam. "The Value of Philosophy in Nonideal Circumstances." *Social Theory & Practice* 34 (2008): 363–87.

Tasioulas, John. "Justice, Equality, and Rights." In *Oxford Handbook of the History of Ethics*, edited by Roger Crisp, 768–92. New York: Oxford University Press, 2013.

Tattersall, Ian. *Masters of the Planet*. New York: St. Martin's, 2012.

Valentini, Laura. "Ideal vs. Nonideal Theory: A Conceptual Map." *Philosophy Compass*, 7 (2012): 654–64.

Vallier, Kevin. "Production, Distribution, and J. S. Mill." *Utilitas* 22 (2010): 103–25.

Vallier, Kevin, and Michael Weber, eds. *Political Utopias*. New York: Oxford University Press, 2017.

Velleman, J. David. *Practical Reflection*. Princeton: Princeton University Press, 1989.

Wachsmann, Shelley. *Seagoing Ships and Seamanship in the Bronze Age Levant*. College Station: Texas A&M University Press, 1998.

Waldron, Jeremy. *Law and Disagreement*. New York: Oxford University Press, 1999.

Walker, Mathew. *Why We Sleep*. London: Penguin, 2017.

Wall, Steven. *Enforcing Morality*. New York: Cambridge University Press, 2023.

West, E. G. "Adam Smith and Alienation: A Rejoinder." *Oxford Economic Papers* 27: (1975) 295–301.

Williams, Bernard. "Internal and External Reasons." In *Moral Luck*, 101–13. Cambridge: Cambridge University Press, 1981.

Williams, Bernard. *In the Beginning Was the Deed*. Princeton: Princeton University Press, 2005.

Wilson, Woodrow. "The Study of Administration." *Political Science Quarterly* 2 (1887): 197–222.

Wittfogel, Karl. *Oriental Despotism: A Comparative Study of Total Power*. New Haven: Yale University Press, 1957.

Wolff, Robert Paul. *Understanding Rawls: A Reconstruction and a Critique*, Princeton: Princeton Press, 1977.

Woodward, James, and John Allman. "Moral Intuition: Its Neural Substrates and Normative Significance." *Journal of Physiology—Paris* 101 (2007): 179–202.

Wright, Gavin. "Slavery and the Rise of the Nineteenth Century American Economy." *Journal of Economic Perspectives* 36 (2022): 123–48.

Zwolinski, Matt, and John Tomasi. *The Individualists*. Princeton: Princeton University Press, 2023.

Index

For the benefit of digital users, indexed terms that span two pages (e.g., 52–53) may, on occasion, appear on only one of those pages.

Figures are indicated by *f* following the page number

human condition (*cont.*)
  Neanderthals and, 228–31
  political economy and, 127, 100–1,
    119, 138, 140
  realistic idealism and, 69, 80, 84,
    85, 86, 87, 91
  reasons and the moral self, 182,
    185, 188
  solipsism and, 41, 45, 52, 63–64
  summary of, 239–41
  trading networks, 231–39
humanitarianism, 29, 30, 44–
    45, 79–80
humanity, 9, 27, 41–42, 79–80, 162–
    63, 220–21, 224, 225, 228–29,
    240–41, 246
human life, 64, 75–76, 112, 180
Hume, David
  on common law, 146–47
  experimental methods of
    reasoning, 3, 13, 17
  human condition, 36
  Is-Ought problem, 11–15
  justice and, 16–30
  moral reasoning and, 11–12
  moral science and, 100–1
  philosophy of moral science,
    3–10, 17
  transfer of external goods, 105–6
Hursthouse, Rosalind, 189
Hypothetical Imperative, 196–97
hypothetical willingness, 172–73

ideal bargainers, 85
idealism. *See also* realistic idealism
  fact-insensitive idealism, 79–80
  political ideals, 20–21, 82, 83
  in political theory, 44
  reasons and the moral self,
    184, 208
  traffic management theory
    and, 79
  utopian idealism, 70, 75, 80, 92

idealizations, 33
ideal theory, xiv, 77–80, 85, 137,
    159, 224
ideals
  moral versus political, 20–21, 82,
    83–84, 243
immorality, 208–9
inalienability rule, 144
incentive, 7–8, 34, 100
incommensurable
    values, 167–68
inconsistency, 32, 114
injustice, 36–37, 75, 76, 81–82, 83–
    84, 224
instrumentalism, 187–89, 202, 203–
    4, 205–6
instrumental rationality, 186, 198
instrumental reason, 186, 187–88,
    189, 201, 203, 205–7
instrumental value, 167–68
intellectual resources, xv
intentional trespass, 145–46, 148
intrinsic value, 167–68
Is-Ought problem, 11–15, 198

Jacque vs. Steenberg Homes
    (1997), 145–46
Juarez, Mario, 109, 118, 126, 129
jumping to conclusions, 13–15
justice
  as adaptation, 221–22
  compliance in, 85–88
  conflict and, 128–29, 137–58, 220
  consensus and, 26–29
  cooperation and, 26
  ecological justice, 219–26
  egalitarian justice, 19
  fact-insensitive justice, 16, 80,
    183
  human condition and, 220–26
  Hume on, 16–30
  injustice and, 36–37, 75, 76, 81–
    82, 83–84, 122, 224